Pictorial History of the United Nations

PICTORIAL

HISTORY

OF THE

UNITED NATIONS

by Jacob A. Rubin

With Forewords

by U THANT and FREDERICK H. BOLAND

Thomas Yoseloff
New York · London · Toronto

Thomas Yoseloff, *Publisher*
11 East 36th Street
New York 16, N. Y.

Thomas Yoseloff Ltd.
123 New Bond Street
London W. 1, England

CREDITS

The author and publisher are grateful to the following photographers, organizations, institutions, and picture services for permission to reproduce their photographs in this book: The British Information Service, the New York Public Library, George R. Rowen, UNESCO Photos, the United Nations Photo Service, and Wide World Photos.

Printed in the United States of America

CONTENTS

of the Secretariat.—Channeling Aid Through the U.N.—New Functions for the U.N.—The Financial Burden.—A Mirror of World Realities.

To My Wife Ella
and My Daughters
Nira and Edna

FOREWORD

By U Thant

Acting Secretary-General of the United Nations

Today, we have a United Nations almost universal in membership, stronger than the League of Nations, more effective and dynamic because of the charter provisions relating to economic and social development and advancement of nonself-governing territories toward independence.

Yet, the United Nations can be no better and no worse than the sum total of what its members choose to make it. At present, especially in the discharge of its political functions, the United Nations may seem weak and inadequate, but it is still our best hope for banishing the threat of nuclear holocaust and for creating the beginnings of a civilized international community.

Ultimately, it is the people of the world who must fashion the kind of United Nations they want. It is true, unfortunately, that while the average citizen usually has some knowledge of his own government, very few know much about the structure, activities, powers and limitations of the United Nations.

For more than sixteen years, the political work of the United Nations has made headlines all over the world, but very little space has been given, for instance, to its fruitful but unobtrusive contributions to economic and social development.

All efforts to help promote a better understanding of the United Nations and its various activities are always welcome.

FOREWORD

What Lies Ahead for the United Nations

By Frederick H. Boland *

The assembly of the United Nations mirrors the world as it is. That is one of its principal functions and, in my view, it is its chief value. It is in the assembly of the United Nations, more than in any other forum in the world, that the intense political pressures and the great economic and social ferments which are slowly but inexorably molding the future destiny of mankind find their fullest, their clearest, and their most authoritative expression.

It is true that, at moments of great tension, expression may become forceful and even vehement. That should not dismay us. It is something which happens in all deliberative assemblies. It happens even in the oldest and most tradition-minded national parliaments. I seem to remember one occasion, many years ago now, on which the Mother of Parliaments—the British House of Commons— had to be hastily adjourned to bring to an end a disorderly scene, in the course of which a member of the Opposition threw a book across the chamber which struck a member of the Government on the head. The member of the Government happened to be the then Mr. Winston Churchill. The debate out of which the disorder arose happened to be about Ireland. The man who threw the book was an Irishman—from the North of Ireland—and the book itself happened to be a copy of the *Rules of Procedure of the House of Commons!*

By themselves, of course, such parliamentary interludes are of little more than passing importance. What are far more important, far more disturbing, are the sharpness of the antagonisms and the intensity of the conflicts of opinion and

policy to which they point, and the feelings of anxiety, resentment, anger, and even desperation of which they are often the outward expression.

It would be difficult, I think, to pick out any previous period in history in which the world situation presented so many dangerous possibilities—so much instability, so many complexities, such a wide variety of problems clamoring so insistently for solution—as it does at the present moment. Many of the major political problems resulting from the last war still remain unresolved today—sixteen years later. They hang over the world scene like a dark and threatening cloud, constantly exacerbating the relations between East and West, embittering the cold war and enhancing the dangers of the ever sharper and more determined competition in armaments.

Nor, when we turn our gaze from the European scene to the other regions of the earth, do we find more comfort. The Far East, ever inscrutable to Western eyes, is in a state of seething unrest. The spirit of anti-imperialistic nationalism, having swept through Asia and the Middle East, is marching through the continent of Africa with an impetus which threatens to explode into violence wherever it encounters obstacles in its path. Tremendous social and economic discontents are creating an atmosphere throughout Latin America which revolutionary fervor may at any moment set aflame. In the meantime, as population pressures continue to increase, the gap between the standards of living and material well-being, in the more developed societies on the one hand and the less developed on the other, grows ever wider and wider; and the measures of mutual co-operation necessary to correct this situation become increasingly difficult to devise and apply according as the antagonisms and resentments dating from

* Permanent Representative of Ireland to the United Nations and President of the Fifteenth Session of the U.N. General Assembly.

subjection and exploitation in the past are constantly revived and sustained by a bitter sense of inequality and underprivilege in the present.

It is against this picture of a world in a state of rapid and revolutionary change and of great and growing tensions that the present position and future prospects of the United Nations must be measured.

And we must begin by facing a basic reality. World society is still a community without a government. The United Nations is in no sense a world government and it was never intended to be. Within our respective national communities, we take the concept of government for granted. Anything else is unthinkable. We believe that the lack of an effective national government would spell chaos and anarchy, and we have dramatic proof of the soundness of our belief in the present situation in the Congo. What we all deprecate and deplore in the case of the Congo, however, we all accept complacently in the case of world society. The fact is that the United Nations represents the furthest point to which the world community has so far shown itself prepared to go toward institutionalizing its common interest in the preservation of peace and in establishing collective control of its common destiny; and if the United Nations is not a stronger and more effective organization than it is, it is because none of our governments have yet shown any disposition or desire to accept the sacrifices of sovereignty required to establish a really effective world government.

Obliged to take that fact as their starting point, the authors of the United Nations Charter had the rather unenviable task of trying to reconcile two somewhat conflicting political realities. One was the fact that all the members of the United Nations wished to retain their full national sovereignty and demanded, on that basis, to be treated on a footing of equality as sovereign states. The other was the fact that, however equal the members of the United Nations might be in theory, they were very unequal in military strength; and that, as a matter of common sense, the preservation of world peace, and the possibility of taking and enforcing effective decisions, was bound to depend in practice on agreement and common action, not on the part of the membership of the United Nations as a whole, but on the part of the four or five members of the organization possessing the greatest military power.

The constitutional structure of the United Nations aims at balancing these two realities. The idea of Great Power agreement and leadership is given expression in the eleven-member Security Council which, on matters involving the maintenance of world peace and security, has power to make decisions binding all members of the United Nations. Such decisions must, however, be agreed to by all the five Great Powers who are permanent members of the council. On the other hand, the principle of the sovereign equality of all members of the organization is given expression in the General Assembly, in which all states, great and small, have an equal vote. The decisions of the assembly are not legally binding on the members of the organization. They have merely the force of recommendations to member governments, and then only if they are adopted by a two-thirds vote.

Of course, much has happened in the sixteen years since the charter was framed. Agreement between the Great Powers has become increasingly difficult to achieve, with the result that on many of the great and urgent issues which have come before it, the Security Council has been unable to act owing to the exercise of the veto. Mainly in consequence of this difficulty, the assembly passed a resolution in 1950—the so-called "Uniting for Peace" resolution—which enables the assembly itself to take up urgent issues of peace and security if the Security Council fails to reach a decision in regard to them owing to the use of the veto power. Not everyone accepts the validity of this resolution. The Eastern European countries, in particular, claim that it is contrary to the charter and therefore unconstitutional. The fact remains, however, that the procedure provided for in the resolution has been followed in a number of concrete cases—among which the cases of Suez and Hungary are conspicuous examples. Thus, the resolution constitutes an important link in a chain of developments which have had the effect, over the years, of gradually shifting the center of gravity of the United Nations from the Security Council, in which the framers of the charter intended that it should reside, to the General Assembly. The result is that it is before the General Assembly rather than the Security Council that most of the major issues of world politics today are brought to trial.

In the meantime, of course, the General Assembly itself has been changing radically, both in composition and in outlook. For one thing, it is far more representative of the world at large today than it was sixteen years ago. Its membership today is twice what it was then. And this increase in membership has inevitably been accompanied by marked changes in the relative voting strengths of the different geographical areas of the world. Of the original fifty-one members of the organization, thirty-two—an absolute majority—were countries of Western Europe, North America, and Latin America. Of the present membership of one hundred and one, forty-one are countries of this area, but no less than fifty-six—a much larger proportion of the total—are mostly neutral or uncommitted countries of Africa, Asia, and the Middle East. And an important consequence follows from this fact. It means that if the countries of the West have exerted a preponderant influence on the decisions of the assembly in the past, they must not be surprised if the assembly speaks more often with an Afro-Asian than a Western accent in the future.

And the difference may be appreciable. People in the West, and especially we Europeans, tend to think of the world situation primarily in terms of the East-West conflict and of problems directly connected with it, such as those of Berlin, German reunification, and European security in general. The countries of Asia and Africa, while they have no desire to become too closely involved in these problems, by no means minimize their importance. But they have problems of their own—problems such as those of racial discrimination, economic underdevelopment and the ending of colonialism—which in their eyes are of equal if not greater importance. Developments over the past sixteen years have made the General Assembly perhaps the most powerful medium of public opinion on the great problems of our times and the critical issues of international politics. It is only natural that the countries of Africa and Asia should seek to use the assembly to focus world attention primarily on the problems which are of the most immediate concern to them.

The existence within the framework of the United Nations of a great deliberative body such as the General Assembly, in which almost every independent country in the world has a voice, has certain undoubted advantages. Being as it is a great forum of free debate, something quite unique in world diplomacy, the assembly affords every government an opportunity to check its own views

and policies against the freely expressed views and policies of others. Moreover, it does tend to exert a moderating influence and to discourage extremism, because delegations trying to capture votes for their proposals invariably find themselves obliged to tone them down in order to secure the support of delegations which are more objectively minded or less emotionally engaged than themselves. The assembly also provides unrivaled opportunities for meetings and negotiations between leading statesmen of the different countries, as well as for that type of quiet diplomacy which, at more than one assembly, has enabled the United Nations to work out *ad hoc* techniques and solutions and, by so doing, to meet great and dangerous challenges.

But it is important not to harbor illusions or lose sight of realities. Great international problems can not be resolved simply by voting on them. No assembly resolution can settle the issue involved in the absence of means of enforcing it. And no enforcement action by the United Nations is practicable without agreement and co-operation between the major military powers. There is nothing to be gained by trying to ignore this basic reality. The fact that in the assembly every country, great or small, has an equal vote means that there is no necessary correspondence in its decisions between voting strength on the one hand and military power on the other. It is essential for the future of the United Nations that that situation should not be exploited or abused. If it were, the result might well put to an end the utility of the United Nations as an instrument for bringing about that measure of agreement and co-operation between the major powers which is and will remain the vital condition of world peace and security.

The United Nations is a living reality; it is also, in a sense, unfinished business. Within the limits assigned to it, it has already managed to achieve much. But it embodies the hopes of men and women everywhere that, in the course of time, it will manage to do more, until at long last the fear of war finally ceases to oppress mankind. To achieve that supreme objective, we need not only imagination, faith, and dogged determination, but wisdom, patience, charity, skill in the handling of men, and, above all, common sense. The great French foreign minister Aristide Briand was said to have been animated throughout his life by "the boldness of the dream tempered by the dictates of common sense." We might do worse than make the same concept the inspiration of our continuing efforts in the United Nations.

PREFACE

The sixteen years of the United Nations Organization's existence are in fact the history of the greatest revolution of all times. It did not start with the San Francisco U.N. Conference on International Organization, where the U.N. Charter was adopted. It did not start at Dumbarton Oaks, where the basic formulations of the principles which guide the international organization were framed. It did not start with the agreement at Yalta of the three major powers, who fought the Axis powers, to have an organization which would deliver humanity from "the scourge of war." It did not start even at the meetings between the wartime leaders of the two Anglo-Saxon nations, President Roosevelt and Prime Minister Churchill, when the Atlantic Charter was proclaimed.

The seeds of the revolution in mankind's history, in relations between nation and nation in solving disputes among themselves by means other than war, had been sown many years before. There were many milestones on the road to the United Nations: the Hague conferences, the Geneva conventions, the international organizations for specific purposes of international co-operation—and foremost of all, the League of Nations.

Admirers and opponents of the United Nations are united in their critical appraisal of the League of Nations. But nothing could change the fact that the League was the first attempt for world co-operation on an international basis, within the framework of a permanent organization, with the clear intent to make it universal to the highest possible degree. In its failure it left not only its concept, but also principles and even organizational forms, some of which were adopted by the United Nations Organization almost without changes.

Viewing from this vantage point of historical perspective the first sixteen years of the U.N., no measure of difficulties or imperfections could impair its importance from the point of view of progress in international relations, and from the point of view of the strivings of men, since time immemorial, to save humanity from the "scourge of war." The success which the United Nations has met, thus far, as compared with that of the League of Nations, justifies fully the beliefs and hopes humanity laid in the U.N. becoming an efficient instrument of international co-operation and conciliation. If not all the hopes bestowed on the U.N. at its inception have been fulfilled, and if even greater strains to its basic precepts are still ahead—as they seem really to be—it nevertheless remains the most noble effort of the human race to replace the language of guns with the language of arguments and persuasion.

It was the Italian philosopher Croce who created the basic theory that human progress follows the pattern of a spiral: after achieving certain heights, it drops back again to its starting point in order to begin from this point an even more accelerated pace toward new stages of perfection.

It is in this spirit that the author tried to review sixteen years of the existence of the world organization for peace. Even though the present stage of international affairs seems not to be best fitting for the expression of confidence in the United Nations, the experiences of the League—even in its failure—which led to the establishment of the United Nations Organization, are a sufficient reason to believe that in spite of all tribulations and obstacles, the ideas and idealism which inspired the League and the United Nations will remain a permanent factor, growing in importance, in the relations between nation and nation.

To make this historic review more vivid and convincing, to show the U.N. in action not only in words, but also in actual pictorial illustration, hundreds of photographs are used in this volume. Every important phase of U.N. activity, every section of the U.N. organization, every specialized agency, is here viewed within a double medium for the presentation of living human history—words and pictures.

The author feels highly indebted to the efficient and most co-operative members of the U.N. photo section, whose assistance and readiness to be of service was a most encouraging factor. The author wishes also to thank some of the U.N. officials who were of assistance in the search for material and sources, and who gave advice unsparingly when asked for it. The author would like to express his special thanks to his wife, Mrs. A. Rubin, for her assistance in checking the material and preparing the index in a most efficient way. He would also like to thank Acting Secretary-General U Thant and Ambassador Frederick H. Boland for their authoritative and interesting remarks presented in Forewords of this volume.

History is a matter of the past, but the history of the U.N. is more than that. It can be viewed as a base on which the future development of relations between nations will be anchored. If this book contributes, even if in a most moderate way, to the dissemination of information on the United Nations Organization, and if it thereby adds something to the efforts to make the U.N. idea convincing to the general public, the author will consider the labor invested in the preparation of this volume worth-while.

JACOB A. RUBIN

Pictorial History of the United Nations

FIRST ATTEMPTS AT WORLD CO-OPERATION

"The League is dead—long live the United Nations," exclaimed the moving voice of Lord Robert Cecil, one of Great Britain's most distinguished statesmen. This statement was made in front of representatives of thirty-four member states of the League of Nations who assembled on the morning of April 8, 1946, in Geneva at the Palace of Nations, to participate in the last assembly of the League.

This assembly was to perform only one function: to proclaim that the League was defunct and that her assets and tasks were to be forwarded to the heir of the League—the United Nations Organization. The eighty-two-year-old Lord Cecil did not deliver a eulogy. The man who inspired, with his vision, the first assembly of the League of Nations, spoke as movingly as he did some twenty-six years before, when he addressed the first assembly of the League. International co-operation, abolition of wars as an instrument of national policy, development of natural resources and their proper distribution among nations—these objectives ranked first in this speech, laden with vision and idealism. And these same objectives also ranked first when expounded emotionally twenty-seven years before, on a snowy and rainy

Palais des Nations, building of the assembly of the League of Nations, and part of the Secretariat Building (*on the left*).

St. Valentine's Day, February 14, 1919, by President Woodrow Wilson.

THE IDEA OF THE LEAGUE OF NATIONS

Even the phrases used by the two statesmen, though uttered over a quarter of a century apart, were almost identical. "A living thing is born," exclaimed President Wilson when he presented the draft of the Covenant of the League of Nations to the most august audience of those days—the plenary conference of the Allied powers assembled for the peace conference, which had to assure nations that there would be no more wars.

The Council Room of the Palais des Nations.

View of Sixth Commission room of the Palais des Nations.

The assembled listened with attention to the twenty-six articles of the covenant. Mrs. Wilson was specially invited to attend this historic gathering and watched her husband's inspiring features as he spoke. After President Wilson finished reading the covenant, the explanatory remarks about the covenant, and the ideas from which the League was born, his wife was the first to break the tense silence with applause.

President Wilson had reasons enough to speak in a mood of self-reliance and exuberance. Here he was, standing first among victors in a global war and proclaiming the implementation of an idea, which, in his opinion, opened a new era in man's life and in relations between nation and nation. Only about a year before, on January 8, 1918, he stood before the U.S. Congress and sounded America's voice of leadership for a better world. And here, after only thirteen months and six days, the most cherished dreams of humanity were presented

in the form of a binding international treaty, to become the guiding beacon of humanity. The last of his fourteen points, fourteen principles for the organization of the postwar world, took practical shape. It read, "A general association of nations must be formed under specific covenants for the purpose of affording mutual guarantees of political independence and territorial integrity to great and small States alike."

President Wilson knew that this was not a completely new idea. There were many of fame who dreamed about having nations accept some kind of order in international relations of the sort individuals have evolved within the organization of states. Dante, Sully, William Penn, Abbé de St. Berre, Rousseau, Bentham, Kant—all have in some form expressed one view that organization of relations between nations, based upon certain unchangeable principles, is not only worth-while, but necessary for the well-being of humanity, and unavoidable in the long perspective of history. Even practical, diplomatic solutions for co-operation between states were not lacking. The "European concert" after the Napoleonic wars implied in itself quite a specific form of organization for the prevention of wars of conquest, and the first international organ invested with some powers of control over individual national administrations, the Danube Commission, was set up as early as 1856 by the Paris Conference.

Nine years later, international organizations for co-operation in specific fields of human endeavor were established: the International Telegraphic Union (1865), the Universal Postal Union, the Interparliamentary Union (1889), The Pan-American Union for Increasing Inter-American Commerce, the International Federation of Trade Unions (1901), the International Institute of Agriculture in Rome (1905), the International Health Office in Paris (1907), not to mention such an outspoken international establishment as the Second Socialist International.

President Wilson knew that these efforts in the direction of international co-operation had been supplemented, in 1898, by a bold proposal of Tsar Nicholas II of Russia, who suggested a conference of all powers possessing diplomatic representatives in Petersburg for the purpose of "assuring all

Library reading room of the Palais des Nations.

peoples the benefit of a real and durable peace, and above all, of putting an end to the progressive developments of the present armament"—a proposal which resulted in the Hague Conference of 1899 and the signing of a Convention for the Pacific Settlement of International Disputes and the establishment of the Permanent Court of Arbitration.

This was not an isolated effort. Eight years later, again on the initiative of the Tsar, a second peace conference was held in Hague. The conference decided to assemble automatically again after eight years, without direct initiative of the caller. And in his native country, the scholar-President could have recalled the League of Nations Societies, as he certainly knew about the British League of Nations Society founded in May, 1915, and was no doubt familiar with the book of the French scholar-statesman Leon Bourgeois, *Société des Nations,* published in 1908. In addition to all these manifestations of growing public sentiment for some form of international organization for peace,

President Wilson must have kept well in mind Theodore Roosevelt's address to the Nobel committee of May 5, 1910: "Finally, it would be a master stroke if those great powers bent on peace would form a league of peace, not only to keep the peace among themselves, but to prevent by force, if necessary, its being broken by others."

Although the United States was not yet involved in World War I, the contending American parties competing for the presidency in 1916 agreed to advocate policies, endorsed by their leaders, for the promotion of an international organization for peace. A great public meeting held in Washington in May, 1916, by the "League to Enforce Peace," local chapters of which were flourishing all over the States, was a bipartisan affair, as it was addressed by the President, Woodrow Wilson, and Henry Cabot Lodge, leader of the Republicans in the Senate.

WILSON'S FOURTEEN POINTS

This unanimity of purpose certainly animated President Wilson's resolve to have the ideas of an organization for peace turned into reality. From

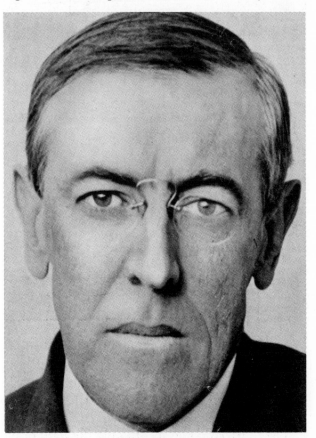

Woodrow Wilson (1856–1924).

The "Big Four" of World War I, left to right: Orlando of Italy, Lloyd George of the United Kingdom, Clemenceau of France, and President Wilson.

advocating peaceful solutions of conflicts among nations pronounced from the pedestal of an observing power, the United States became a partner in the world struggle. After entering the war on the side of the Allies, in August, 1917, the United States could not only express its pious wishes and suggest its good offices and advice, but, also, it could use its overwhelming influence to assure that the postwar world would set a course toward peace, and that the prevention of wars would become not only a wish, but also a reality. In this full consciousness of historic responsibility and opportunity, President Wilson formulated his famous fourteen points for a better world.

The address which expounded the fourteen points was a revolution in the whole concept of American national policy. It was a declaration of departure from the traditional tenets of American isolationism. One of the opposition papers stated, "In a single speech he [President Wilson] has transformed the whole character and broken with all the tradition of American policy. . . . Today as never before, the whole nation marches with the President certain alike of the leader and the cause."

The fourteen points mentioning the right of nations to self-determination, and the enthusiastic endorsement of the revolutionary policy of the President of the United States was a true expression of the basic lines of thinking in the Allied camp. Three days before President Wilson's address, in another capital of another major ally, a similar plan for solution of world problems after the war was voiced. British Prime Minister Lloyd George, speaking before delegates of trade unions about the war aims of his government said: "First, the sanctity of treaties must be re-established; secondly a territorial settlement secured, based on the right of self-determination or consent of the governed, and lastly we must seek creation of some international organization to limit the burden of armaments and diminish the danger of war."

SHAPING THE ORGANIZATIONAL FORMS OF THE LEAGUE

There seemed to be a widespread meeting of minds among the Allies. A member of the British War Cabinet, the leader of the South African Dominion, Field Marshal Jan Smuts, did not limit himself to expressions of favor for the idea of an international organization for peace, but prepared a pamphlet which outlined in detail the implementation of the idea: *The League of Nations—a Practical Suggestion*. The League should be thought of, Smuts wrote in this pamphlet, "not only as a possible means of preventing future wars, but much more as a great organ of the ordinary peaceful life of civilization, as the foundation of the new international system which will be erected on the ruins of this war. . . . The greatest opportunity in history would be met by the greatest step forward in the government of men."

Even details for the organization of the organs of the League were included in Smuts's pamphlet. He suggested a council of nine members to represent all great powers and stressed explicitly that to give this institution real political weight it should consist of prime ministers or foreign ministers, and that at least one annual meeting should be attended by them all.

In this general atmosphere of strivings for world co-operation, and on his arrival in Paris as the head of the United States delegation to the peace conference, President Wilson had no special difficulty getting the League idea into the center of political attention of the conference.

On January 28, 1919, a plenary session of representatives of thirty-two states and dominions adopted a resolution about the League and appointed a committee to be headed by President Wilson. Together with his closest associate, Colonel

Léon Bourgeois, a leading French statesman, and one of the founders of the League of Nations.

House, whose short figure was soon to become the most familiar personality in the chambers of peace diplomacy, President Wilson set out for a killing

In World War I, President Wilson appeared at war rallies with Franklin D. Roosevelt (*standing, right*), his assistant secretary of the Navy, who later became an architect of the U.N.

pace of consultations for the preparation of the League's covenant.

Together with the other members of the committee, Lord Cecil and Field Marshal Smuts for the British Empire, Leon Bourgeois for France, Roman Dmowski for Poland and Venizelos for Greece, President Wilson accomplished the almost impossible. After ten meetings, totaling about thirty hours of working time, a constitution for the entire world was put in its first shape. And these were not working days completely devoted to the League. The committee used to meet after a day's work at the peace conference to discuss the paragraphs of the covenant. They worked until the late hours of the night, and even the early hours of the morning. The spacious quarters of Colonel House, Room 315 of the Hotel Crillon, a magnificent building overlooking the pride of Paris planning—Place de la Concorde (the Square of Accord)—served as the meeting place of the committee.

There was reason for the speed with which the committee worked. It was President Wilson's contention, fully supported by other members of the committee, that to assure the acceptance of the League idea and its existence, it was necessary to make the covenant of the League an integral part of the peace treaty, something which should be so interwoven within the framework of peace arrangements, that nothing could be done to extricate it from the general solutions of problems of the postwar world.

The general propositions of the League—collective security, arbitration, economic and social cooperation, reduction of armaments, and open diplomacy—had to become effective through the creation of a great international organization, charged with the duty of applying them and invested with powers necessary to that end.

The proposed draft of the covenant included not only the ideas of Field Marshal Smuts. One of Smuts's central ideas about the protection of national minorities was included in the covenant, and became later one of the most controversial and

President Wilson arrives in Europe for the peace conference with the blueprint of the League of Nations.

The Wilsons and Colonel House in Paris.

strife-inducing problems which kept the League busy, but also gave protection for minorities which wanted to struggle against the suppression of their rights. The second idea, that of entrusting the League with the function of supervision and guidance of territories which were to become the beneficiaries of the adoption of principles of self-determination of nations, was also a brainchild of Smuts to which President Wilson gladly and quickly subscribed. The new states to arise on the ruins of the dismembered three empires, Austria-Hungary, Tsarist Russia, and Ottoman Turkey, were understood to be deficient in the qualities of statehood. Their guidance, believed Smuts, should fall to the League, and not to the conquerors, the bled-white victors of the war. Of all leagues, wrote Smuts, which made up former empires, only the British Commonwealth remained "the embryo league of nations based on true principles of national freedom and decentralized political federation. Europe is being liquidated and the League of Nations must be the heir to this great estate."

Wilson was attracted to this idea. It was shaped into the form of mandates and a special body, within the League, to supervise the implementation of the trust vested in victorious powers to administer these territories until they reached a stage when they would be ripe for complete independence. Wilson believed that this would give the League some specific and important task from the very start. Perhaps he remembered that the American Union had been held together from 1781 to 1789 in part because the weak government under the Articles of Confederation was charged with the trusteeship of a vast area of public lands.

The Wilson enthusiasm so fully complemented by that of Smuts was not dampened by the rather skeptical attitude of the French "Tiger," Clemenceau. The Wilsonian vision was completely acceptable for him, but the French did not look for visions, but for firm guarantees of the security of their nation before another attack by their neighbor on the east, the Germans. Wilson appeared to him too much of an idealist and too much obsessed with the idea of the League as such to talk to him in practical terms. Clemenceau preferred Wilson's able and devoted lieutenant, Colonel House, before whom he once confided: "I can get on with you. You are practical. I understand you, but talking to Wilson is something like talking to Jesus Christ." In another confession of skepticism about the practicality of Wilson's idealistic approach to international problems, Clemenceau said: "God gave ten Commandments and we broke them. Wilson gives us fourteen points. We shall see."

UNITED STATES OPPOSITION TO WILSON'S LEAGUE

But the real test for Wilson's plans was yet to come. While the President of the United States was in Paris struggling to have the League shaped

Paul Hymans, Belgian statesman, co-founder of the League, and president of the first session of the assembly of the League.

President Wilson returns from France.

in his image and fully interwoven into the peace treaties, clouds started to gather on the home front. A cable of twenty-six Democratic members of the Massachusetts Legislature calling President Wilson to come home to reduce the cost of living ". . . which we consider far more important than the League of Nations," was one of the minor signs of the difficulties the opposition started to shape against Wilson's League of Nations and United States involvement in it. "I decline to set up any Government greater than the Government of the United States of America," argued Senator Reed of Missouri; and Republican Senate leader Henry Cabot Lodge, who had only recently manifested openly his support for the conception of a League, started a campaign of criticism which was clearly aimed at the working of the entire structure of the League which President Wilson so laboriously put together.

Personal animosity and partisanship played quite an important role in this development. It is certainly characteristic of this kind of feeling, Senator Lodge suggested, that the amendments to the original draft of the League's covenant also numbered fourteen, a kind of symbolic countermeasure to Wilson's fourteen points. And when on March 4, 1919 Senator Lodge published a document, the so-called "Round Robin," signed by thirty-nine senators and representatives, everybody understood that a deathblow was aimed at the League, or at least at complete United States involvement in it. The *New York Sun* rejoiced, writing, "Woodrow Wilson's League of Nations died in the Senate tonight." In the same tone another paper wrote about the "League of Denationalized Nations."

Although the Round Robin announced first to the Paris conference and then to the world that the signatories, thirty-nine senators and representatives, did not find the covenant acceptable "in form now proposed," Wilson refused to change even one phrase in the covenant's wording. The reservations quoted by the opponents of the League concentrated basically on the following amendments to be introduced into the covenant: (1) the right to refuse the acceptance of a mandate, (2) exemption of domestic questions, especially questions as to immigration and tariffs, from the League's jurisdiction, (3) the procedure and right of withdrawal, and (4) a reservation safeguarding the Monroe Doctrine. Special opposition was voiced against article ten which reads: "The members of the League undertake to respect and preserve as against external aggression the territorial integrity and existing political independence of all members of the League. In case of any such aggression or in case of any threat or danger of such aggression the Council shall advise upon the means by which this obligation shall be fulfilled."

Of course some of the amendments were completely acceptable to Wilson and some were immaterial, as the covenant provided for them anyway—but in the heated atmosphere of partisan contest, not reason counted, but the will to have one's argument, one's point of view, prevailing. The Wilson idealism was supplemented by a public romanticism which the President proudly proclaimed: "If I think it is right to accept it I shall do so regardless of consequences. As for myself I can go down in a cyclone cellar and write poetry the rest of my days, if necessary."

Formally, President Wilson had the country's public opinion behind him. In an inquiry sent to all newspapers in the United States by the *Literary Digest,* asking, "Do you favor the proposed League of Nations?" 718 answered Yes; 181, No; and 478 were in favor under certain conditions. As far as circulation was concerned: 9,886,449, Yes; 4,326,-882, No; 6,792,461, conditional. But the Senate majority, forty-nine Republicans, and the Senate majority leader Lodge, were not impressed by this show of popular support for Wilson's policies on the League. A witty remark of those days defined well the situation: "The President proposes, the Senate disposes, while the country dozes." Nothing was left but to go to the people. Wilson was ready for the fight. "I am ready to fight from now until all the fight has been taken out of me by death, and redeem the faith and promises of the U.S."

Wilson went on a tour of the country to mobilize support for his program. It was a grueling undertaking. Eight thousand miles of travel, innumerable conferences, a dozen or so wearying parades, thirty-six set speeches, averaging an hour in length, to say nothing about rear platform addresses at almost every stop. The reception was enthusiastic, the applause unforgettable. It strengthened Wilson's belief in the righteousness of his vision: "I would rather lose in a cause that I know someday will triumph, than triumph in a cause that I know someday will lose."

But the tension was too demanding. In the midst of this tour the President was stricken and incapacitated. The great cause lost its great fighter. Wilson's resounding appeal "Dare we to reject it [the League] and break the heart of the world?" did not change the opinion of the League's opponents. The opposing Senators proudly paraded the names they had been called because of their opposition to the covenant—"bitter enders" and "battalion of death"—and finally triumphed, thanks to parliamentary maneuvers and President Wilson's unfailing faithfulness to the original version of the covenant, in which he was not ready to accept any compromise, any amendment.

If one takes into account the reawakening moods of isolationism in the United States, the picture becomes clear: the United States of America, the country which proclaimed the League's idea, the country which used all its prestige and influence to have other skeptics of international co-operation support the idea and work for its implementation, was the first country to abandon the idea when implemented. One paper hastened to comment: "Until the League proves itself we had better beat our swords into convertible plowshares." And the Senate majority report boasted: "The other nations will take us on our own terms, for without us their League is a wreck and their gains from a victorious peace are imperiled."

FIRST STAGES OF THE LEAGUE'S ACTIVITY

It took nineteen years to find out whether the assertion of the United States Senate majority would turn out to be correct. The covenant was an integral part of the Treaty of Versailles, section I, with its final text adopted April 28, 1919. A unanimous decision of the peace conference stated in its preamble:

Signing the peace treaty after World War I at the Hall of Mirrors, Versailles.

The High Contracting Parties, in order to promote international co-operation and to achieve international peace and security by the acceptance of obligations not to resort to war, by the prescription of open, just and honorable relations between nations, by the firm establishment of the understandings of international law as the actual rule of conduct among governments, and by the maintenance of justice and a scrupulous respect for all treaty obligations in the dealings of organized people with one another, agree to this Covenant.

The League could not begin to function formally and officially until the treaty came into effect. This did not happen until January 10, 1920, and that date is therefore the official birthday of the League.

Many formal problems had already been solved and many had still to wait for time and experience to determine the solutions. The "Body of Delegates," the name for the assembly of representatives of all member states, was changed in the final draft into Assembly (which was supposed to meet each year in September), and Executive Council was changed to Council (which normally met thrice yearly).

Similarly, the names of other organs of the League: the Mandates Commission, the Committee on Intellectual Co-operation, and the Secretariat were finally established. Thirty-two Allied states and dominions and thirteen neutral states had the right to become the original members of the League, which provided for admission of new members by a two-thirds majority of the assembly and for the withdrawal on a two years' notice. A director general, later called secretary general, was appointed. Mr. Eric Drummond, a career official of the British Foreign Office, was entrusted with the important task of organizing the League, of translating the stipulations of the covenant into practical forms for an international organization. One hundred thousand pounds sterling was the first budget put at the disposal of the secretary general. The League had no place to be housed, no civil service to run its offices and its agencies.

Even the city of the permanent seat of the League had yet to be chosen, with Brussels, competing unrelentingly with Geneva to become the seat of the League's headquarters. No time could have been lost. The Hotel National in Geneva, Switzerland, with two hundred rooms, was bought for 5.5 million francs and on November 1, 1920, the secretary general and his small staff took possession of the hotel. They were left with only a very short time to prepare for the opening of the first General Assembly at which forty-two delegations were to participate.

The agenda of the assembly mirrored truly the scope of problems the League intended to deal with: (1) general organization, (2) economic, social and technical work, (3) establishment of a permanent court, (4) budget and staff, (5) admission of new members, and (6) mandates and disarmament.

The five weeks of the first assembly session did not solve many problems but laid the foundation for the League's activities. The first formal budget, for May, 1919 through December 31, 1920, for the League and the International Labor Organization (ILO) in the amount of 550,000 pounds sterling, was almost doubled for the coming year and put at 1,060,000 sterling.

But this growth in budgetary expenses was not progressing geometrically. Economy was rather the rule of the day. Within the years of the League's functioning from 1920 until 1939 the average annual cost of the League, ILO, Permanent Court, including the cost of building of the Palais des Nations, amounted to about 27 million gold francs, or about $5,400,000.

THE MANDATES

The League had, from the start, to undertake certain functions which gave it direct administrative tasks in certain territories. A direct responsibility for the administration of territories was one of the specific features of the international organization at the very beginning of its existence, something which the United Nations' role in the Congo, for instance, resembles only in a very slight degree. The Saar region was directly ad-

Ninety-first extraordinary session of the League's council at St. James Palace, London (March, 1936).

The one hundredth session of the council, in the new Council Room (January, 1938). Mustafa Adle of Iran presides.

Pierre Laval, French foreign minister, addresses assembly session.

Sir Eric Drummond, first secretary general of the League, and organizer of its secretariat as well as of its entire machinery.

ministered by the League's commissioner who had executive powers, and the Free City of Danzig also had a League commissioner. These two functions beset the League at the very outset with problems which its opponents used as a proof that ultimately the League was bound to become a kind of superstate, or supergovernment.

But in the framework of postwar problems, this was rather a less acute one. National upheavals swept all over Europe. Nations which drew hope and encouragement from the principles of self-determination proclaimed by President Wilson and implemented in the League's covenant, declared their independence. The first to do this were some of the nations conquered by Tsarist Russia and incorporated into the Russian empire as the Ukraine, Azerbaijan, Georgia, and Armenia. All of them looked to the League as a guarantor of their newly won independence, but could not be helped as they were overrun and reincorporated into Russia—this time by the victorious Red Army. The empires which had lost their territories were the German and Ottoman and their administra-

The first session of the assembly of the League (November, 1920).

Some leading diplomats of the League, left to right: Thanassis Aghnides, undersecretary of the League; Nicolas Politis, foreign minister of Greece; Arthur Henderson, foreign secretary of the United Kingdom; and Edward Beneš, foreign minister and later president of Czechoslovakia.

tion was entrusted, in the name of the League, to the victorious Allied powers. The system of mandated territories, put under the administration of the Allied powers with Great Britain and France as the chief benefactor of this solution, had to provide the form of fulfilling one of the basic principles adopted at the conclusion of World War I, that there would be no annexation of territories and no rule without the consent of the people. Article 22 of the covenant stated that "countries inhabited by peoples not yet able to stand by themselves under the strenuous conditions of the modern world," were to be entrusted to "advanced nations."

According to the stage of their development the parts of the Ottoman empire in Asia and the German colonies in Africa and the Pacific were divided into three categories: "A," mandated terri-

tories, the most developed of which had to gain their independence quickly; "B," mandated territories in need of a longer period of tutelage; and "C," territories inhabited by primitive people, who had to pass various stages of development before they could be considered ripe for self-determination.

Of the A-territories, Iraq was the first to achieve independence. The mandate of Palestine, although formally in the A-category had to be administered in accordance with provisions which obliged the mandatory power, Great Britain, to take such steps as would be necessary to facilitate the establishment of a Jewish National Home. The fact that the mandatory power was obliged to submit annual reports on the administration of the mandated territories served as a kind of precaution against the League's trust being turned unscrupulously into an outright annexation—although not once were the recommendations of the League's Mandate Commission left completely unheeded or only formally implemented.

The mandates nullified, as Wilson had hoped, his worries that the League was in danger of becoming a body without practical tasks which would keep it alive. But the worry as such proved unjustified. Within its nineteen years of existence the League never was in need of some "issue" to make its existence a vivid component of the international scene.

Unfortunately crises were in abundance. The fate of the Armenians and the Armenian Republic, which was envisaged as a coming mandated territory to be administered by the United States; the Turkish-Greek war and its aftermath, the mass refugee problem, involving about half a million Greeks who had to leave Asia Minor and resettled in Greece (one of the glorious accomplishments of the refugee commissioner); the permanently smoldering conflict between the republics of Poland and Lithuania over Wilna, which always threatened to erupt into open, armed conflict; the never ending complaints of national minorities in Europe which took the covenant's provisions for the protection of their national rights seriously and demanded action from the League, which had not always been forthcoming, although the League had always provided a public forum for the airing of complaints and must have curbed the nationalistic fervor of the majority nations; the grand-scale economic rescue operations which saved Austria, Hungary, and Greece from complete economic collapse and had put those countries on their way to economic recovery—all these and many other

Opening session of the assembly of the League (September, 1924). The British delegation—Premier MacDonald, Lord Parmoor, and Arthur Henderson—is in the center.

How the cost of the League is apportioned

THE SCALE FOR 1926

Albania	1	Ethiopia		Norway	9
Argentine	29	(Abyssinia)	2	Panama	1
Australia	27	Finland	10	Paraguay	1
Austria	8	France	79	Persia	5
Belgium	18	Greece	7	Peru	5
Bolivia	4	Guatemala	1	Poland	32
Brazil	29	Haiti	1	Portugal	6
British Empire	105	Honduras	1	Roumania	22
Bulgaria	5	Hungary	8	Salvador	1
Canada	35	India	56	Kingdom of the	
Chile	14	Irish Free State	10	Serbs, Croats	
China	46	Italy	60	and Slovenes	20
Colombia	6	Japan	60	Siam	9
Costa Rica	1	Latvia	3	South Africa	13
Cuba	9	Liberia	1	Spain	40
Czechoslovakia	29	Lithuania	4	Sweden	18
Denmark	12	Luxembourg	1	Switzerland	17
Dominican		Netherlands	23	Uruguay	7
Republic	1	New Zealand	10	Venezuela	5
Esthonia	3	Nicaragua	1		937

The sum authorized to be raised from contributions by members being $4,424,542.31, $\frac{1}{937}$ of that amount $4,722.03 = the unit of contributions.

The scale of contributions to the League budget for 1926.

operations had put the League to tests which it passed with outstanding achievements.

REDUCTION OF ARMAMENTS

There had been one paramount issue which absorbed the League from its very beginning: the reduction of armaments. In this respect the League's covenant did not indulge in enthusiastic idealism. It did not speak about complete disarmament. Article eight authorized the council to formulate plans for the reduction of armaments, and article nine provided for a permanent commission on military, naval, and air problems. Not only on problems concerning armaments had the authors of the Covenant demonstrated earthbound realism. Although articles ten and eleven had dealt with the preservation of territorial integrity and measures against external aggression directed against members of the League—making any war or threat of war a matter of concern of the entire League, to result in the League taking action which it deemed wise and effectual in safeguarding the peace of nations—article twelve did not exclude a declaration of war. Although members of the League were bound to submit disputes to arbitration or to inquiry by the council, nonetheless this article stipulated that members of the League "agree in no case to resort to war until three months after the award by the arbitrators or the report by the Council."

The efforts for the limitation of armaments seemed to become a kind of bridge to bring the League closer to the power from whence it originated—the United States of America. On July 7, 1921 an announcement from the White House revealed that consultations with Great Britain, France, Italy, and Japan were in progress concerning the holding in Washington of a conference to consider limitation of armaments. On August 11, formal invitations had been issued.

The Washington Disarmament Conference, which lasted from November, 1921 till February, 1922, brought about an agreement concerning limitations of naval armament (seventy capital ships were scrapped, including thirty of the United States) while land and air armaments were not touched. But even this limited agreement was not too lasting and the late thirties saw an intense rivalry in building of new vessels of war, with Italy demanding parity with France and with France withdrawing from the agreement, renewed later, in 1930, in the London treaty.

This was not an isolated effort for the reduction of armaments. A Temporary Mixed Committee for Reduction of Armaments was established. A Preparatory Committee for the Disarmament Conference came into being. From 1922 to 1933 the question of disarmament became central among the aims and activities of the League. Members of the League looked to the council to draw up a general plan for arms reduction. During these consultations an interesting plan was suggested by Lord Esher. According to this plan military forces had to be reckoned by units of thirty thousand men of all ranks, of which France was to retain six, Italy and Poland four, etc.

The negotiating powers included first of all those very powers which were on the Allies' side during the war. Germany was the first example of disarmament, even though an imposed one, and Soviet Russia was still occupied by internal upheavals in the wake of the October revolution. If one takes into consideration that the disarmament negotiations were in fact conducted between Allied powers, the results achieved could not be considered too encouraging.

Women at the League of Nations, left to right: Dr. Kristine Bonnevie, substitute, Norway; Anna Bugge-Wicksell, substitute, Sweden; Henni Forchhammer, technical expert, Denmark.

During the negotiations, two basic problems—*arbitration* and *security*—emerged as the conditioning factors of any disarmament, or rather arms reduction agreement. This was the sequence *arbitration, security,* and *disarmament.* A draft of a general disarmament treaty prepared by a commission of the League and submitted finally in 1930 after five years of negotiations ran into opposition from various governments. It provided not only for limitations of military personnel and military aircraft, but also for the limitation of the total military expenditure.

The Geneva protocol was a highly ingenious, and in the opinion of many, successful attempt to translate into a formal system the formula of arbitration, security, and disarmament. The manufacture of poison gas for use in war was given special attention. During these deliberations, the representative of Soviet Russia, M. Litvinov, remarked in 1927, two years after the start of discussions on disarmament, that the Soviet Union had no confidence in what was done till then. Litvinov brought before the assembled the first version of the Russian "total and complete dis-

armament" repeated after thirty-three years by the Russian Premier Khrushchev at the United Nations. If disarmament is desired, stated Litvinov "let all military, naval, and air forces be disbanded, all arms, warships and war planes destroyed and let us have no weapons except those in the hands of police and custom services of each State."

As this statement was made, the Treaty of Locarno, a series of mutual security agreements between Great Britain, France, Italy, Germany, Poland, and Czechoslovakia had already been signed (October 16, 1925) and the Russian proposal did not receive serious consideration.

Another disarmament effort was made when a disarmament conference was held in Geneva, on February 2, 1932. All sixty-four recognized states of that time, except for the smallest Latin American republics, were present. Again the problem of security was the stumbling block. France refused to disarm unless guaranteed security. Developments in Germany have fully justified France's point of view. Germany withdrew from the League; German rearmament started, leaving

Professor William Rappard, director of the Mandate Commission of the League.

The third session of the assembly (September, 1922). W. S. Fielding of Canada presides.

no doubts what the future held. After several adjournments the conference reached a deadlock and adjourned for the last time in 1934.

There were some United States initiatives in this field: the Kellogg-Briand Pact for the Renunciation of War, signed in Paris, August 2, 1928, and later, in June, 1932, President Hoover's proposal for the abolition of specifically offensive weapons and reduction of the rest by one third. But the tide had already turned and the arms race was in full swing.

PRELUDE TO WORLD WAR II

The failure to reduce armaments was not the only failure of the League. The Japanese aggression against China in 1931 had put the League machinery in motion, but unhappily the means of communication of those days made the immediate arrival on the scene of the League's commission of inquiry, under Lord Lyttelton, impossible, and at the commission's arrival the aims of the aggression were almost an accomplished fact. The rise of Hitler to power, which started the rapid rearmament of Germany, and the seizure of the Ruhr district and its remilitarization, shook the League to its foundations. And when it rose in

1935 to defend the victim of Mussolini's aggression, the kingdom of Ethiopia, whose emperor Haile Selassie came personally to Geneva to arouse the world, many thought and hoped that the aggressor would be stopped by concerted action of the League's members.

Resolutions short of military intervention were adopted. Economic sanctions preventing the delivery of strategic goods to Italy were voted. But this first collective action against an aggressor under the covenant collapsed soon afterward, revealing the League's incapability of punishing lawlessness and aggression. Civil war in Spain, Hitler's threats of war, and aggressions ending in conquest of free cities and countries such as Memel, Danzig, Austria, Czechoslovakia—all these acts of aggression were accomplished without the League being ready or able to act against them.

The only action considered feasible in the given state of affairs—the expulsion of the aggressor from the League—was made immaterial through the acts of the aggressors who left the League ostentatiously, slamming the door behind them with contempt.

It is an amazing proof of how deeply the League was identified with peace and its preservation, that

Sixth Commission (Political) under the chairmanship of P. Hymans of Belgium, at the fourth session of the assembly of the League.

even the people who wrecked the League and set the world afire—the leaders of Nazi Germany—saw in their decision to leave the League the turning point in the history of their nation toward military adventures. In burning Berlin, a few days before his suicide, Hitler's right-hand man, Goebbels, said to Fritzsche: "After all, the German people did not want it otherwise. The people, by a great majority, decided through a plebiscite on the withdrawal from the League of Nations and against a policy of yielding, and chose instead a policy of courage and honor; thereby the German people themselves chose the war which they have now lost." There was only one aggressor whom the League expelled: Soviet Russia was voted out of membership in the League after its aggression against the little republic of Finland, late in 1939.

The League, already beleaguered by the declared war in Europe, but not yet completely paralyzed, made a last effort to prove its worth. Poland did not appeal to the League after the German attack, and so when Finland lodged an appeal against the Russian aggression on December 2, 1939, Secretary General Avenol called the council on December 9, and the assembly was convened on December 11. On December 14, the

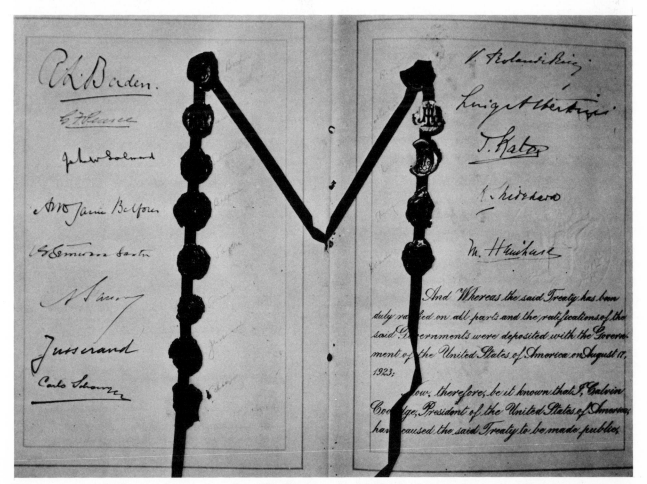

Treaty on naval disarmament, signed in Washington in 1922. At this conference, called by the United States, the United States and the United Kingdom agreed to keep their navies down to 525,000 tons of combat ships. Japan agreed to 515,000 tons and France and Italy to 175,000 tons each.

Secretary of State Hughes signs the treaties on the limitation of naval armaments. They were brought about by the administration of President Harding who was elected on a platform that opposed the United States' joining the League.

council exercised for the first and only time in its history the power granted it under article 16—to exclude from the League a member which violated the covenant. No member voted against, but a considerable number abstained (seven out of fourteen members of the council).

These final and tragic hours of the League's existence were preceded by many acts of international co-operation (in addition to the successful solution of many political problems which helped to avoid wars). These acts cannot be discounted in determining the value of the League's activities. Invaluable work was done by various agencies of the League in the field of social progress, combating of diseases, technical assistance, and cultural co-operation. The Committee on Intellectual Co-operation, which was composed of the greatest minds of those times, and which was presided over by the great French philosopher Henri Bergson, together with such personalities as Madame Curie and Professor Albert Einstein; the International Labor Organization; the International Court—all of these organizations became a foundation for future endeavors in the field of international co-operation, which was to mature in the U.N. era.

Organizational forms and many rules of procedure of the League proved to be of lasting importance since they were later copied almost

unchanged into the framework of the United Nations Organization. The council with its permanent members, the great powers Great Britain France, Italy, and Japan, and with the vacated and never-filled seat of the United States of America, adjusted itself to changing conditions. In 1926 the membership of the council was raised from ten to fourteen with Germany attaining the status of a permanent member and the number of elected members of the council being increased from six to nine. The provision allowing re-election introduced a new kind of permanent member of the council: one which was elected, but permanent *de facto*. The tenth assembly of the League opened in September, 1929, and was attended by representatives of fifty-three delegations, with thirty prime ministers and foreign ministers present. Looking at this assembly from the background of present-day developments, this was rather a history-making assembly. India's delegation was for the first time led by an Indian and this delegate, together with the delegate of Persia (Iran) demanded that the assembly begin to think seriously about Asia.

Sixteenth session of the assembly of the League (September, 1935). In the presidential chair is Beneš of Czechoslovakia. At his left is Secretary General Avenol.

The laying of the cornerstone for the permanent quarters of the League, which took place in that year (the building was finished only after seven years, in 1936, when the Secretariat moved into its own quarters), was intended to symbolize the permanence of the world organization, from which only two states permanently stayed out— the United States of America and Saudi Arabia.

The first plenary session of the Five Power Conference opened in the Locarno Room of the Foreign Office (1935). Stanley Baldwin, British prime minister, opened the conference, and is seen here at the extreme left behind the first microphone.

As far as other states were concerned, the membership in the League could be compared with a revolving door—states joined the League, left it, and rejoined it as they pleased.

But even in this unstable state of affairs the League was a center of diplomatic contacts, of permanent efforts for easing of world tensions, and quite often for the solution of problems which either already had turned into military conflagrations, or were on the verge of becoming a threat to peace and security. One and a half billion people were represented in the League membership, which reached a peak of fifty-eight states. The delegations to the League of Nations had turned by 1932 into permanent diplomatic missions, with all the organizational forms of a diplomatic corps. They had a dean of the corps, and requested the

secretary general to receive them at regular intervals as a corporate body.

Sir Eric Drummond, the secretary general, became an institution in himself. During the thirteen years of his office (1920-1933) Drummond symbolized stability, faithfulness to the principles of the covenant, and objectivity in most trying circumstances. His successor, Avenol, had to encounter the most difficult period of the League, when war became rather the regular state of affairs all over the world, with the League in the position of an outside observer.

The withdrawal of Germany from the League in October, 1933 signaled the coming of an era of increasing international tension which erupted finally into World War II. The fact that three months after Germany's withdrawal, Stalin ex-

THE COST OF ARMAMENTS

The Nations of the world are annually expending on military, naval and air forces, a sum equivalent to

2.700.000.000 dollars U.S.A.

The League of Nations budget averages 4.500,000 dollars U.S.A.

The world expenditure on armaments in a single year would support the League of Nations for six hundred and thirty years.

The rising clamor for disarmament and for putting expenses for armaments to better use, was echoed in the League's efforts at visual illustration of the problem. In this photograph, cost of armaments is compared with cost of supporting the League of Nations.

Principal delegates of Russia to the conference on reparations in Genoa (1922). From left: Maksim Litvinov, later Russia's first representative in the League, and long-time Russian foreign minister; and Worowsky and Joffe, leading members of the Communist hierarchy.

pressed readiness to support the League, and that Russia joined the League, in September, 1934, did not turn the League into a more potent instrument for the preservation of peace.

January, 1940, witnessed the last appeal to turn the League into a practical instrument against aggression. In that month, Churchill asked European neutrals whether they might not do their duty by

Sir Austen Chamberlain, a most ardent supporter of the League. As British secretary for Foreign Affairs, he was instrumental in bringing about the signing, in 1925, of the Locarno treaties, and was awarded the 1925 Nobel Peace Prize.

Joseph Avenol, the second and last secretary general of the League of Nations.

First session of the council of the League, Quai d'Orsay Palace (January, 1920).

Signing of the Locarno Pact. Left to right: Dino Grandi (*with beard*), Italy; Hans Luther (*wearing glasses*), Germany; Benito Mussolini (*seated in background*), Italy; Gustave Stresemann (*facing camera in front and to right of Mussolini*), Germany; Sir Austen Chamberlain (*wearing monocle*), England; and (*seated at table, extreme right, with cigarette*) Aristide Briand, France.

President Hoover in the historic East Room of the White House proclaims before representatives of the nations of the world the coming into force of the Kellogg-Briand Treaty, renouncing war as an instrument of national policy.

Wilson's contribution to the first attempts at organized international co-operation was perpetuated in many ways all over the world. Shown here is a plaque in Wilson's memory in front of the Palais Wilson in Geneva. This building is today the headquarters of the International Telecommunication Union. The plaque reads, "In memory of Woodrow Wilson, President of the United States, founder of the League of Nations."

Aristide Briand, French foreign minister, signs the Kellogg-Briand Pact. The pact was signed by fifteen nations in Paris (August 27, 1928).

King George V of England opens the 1930 London Conference of the five powers. The treaties were later amended after signatories started competing in the construction of vessels 10,000 tons and under, which were not limited by the treaty.

Plenary session of the assembly, 1937. This, the eighteenth session, was the first in the new hall. The Aga Khan is in the presidential chair, and on his right is Secretary General Avenol.

resisting military aggression in accordance with the covenant. No response was given whatsoever. Europe was engulfed in flames of war.

When, in June, 1940, the Princeton Institute of Advanced Studies, and the Rockefeller Foundation invited the Secretariat of the League to move the technical services to Princeton, the secretary general accepted the invitation. The Financial and Transit departments crossed the Atlantic late in the summer. The Treasury moved to London, the International Labor Organization to Montreal, Canada, and in spring, 1941, the Drug Traffic department was officially invited to Washington.

On August 31, 1941, Secretary General Avenol resigned. There was no budget; there was nobody who could provide the budget. Sean Lester of the Secretariat carried the burden of office until the formal dissolution of the League, which merged into the prehistory of the United Nations. The final act of the League—its formal decision of dis-

solution and transfer of its assets to the successor organization, the United Nations, became a fact on April 18, ten days after the Assembly of the League of Nations met for the last time in Geneva. Representatives of thirty-four nations who met in Geneva wrote with unanimity the act dissolving the League, in the deep conviction that they were paving the way for a new form of international organization which would draw its lessons from the League's experiences, avoid its pitfalls, avoid indulging in too daring hopes and expectations, and base the future of international co-operation on sound foundations.

The spirit of President Wilson was there as the delegates recalled the proud statement made by President Wilson when the first draft of the Covenant of the League of Nations was adopted: "A living thing is born." This time they hoped not only a living thing was born, but also a long-lasting one.

TOWARD THE UNITED NATIONS ORGANIZATION

The failure of the League to fulfill the basic purpose of its establishment—the prevention of war—did not cause a complete departure from the idea it represented. The fate of the United States attitude toward the League was haunting the American public figures, while the leaders of the European countries, especially the two leading powers Great Britain and France, did not conceal their conviction that had it not been for the reversal in United States policies which resulted in its abandonment of the League, the League's fate could have been different, as could have been different the fate of peace and the efforts for its preservation in general.

Although a great deal of talk was heard about the "failure of the League," even United States leaders turned time and again not only to the idea of an international organization for peaceful cooperation between nations, and for prevention of war, but concentrated their attention upon finding some organizational forms which could assure the implementation of those ideas.

THE SEARCH FOR NEW FORMS OF INTER-NATIONAL ORGANIZATION

These opinions were not limited to the political thought of the United States alone. In the midst of the growing crises in Europe, after the great

Prime Minister Churchill strokes the black cat of H.M.S. *Prince of Wales* while on his way to a meeting with President Roosevelt. About five months later, in December, 1941, the *Prince of Wales* was sunk by a Japanese torpedo.

President Roosevelt and Prime Minister Churchill attend religious service on board the _Prince of Wales_.

After the service, President Roosevelt and Prime Minister Churchill continue their consultations, their prayer books still with them.

President Roosevelt, Prime Minister Churchill, Mackenzie King, prime minister of Canada, and members of their party on the terrace of the Citadel, overlooking the city of Quebec. In the background can be seen the Château Frontenac.

serious effort of the League to stop aggression failed, President Roosevelt considered, in 1937, a dramatic announcement of a proposal for an international conference and agreement to support certain principles of international conduct, the expansion and stabilization of world economy, peaceful revision of treaties, reduction of the burden of armaments, the rights of neutrals, and the laws and customs of warfare.

A memorandum on discussions in the State Department stressed the importance of some machinery for political decisions and further stressed that "this agency should also be responsible for the operation of an international military force which could enforce the peace." An interesting situation developed. While embracing the idea of the

League, which continued formally to exist, American leaders thought it advisable to avoid mentioning the name of the League in discussions about the future of international relations. Not only the so-called "failure of the League" played its role here. The fate of the League in American history —the fate of President Wilson's struggle to have the United States adhere to the League and become one of its members—became a kind of an obsession for American political figures who saw in this chapter of history not only a tragic experience of a great American president, but even more, a warning for the future to all who understood the importance of an international organization and knew well that without the United States in it, such an organization must be deprived of the main factor of

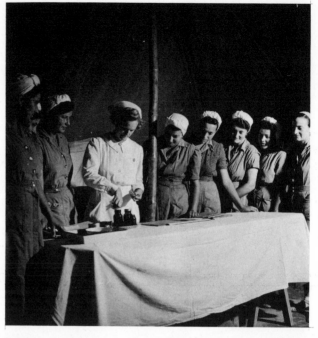

Allied powers fighting the Axis in World War II adopted the name United Nations before final decisions were taken concerning the U.N. Organization. The first U.N. agency, the United Nations Relief and Rehabilitation Administration, started relief operations almost two years before the official establishment of the U.N. Here refugee youngsters, to whose needs "UNRRA" ministered, are shown learning to sing.

United Nations Relief and Rehabilitation Administration refugee camp in a desert in the Middle East. An UNRRA nurse gives instructions in handling hypodermics.

In addition to taking care of the physical well-being of victims of war, UNRRA also gave attention to cultural needs. A camp newspaper, hot off the press, is here scanned eagerly.

View through the main archway of the UNRRA tuberculosis sanatorium at Giessen, Germany.

A course being given at UNRRA's training center at the University of Maryland.

its influence on world affairs.

While talking about an international organization they were most careful in the choice of phraseology. They were very much concerned with the creation of an atmosphere in which public opinion would support the idea of such an organization. In January, 1940, Secretary of State Cordell Hull stated that "if peace comes it would be essential in America's own best interest to throw the weight of our country's moral and material influence in the direction of creating a stable and enduring order under law." This goal, Hull declared, obviously meant a world organization.

United States envoys leaving for their assignments in foreign countries were instructed to present their views accordingly. A memo to Myron C. Taylor, before he left on his way to the Vatican City, contained the following directions: "In the present complete world confusion it is not thought advisable at this time to reconstitute a League of Nations, which because of its size makes for disagreement and inaction. There should be a meeting place of nations for the purpose of full discussion, but for management there seems no reason why the principle of trusteeship in private

affairs should not be extended to the international field. Trusteeship is based on the principle of unselfish service."

But with all the reluctance to spell out what form the idea of preservation of peace was to assume, plans for such an organization had to be made, tasks set, aims defined. In the very midst of the German "blitz" attacks an Interrallied Declaration was signed in London (June 12, 1941). The list of signatories was not too imposing. Besides the United Kingdom and the British Dominions, Canada, Australia, New Zealand, and the Union of South Africa, only governments in exile were among the signatories: Belgium, Czechoslovakia, Greece, Luxemburg, the Netherlands, Norway, Poland, Yugoslavia, and France, represented by General De Gaulle. The text of the declaration implied the hopes for some kind of an international organization by stating: "The only true basis for enduring peace is the willing cooperation of free peoples in a world in which relieved of the menace of aggression, all may enjoy economic and social security; it is our intention to work together, and with other free peoples, both in war and peace to this end."

Refugees of various nationalities, stranded in Rome, drawing UNRRA rations.

Some two months later a meeting between the leaders of the Anglo-Saxon world in the struggle against the Axis powers gave ample occasion for a new formulation of this desire. The acknowledged necessity of such a formulation gave birth to the Atlantic Charter, a declaration signed on August 14, 1941 by President Roosevelt and Prime Minister Churchill after a series of conferences aboard a warship in the North Atlantic, off the coast of Newfoundland. The eight-point charter dealt with all the aspects of war and postwar settlements. In almost all of them one central idea was repeated, that of "fullest collaboration between all nations." In the economic field, the object was to secure for all, improved labor standards, economic adjustment, and social security (point five

The United Nations Relief and Rehabilitation Administration also took care of some special food needs. Here kosher meat is approved for use of Jewish refugees.

Young Greek boys, caught begging on a street in Athens, were later taken care of by UNRRA.

of the Atlantic Charter). Another objective was the abandonment of use of force, accompanied by disarmament "pending the establishment of a wider and permanent system of general security" (point eight of the charter).

Some months later, on January 1, 1942, at a conference in Washington at which Churchill and the ambassadors of Russia and China participated, twenty-six governments at war with the Axis powers stated that they subscribed to a common program of purposes and principles embodied in the joint declaration known as the Atlantic Charter. This statement called the United Nations Declaration was later signed by most of the free nations of the world, and was to become later the basis of the United Nations Organization.

The declaration reads:

The Governments signatory hereto, having subscribed to a common program of purposes and principles embodied in the joint Declaration of the President of the United States of America, and the Prime

Mules supplied by UNRRA, hoisted on board in pairs, start their voyage to Greece to replace draft animals lost in the war.

Minister of the United Kingdom of Great Britain and Northern Ireland dated August 14, 1941 known as the Atlantic Charter.

Being convinced that complete victory over their enemies is essential to defend life, liberty, independence and religious freedom, and to preserve human rights and justice in their own lands as well as in other lands, and that they are now engaged in a common struggle against savage and brutal forces seeking to subjugate the world, declare:

I. Each government pledges itself to employ its full resources, military and economic, against those members of the Tripartite Pact and its adherents with which such government is at war.

II. Each government pledges itself to co-operate with the governments signatory hereto and not to make a separate armistice or peace with the enemies. . . .

The foregoing declaration may be adhered to by other nations which are, or may be, rendering material

A baby receives a piece of bread in Warsaw.

Two little Estonian girls being fitted with new clothes in a camp near Kummelnas.

Displaced persons camp. Women do the family washing in huge laundry rooms in the basement of the barracks.

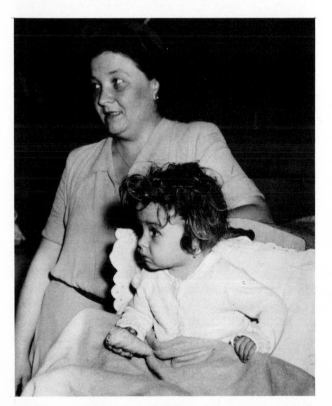

Fourteen-months-old Adrian Buntova received daily aid from UNNRA at a children's clinic in Prague.

assistance and contributions in the struggle for victory over Hitlerism.

The signatories were the United States of America, the United Kingdom, the Union of Soviet Socialist Republics, China, Australia, Belgium, Canada, Costa Rica, Cuba, Czechoslovakia, the Dominican Republic, El Salvador, Greece, Guatemala, Haiti, Honduras, India, Luxemburg, the Netherlands, New Zealand, Nicaragua, Norway, Panama, Poland, the Union of South Africa, and Yugoslavia. As time passed new states adhered to the declaration, sometimes induced to do so in the wake of the changing fortunes of war, when it became ever clearer that the Allied Powers were almost sure of victory. The order of the following is based on the order of the dates of adherence: Mexico, Philippines, Ethiopia, Iraq, Brazil, Bolivia, Iran, Colombia, Liberia, France, Ecuador, Peru, Chile, Paraguay, Venezuela, Uruguay, Turkey, Egypt, Saudi Arabia, Syria, and Lebanon. It was at the signing ceremony that in spite of the accepted principles of equality of all states, large and small alike, consideration for the real power relationship between nations had been given. At that occasion, not the alphabetical order decided —the "big four" signed first. President Roosevelt acknowledged that this priority based on strength and military contribution to the war effort was somewhat contrary to the high principles of equality, and he felt obliged to give some explanation of the order chosen. Said President Roosevelt, "I have a feeling that the U.S.S.R. would not be pleased to see their names following some of the countries which realistically are making a minor contribution."

BLUEPRINTS FOR A WORLD BODY

There is no doubt that this order of putting signatures signaled future developments in the thinking about the international organization to replace the League of Nations. Although the contracting powers were far from spelling out what the role of the big powers in the leading body of the international organization was to be, there is no doubt that this order of signing of the Atlantic Charter foretold the forthcoming establishment of the central body of the United Nations Organizations—the Security Council.

But for the time being no specific commitments had been made and no specific principles set. The main power and the most concerned with the establishment of the international organization, the United States, had still to move most cautiously to avoid a repetition of its experiences at the time of discussions about the League of Nations. The preparatory work started in State Department committees entrusted with the formulation of papers on

One of the fifteen hundred tractors sent to Greece by UNRRA.

Chinese model of Yellow River dike reconstruction project.

At Kloster Indersdorf, member of an UNRRA team adjusts clothes of lad about to meet the UNRRA director.

forms of an organization which would make the preservation of peace feasible. Trial balloons were then tossed into the public discussion through speeches of leading members of Congress, of government officials, and even through publication of articles in magazines and newspapers. The most outspoken of these was in the *Saturday Evening Post* under the title "Roosevelt's World Blueprint." The article, considered by many as reflecting President Roosevelt's thinking and by others even as inspired by Roosevelt, included a quite outspoken

Orphanage in Hengyang which took care of 590 children with UNRRA assistance.

Herbert H. Lehman, former governor of New York, who was appointed director general of UNRRA.

At the Cairo Conference (August, 1942), front row, are Generalissimo Chiang Kai-shek, President Roosevelt, Prime Minister Churchill, and Madame Chiang Kai-shek. In the back row are military commanders.

The leaders of the United States, China, and Great Britain, with their advisers. Among the latter are Anthony Eden and Averell Harriman.

At Cairo, President Roosevelt and Prime Minister Churchill met President Inonu of then neutral Turkey.

At the gardens of the British embassy in Cairo, Churchill is seen conferring with Field Marshal Jan Smuts.

Signers of the historic Moscow Tripartite Conference Agreement at Speridonovka Palace smile as they bring the momentous meeting to a close. Signers (*left to right*) are Secretary of State Cordell Hull, Soviet Foreign Commissar Vyacheslav Molotov, and British Foreign Secretary Anthony Eden.

Allied leaders of the United States, Britain, and Russia met in Teheran, the capital of Persia, to discuss the war against Germany and a number of political questions. Mr. Churchill is seen at a private dinner party in Teheran, celebrating his sixty-ninth birthday, which occurred during the conference.

The Soviet Legation in Teheran where President Roosevelt met with Marshal Stalin. United States military policemen stand guard in front.

During the Teheran Conference, Churchill presented the Stalingrad Sword to Marshal Stalin. The sword was a gift of King George VI to Stalingrad.

Marshal Voroshilov shows the Stalingrad Sword to President Roosevelt while Churchill and Stalin look on.

The Big Three on the steps of the Soviet Legation in Teheran.

Here the three Allied leaders pose with some of the leading members of their governments.

Prime Minister Mackenzie King, President Roosevelt, and Prime Minister Churchill on the terrace of the Citadel, at the Second Quebec Conference (1944).

Prime Minister Churchill and President Roosevelt met on their way to the conference in Quebec.

sentence: "Roosevelt opposed reviving the League of Nations because of its aura of failure—he favored retaining and developing certain of its instrumentalities."

The degree of caution observed by Roosevelt in this delicate matter of committing the United States to membership in an international organization, was demonstrated in January, 1943, when at a press conference Roosevelt refused to answer a basic question as to how, in his opinion, peace could be maintained, and stated somewhat angrily: "No, no—you are talking about details. I am talking about objectives."

Nevertheless these objectives had to be spelled out at least vaguely by other influential people in the government. In July, 1941, Undersecretary of State Sumner Welles wrote: "Some adequate instrumentality must unquestionably be found to achieve such adjustments when the nations of earth again undertake the task of restoring law and order to a shaken world: (1) abolition of offensive armaments (2) equal economic enjoyment."

A year later Roosevelt's Secretary of State Cordell Hull saw fit not only to speak about some international agency but even leveled a direct attack on the American isolationism. Speaking in July, 1942, Hull stated that the United States was at war "because we ignored the simple but fundamental fact that the price of peace and of the preservation of rights and freedom among nations is the acceptance of international responsibilities." About the future he said: Some international agency capable of using force when necessary "would have to be organized" and "regulation of armaments, peaceful settlement of disputes between nations, which would necessitate a vital international court" will become imperative.

The fear of interparty rivalry was removed when a conference of Republican leaders adopted a unanimous resolution in favor of "responsible participation by the U.S. in a postwar co-operative organization among sovereign nations to prevent military aggression and to attain permanent peace with organized justice in a free world." Senator Vandenberg, the Republican spokesman on international affairs whose zeal for bipartisanship in setting foreign policy principles was credited for many political decisions of the Democratic administration, did his best to "end the miserable notion that the Republican Party will return to its foxhole when

On the terrace overlooking Quebec, Mackenzie King, Churchill, Roosevelt, and the Earl of Athlone, Governor of Canada.

Churchill toasts a group of French boys who crossed the English Channel in two canoes from occupied France to join the Free French Forces of General De Gaulle.

General view of the opening of the conference at Dumbarton Oaks (August, 1944).

the last shot in this war has been fired and will blindly let the world rot in its own anarchy." The Fulbright resolution, adopted with a majority of 360 against 29, affirmed overwhelmingly the principles of United States participation in a world organization. The resolution reads: "The Congress hereby expresses itself as favoring the creation of an appropriate international machinery, with powers adequate to establish and to maintain a joint and lasting peace among nations of the world and as favoring the participation by the United States of America therein through constitutional process."

The public statements and resolutions fell on fertile political soil. Wendell Willkie, the Republican candidate for the Presidency's book *One World* was one expression of a man of ideals. But it was the general feeling of the public that something tangible had to be done to make a new war impossible. The vague declarations about international co-operation which started with the Atlantic Charter and which also appeared later in the United Nations Declaration, in which we find the

first formal usage of the term "United Nations," had to be followed by exploratory negotiations between the major powers fighting against the Axis.

Difficulties were towering. Soviet Russia was rather reluctant to accept far-reaching obligations relating to postwar problems. The Russians were concerned with winning the war and with United States aid in the conduct of war. Marshal Stalin was more interested in one problem than in any other aspect of international security and international organization for security—efficient control of Germany. But the United States and Great Britain pressed incessantly for some form of commitment, by Russia, to subscribe to the idea of an international organization. Field Marshal Smuts, seized with the problems of such an organization, appeared again in the center of the political activity. In an address to the British Empire Society, Smuts stated emphatically, "The future belongs to larger human groupings. The pressure of the times has already welded the free democracies, representing Western civilization, into one group. Similar pres-

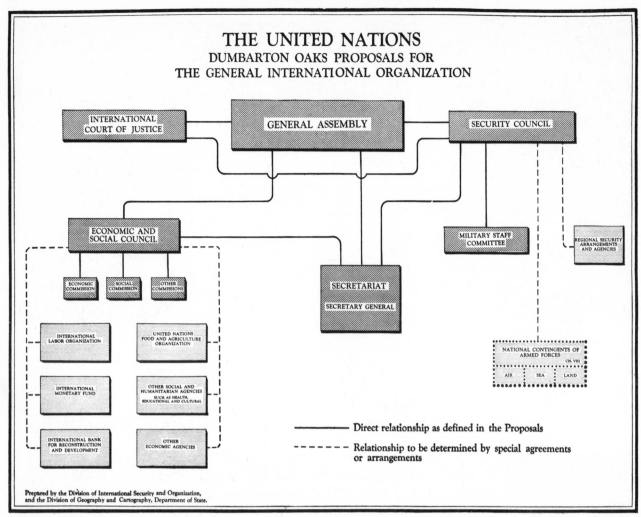

Chart prepared by the State Department subsequent to the Dumbarton Oaks Conference, showing proposed structure of international organization.

About two weeks before the opening of the U.N. Conference on International Organization, international jurists assembled in Washington to complete the basic design of the Dumbarton Oaks security plan.

Acting Secretary of State Dean Acheson (*standing, center*) addresses representatives of twenty-eight nations gathered at the State Department in Washington, D.C., to sign the Bretton Woods Monetary Agreement. United States Secretary of the Treasury Fred M. Vinson (*hands folded, right center*) and the Earl of Halifax, British ambassador to the United States (*at Vinson's left*) sit with the group.

President Roosevelt and Prime Minister Churchill have a private word after one of the meetings at Yalta, in the Crimea (February, 1945).

Churchill with Molotov, People's Commissar of Foreign Affairs of Russia, at Yalta.

The Big Three with some of their aides pose on the grounds of Livadia Palace, United States headquarters at Yalta.

The room in Livadia Palace where meetings of the Yalta Conference were held.

sure will bring together all nations into one great world organization. This association will not be a mere repetition of the League, although there will be various degrees of affinity."

Cordell Hull favored promoting world security on the basis of a type of institution similar to the League of Nations. Under his supervision an agenda group in the State Department worked on a plan for a global organization to combine the negative function of preventing or punishing aggression with the positive function of promoting conditions conducive to peaceful relations among

View of British Headquarters for the Yalta Conference, Vorontsov Palace.

nations. President Roosevelt had in this respect a clear plan. He envisaged a small centralized organization for enforcement of peace, combined with much looser, decentralized organizations for handling other aspects of international relations.

By June, 1943, a subcommittee directed by Undersecretary Welles developed the first reasonably complete plan for a postwar institution—the Draft Constitution of an International Organization. A revision of this first plan was called the New Draft Charter of the United Nations. Thus when the foreign ministers of the United States, Great Britain, and Soviet Russia, and the Chinese ambassador met in Moscow in October, 1943, the formulation of specific plans for the establishment of the United Nations as a permanent international organization was initiated, and the conference adopted the Moscow Declaration, published in the same month and signed by these same powers.

Vorontsov Palace, erected for Prince Vorontsov in 1837 at the cost of three million rubles (1.5 million dollars) from plans of the English architect Blore, who adopted a combination of Gothic and Moorish styles.

The signatories pledged united action for peace and security after the conclusion of World War II, and a formal commitment was obtained from the Soviet Union to follow a policy of postwar co-operation and specifically support an international security organization.

The conference went even further: a seven-member group was envisaged, to consist of the United States, Russia, Great Britain, China, Canada, the Netherlands, and Brazil, with powers to: (1) recommend plans for a permanent over-all economic organization to co-ordinate existing and future

President Roosevelt and Prime Minister Churchill arrive in Yalta for the conference with Stalin.

Delegates and visitors on their way to the United Nations Conference on International Organization met briefly at the Inter-Departmental Auditorium, Washington, D.C., prior to departure for San Francisco (April, 1945).

President Harry S. Truman in the White House, April 25, 1945, at microphones over which he broadcast message opening the U.N. Conference on International Organization at San Francisco. He told the delegates, "You are to be the architects of a better world. In your hands rests our future."

specialized agencies, (2) to fix a schedule for further discussions, (3) to decide whether boards of allocation of strategic materials should be integrated into postwar planning activities. Clause four of the Moscow Four-Nation Declaration on General Security proclaimed that "they [the four governments] recognize the necessity of establishing at the earliest practicable date a general international organization, based on the principle of the sovereign equality of all peace-loving states and open to membership by all such states, large and small, for the maintenance of international peace and security."

THE TEHERAN CONFERENCE

The stage was therefore set when the leaders of the three principal members of the United Nations gathered for their meeting in Teheran (No-

vember 28 through December 1, 1943). It is indicative of the then prevailing sincere desire of the United States government to strengthen United States–Russian friendship, that the United States Secretary of State Cordell Hull, refused to meet on his way to Moscow, the British Foreign Minister Eden, in order, as was openly stated, to avoid Russian suspicion that the United States and Great Britain were prearranging positions prior to their meeting with their Russian counterpart. Winston Churchill spelled out this situation clearly: "There was a strong current of opinion in the American Government circles which seemed to wish to win Russian confidence even at the expense of co-ordinating the Anglo-American effort."

On their way to Teheran President Roosevelt

Delegates to the U.N. Conference on International Organization listen to the voice of President Truman, whose radio address opened the first plenary session of the conference at San Francisco.

Wounded veterans arriving at the Opera House, San Francisco, for the second plenary session of the conference.

Servicemen attend plenary session at the Opera House.

President Truman visiting veterans.

and Prime Minister Winston Churchill stopped in Cairo to meet the Chinese leader Chiang Kai-shek to discuss the problems of the Far East. The conference was open to the Russians, but Stalin, who refused to travel to places distant from Russia, wanted instead to have a Russian general participating in the meeting. Churchill's opposition to this Russian demand was definite. The Declaration of Cairo which emerged from this meeting, dealt with the punishment of Japan, and resolved to deprive her of all conquests and to establish a free Korea.

When the two leaders left Cairo on their way to Teheran to meet Stalin, they were firmly resolved to center the discussions not only on strategic plans for the conduct of war, but also on problems of postwar measures for the preservation of peace. Churchill promoted an original idea of having the peace enforcement authorities separately for each area, for Europe, the Far East, etc. This idea, which in fact was conceived to complement the institutions of the global organization, found in Stalin a staunch supporter, but did not find favor with President Roosevelt.

But this was not the central problem of the discussions. The three participants agreed that enforcement authorities for any agreement for the preservation of peace were essential. Thus the idea of "four policemen," the United States, Russia, Great Britain, and China came into being. It is ironical, from the point of view of later Russian demands that the United States liquidate its overseas bases, that according to Marshal Stalin, the "four policeman" idea would require sending of American troops overseas and the establishment of strategic bases throughout the world. President

Clark Eichelberger (*center*), executive director of the American Association for the United Nations at the Lions Club dinner for consultants to the United States delegation.

Roosevelt opposed such suggestions resolutely, speaking only about United States naval and air forces, and suggesting that land forces be supplied by Great Britain and Soviet Russia. Toward countries starting hostilities President Roosevelt had a ready-made solution—the idea of a "quarantine," an idea he had voiced once, prior to the outbreak of World War II; but in case of aggression by a major power, Roosevelt suggested an ultimatum of the four policemen. The problem of handling an aggression by one of the policemen was never mentioned. Such a thought did not occur at that time.

All were excited with the conference and the resolutions adopted. This general atmosphere found its expression in the communiqué of the conference which stated: "We came here with hope and determination. We leave here friends in fact, in spirit, in purpose." And on the question of future peace the Teheran Conference declared: "We are sure that our concord will win an en-

Meeting of Commission I, General Provisions, Committee 1, on preamble, purposes, and principles of the United Nations. Henri Rolin of Belgium was chairman of the committee.

Meeting of General Provisions Committee on preamble, purposes, and principles. Interpreters listen to speech of Raporteur Farid Zeineddine of Syria.

during peace. We recognize fully the supreme responsibility resting upon us and all the United Nations to make a peace which will command the goodwill of the overwhelming masses of the peoples of the world and banish the scourge and terror of war for many generations."

When President Roosevelt returned from Teheran he reported to the nation over the radio, on Christmas eve, concerning the objective of an organization to keep world peace: "On the basis of what we did discuss I can say even today, that I do not think any insoluble differences will arise among Russia, Great Britain and the United States. . . . As long as the four nations stick together in determination to keep peace, there will be no possibility of an aggressor nation raising another war."

Votes are counted at a meeting of Commission I.

Meeting of the officers of Commission I, General Provisions.

This general spirit of the alliance and especially this conviction that co-operation among the four is the best guarantee for peace, was prevailing even in times of stress and trial in relations with Soviet Russia. On this confidence was based the entire structure of the new international organization. The leaders of the great alliance were fully aware that this confidence would be conditioned by the kind of peace they would be able to assure. Senator Vandenberg, the initiator of the Republican support for a policy of United States participation in a world organization, wrote "No matter how acceptable this program for a new League might be, everything depends upon the kind of peace, whether it is a just peace, which this new international organization will implement."

Members of the Executive Committee of the conference, with their advisers, stand for a minute of silent meditation upon the end of the war in Europe, at their meeting of May 8, 1945.

DUMBARTON OAKS

The discussions on principles of the international organization were again injected into the United States presidential campaign of 1944. Thomas Dewey, the Republican candidate for the presidency, declared that he was disturbed by reports indicating that the forthcoming Dumbarton Oaks conversations were intended to "subject the nations of the world, great and small,

First meeting of Committee 2, the General Assembly Committee of the conference.

Andrei A. Gromyko and James Farley, U.S. Postmaster General, shake hands at a Russian reception at St. Francis Hotel in San Francisco, in celebration of victory over Germany.

Meeting of Commission II, General Assembly, Committee 3, on economic and social co-operation.

permanently to the coercive power of the four nations holding this conference," but Cordell Hull, the secretary of state, assured Mr. Dewey that his worries were utterly unfounded, because "the Dumbarton Oaks meeting is for the purpose of discussion among the signatories of the Moscow Declaration as to the most feasible and desirable methods of establishing the kind of organization envisaged in that Declaration and in the Senate resolution."

The Dumbarton Oaks conference was held in two phases. The first was from August 21 to September 28, 1944, between Russia, the United States, and the United Kingdom. The second, from September 29 to October 7, 1944, between the United States, the United Kingdom, and China (Russia withheld participation to respect her neutrality in war against Japan) revealed many serious misunderstandings. The pleasant environment of a mansion on the outskirts of Washington, D.C. did not convey its atmosphere to the assembled diplomats. The discussion stage was over. The time had arrived for serious formulations and

Martin H. Miller addresses a meeting of consultants to the American delegation.

Dr. Charles F. Gross of the Federal Council of Churches addresses the chairman of the consultants meeting (May, 1945).

decisions. Among the many snags that developed, two assumed such serious dimensions that at times they seemed to threaten the entire conference and its outcome. The problem of the voting system in the Security Council and the question of membership in the international organization caused a serious stalemate.

Dr. Mary McLeod Bethune of the National Association for Advancement of Colored People questions the speaker at a consultants meeting.

How serious the situation appeared to those present at the conference could be judged from one of the remarks made at the occasion: "The alternative to a creation of such an international organization, a third world war within our lifetime, seems unthinkable." At the height of the crisis, Stalin emphasized in a cable to Roosevelt that the principle of great-power unanimity on all questions presupposed absence of mutual suspicion—and that any departure from it would deviate from the understanding reached at Teheran.

On this question of unanimity, which, translated into simple language, meant to accord each great power the right of blocking any decision through a simple veto, the negotiating powers were more agreeable to an accommodation than on the question of representation. Soviet Russia demanded that all the republics of the Soviet Union become members of the international organization. "They are no less sovereign than the British Dominions," argued the Russian delegation. At this point there was no readiness to acquiesce with Russian demands. "A quick compromise on Russian terms might conceivably imperil the success of the organization"—this was the conclusion at which the United States delegation arrived. President Roosevelt reacted most vehemently stating that if the Russians stuck to their position he would demand right of membership for all forty-eight States of the Union.

With the exception of these two questions the Dumbarton Oaks conferences proceeded smoothly with their work. Agreement was easily reached on nomenclature of main organs of the international organization: General Assembly, Security Council, Economic and Social Council, Secretariat, Secretary General, International Court of Justice—names which had an established meaning in the practice of the League of Nations. Conspicuously, the name of the Trusteeship Council was not easily agreed upon because the League name "Mandate Commission" seemed irrelevant in view of ideas which had developed on the administration of territories which had not attained their independence. There were of course various suggestions as far as the names of these organs were concerned. The Soviet delegation suggested "The International Security Organization" and after accepting the name "Security Council" they proposed "World Union" for the general name.

Commander Harold Stassen of the United States delegation at a meeting of consultants at the Fairmont Hotel, San Francisco.

Although the Dumbarton Oaks proposals included not only the names of the organs in the first blueprint of the United Nations, but also, among other resolutions, the decision that the task of preservation of world peace had to be entrusted to the Security Council composed of the "Big Five" (after France was admitted to the councils of major powers), it was emphasized that the proposals were not the approved draft of a charter to be accepted on a "take it or leave it" basis by smaller United Nations. The voting procedure in the Security Council was left open, to be taken up

in Yalta at the second conference of the three world leaders, President Roosevelt, Marshal Stalin, and Prime Minister Churchill.

THE YALTA CONFERENCE

The problems of the world organization were not the exclusive matter the conference had to deal with. The retreat of the German armies and near collapse of the German war machine gave

Dr. Helen Reid of the American Association of University Women addresses the speaker at the consultants meeting.

Hamilton Fish Armstrong of the United States delegation proposes an amendment at the meeting of Commission I, Committee 2 (June, 1945).

Herbert Evatt of Australia and Harold Stassen argue a point after a session of Commission I, Committee 2.

Meeting under the auspices of the National Committee for India's Freedom, a group active during the conference.

Members of the delegation of Panama.

ample occasion to reveal the real intentions of the principal allies. There had already been certain misgivings about Russia's treatment of one of the United Nations' members—namely Poland. Other Eastern European countries were in line to be, or had already been liberated. Their fate, the preservation of their independence, was at stake. Regarding this matter it was Churchill's desire to have Russia presented with an agreed point of view of the two Western allies. And problems of the international organization which had been left open at Dumbarton Oaks could not, in Churchill's opinion, wait for their first examination at a meeting with Stalin. Churchill demanded preliminary talks between the Foreign Ministers, Stettinius and Eden, at least for a preparation of the agenda for the forthcoming meeting with Stalin. President Roosevelt was opposed. His concern not to arouse

Russian suspicions of a Western "frame up" persisted. In Roosevelt's opinion the Yalta conference should not last longer than "five or six days." Churchill persisted that ample time had to be given for thorough discussion, arguing that he did not see any way "of realising our hopes about a world organization in five or six days. Even Almighty took seven."

The conference itself was preceded by a meeting of Roosevelt and Churchill at Malta (January 30 to February 2) and after two days the three leaders met at Livadia, close to Yalta. The pleasant Russian resort area, with its agreeable climate and magnificent palaces built for the Russian aristocracy, created an appropriate atmosphere for leisurely confrontation among the three world figures. The destruction left by the German invading forces served as a good reminder of the

Pan-American picnic and tour given in honor of the delegations of states of the Americas.

horrors of war. And the realities to be faced could not be avoided either. The first and most challenging was the fate of Poland. The discussion about it was most indicative of the general atmosphere which prevailed.

When Roosevelt demanded that steps be taken "to facilitate if necessary the holding of elections," Stalin replied quickly, "I accept that." Encouraged by this seemingly easy success Roosevelt continued "Poland will be the first example of operating under this declaration. I want the elections in Poland to be beyond question, like Caesar's wife. I did not know Caesar's wife, but she was believed to have been pure"—to which Stalin smilingly replied: "It was said so about Caesar's wife, but, in fact, she had certain sins."

Whether this remark foreshadowed that the future elections in Poland would also have "certain sins," nobody seemed to consider. The three

leaders were preoccupied with the idea of preserving peace and in this case the particulars about the standing of one nation seemed to be of secondary importance. Churchill kept on repeating, "The peace of the world depends upon the lasting friendship of the three great powers," and, "We would like to secure the peace for at least fifty years." Stalin proved not less aware of what was at stake. After Churchill's statement Stalin said: "It is not difficult to keep unity in time of war since there is a joint aim to defeat a common enemy, which is clear to everyone. The difficult task will come after the war when diverse interests tend to divide the Allies. It is our duty to see that our relations in peacetime are as strong as they have been in war."

It was in this spirit that the decisions on the international organization had been adopted. On February 11, 1945 the three leaders declared, "We

Another view of the picnic, which was held in late May, 1945.

are resolved upon the earliest possible establishment, with our Allies, of a general international organization to maintain peace and security.... We have agreed that a conference of United Nations should be called to meet at San Francisco in the United States on 25 April, 1945, to prepare the charter of such an organization along the lines proposed in the informal conversations at Dumbarton Oaks." The declaration also included a statement that problems relating to voting procedure in the future organization had been resolved. No details were given, but, as it became evident later, the contracting parties had agreed to incorporate into the charter of the United Nations the provision that the Security Council could adopt binding decisions only by a unanimous vote of its permanent members. The problem of Russian representation was also resolved. Although the maximum Russian demand (to have

the Ukrainian, Byelorussian, Moldavian, Lithuanian and other republics afforded a status equal to that of sovereign state members of the United Nations) had been rejected, nevertheless, for the sake of unity and amity, it was decided that two of the republics, the Ukrainian and Byelorussian, would be admitted to membership in the United Nations.

Francis Michael Forde, Deputy Prime Minister of Australia; Herbert Evatt, attorney general; and members of the Australian delegation.

Members of the delegation of China during the dedication of Chinese aircraft.

René Pleven, French delegate, talks with Paul Verdier, owner of the City of Paris store, while on a visit to the Kaiser shipyards.

But even with this compromise no illusions prevailed. President Roosevelt cautioned optimists saying: "We delude ourselves if we attempt to believe wishfully that all these problems can be solved overnight. . . . Perfectionism, no less than isolationism or imperialism or power politics, may obstruct the path to international peace. Let us not forget that retreat to isolationism a quarter of a century ago was started not by a direct attack against international cooperation, but against the alleged imperfections of the peace."

Senator Vandenberg, the Republican leader went even further when he stated that "Russia's unilateral plan appears to contemplate engulfment, directly or indirectly of a surrounding circle of buffer states, contrary to our conception of what we thought we are fighting for."

UNITED NATIONS CONFERENCE ON INTERNATIONAL ORGANIZATION

But in spite of these misgivings the Yalta agreement appeared as the best compromise possible. The American press was elated. The *Philadelphia*

Dmitry Z. Manuilsky of the Ukrainian delegation speaks at the anniversary celebration of the Anglo-Russian Pact at the Mark Hopkins Hotel, San Francisco. Seated are Bartley Crum, member of the Anglo-American Palestine Commission, and Governor of California Earl Warren.

Record called the conference the "greatest United Nations victory of the war." *Time* wrote: "All doubts about the Big Three's ability to co-operate in peace as well as in war seem now to have been swept away." The stage was set completely for the conference to prepare the charter of the international organization.

Not too many practical problems had been left unsolved for the San Francisco conference. Ample provisions had been made to have basic principles of the organization fixed, and set above any discussion. The Atlantic Charter, the Declaration of the United Nations, the Moscow Declaration, the Teheran Declaration, Dumbarton Oaks, the Yalta Declaration—all were milestones on the way toward the establishment of an international organization. But even in these conditions, after such thorough preparation, the San Francisco conference worked for two months until it had adopted

the Charter of the United Nations and the Statute of the new International Court of Justice. Compared with the ten sessions, the 30 hours, in which the Covenant of the League of Nations was compounded, after only some vague preparatory work, the United Nations Charter should have included every possible provision to make it a most farsighted basis for international co-operation within the framework of the United Nations Organization. The 1200 amendments which had been submitted by the participating delegations together with the existing documents on the international organization, served as the basis for discussions on the U.N. Charter.

Chiefs of delegations, comprised of prime ministers, foreign ministers, and ambassadors, accompanied by swarms of advisers, filled the halls of the San Francisco Opera House, and committees on various specific aspects of the international

Earl Warren talks with T. V. Soong, premier of China, and Madame Soong.

organization spread all over the city of the Golden Gate. The United States delegation was carefully selected on a bipartisan basis. With Secretary of State Stettinius as chairman and Cordell Hull as senior adviser, it included Republicans of the highest standing, such as Senator Vandenberg and Commander Harold Stassen. In addition, there was Tom Connally, Chairman of the Senate Committee on Foreign Relations; Sol Bloom, Chairman of the House Foreign Relations Committee; and Miss Virginia Gildersleeve, Dean of Barnard College in New York City. Here again was Field Marshal Smuts, the architect of the League of Nations, who influenced greatly the wording of the preamble of the United Nations Charter; here was the arch-representative of Stalin's politics on the international scene, Vyacheslav Molotov; here was Clement Attlee, Deputy Prime Minister of Great Britain to become soon the First Minister

of the Crown, after the early postwar defeat of Churchill in general elections.

But the man who believed more than all present that the international organization would become a lasting guarantee of peace, the President of the United States of America, Franklin Delano Roosevelt, was not among them, for he had died on April 12. Only some weeks prior to the opening of the United Nations Conference on International Organization, President Roosevelt had confided to his closest friends that he would leave on April 20 for San Francisco to open the conference on April 25, as scheduled at Yalta. With all his vigor Roosevelt sought to have the conference open on time in spite of difficulties which started to arise with Russia as to the interpretation of certain details of the Yalta agreement. It was on April 2 that Roosevelt approved the issuance of a statement by the secretary of state saying that the United States

Academic procession at the Greek Theatre of the University of California, during a ceremony extending honorary doctorates to some delegates to the conference.

would not press at San Francisco for three delegates in the Assembly of the United Nations Organization, as did Russia, which based its demands on her interpretation of the Yalta agreements.

President Harry S. Truman was afforded the greatest honor possible—to inaugurate the Conference on International Organization. As about a quarter of a century ago, when the League of Nations was established, it was again the President of the United States who presided over the maximum effort for organization of co-operation between nations and the preservation of peace. Two months of discussions sufficed to have the Charter of the United Nations Organization signed. Although a symbol of prevailing realities on the international scene, becoming evident even before the war was over, could not be avoided (there was no one to sign in the name of Poland, concerning which the first serious controversy between the Allies about the composition of the Polish government arose) nonetheless the signing ceremony was not delayed. The fifty delegates, representing the fifty nations, consisted of (1) original signatories of the Declaration of the United Nations, (2) adher-

Color guard at the University of California ceremony.

Chairmen of delegations remain standing after their unanimous approval of the United Nations Charter in San Francisco (June 26, 1945).

Edward R. Stettinius (*seated*), former United States Secretary of State, signs the United Nations Charter, which joined the United States with forty-nine other nations in the creation of the United Nations.

S. K. Tsarapkin signs the United Nations Charter for Russia. Standing at his left are Andrei A. Gromyko and other members of the Russian delegation.

V. K. Wellington Koo (*seated*), Chinese Ambassador to the Court of St. James, signs the U.N. Charter.

Field Marshal Jan Smuts (*seated*), prime minister of the Union of South Africa, signs the U.N. Charter.

ents to the declaration before the Dumbarton Oaks conference, (3) states which were designated as Associated States after breaking with the Axis powers and had attended United Nations economic conferences, and (4) other states adherent to the United Nations Declaration at later dates. All these approved unanimously the Charter of the United Nations Organization, and on June 26, the San Francisco United Nations Conference on International Organization was declared adjourned. The space left open for the signature of Poland was filled on October 15, and on October 24, 1945, the charter was already ratified by the five major powers, China, France, Russia, the United Kingdom and the United States, and a majority of the other signatories. The condition for the ratification of the charter had been fulfilled. The United Nations Organization came into being.

SETTLING INTERNATIONAL DISPUTES

At the time when the Charter of the United Nations Organization was ratified, the Preparatory Commission established at San Francisco had already reached an advanced stage in its work. Composed of representatives of all member states, the commission succeeded in drafting, within about half a year (June 27–December 23, 1945), a detailed plan for the functioning of the U.N. organs. Simultaneously arrangements had been made for the first meeting of the General Assembly.

When the assembly convened in London, in January, 1946, the initiators of the United Nations Organization did not conceal their pride. Within six months the U.N. started to function. And those who remembered the dragging processes into which the League of Nations was drawn before it was able to hold its first meeting—after almost a full year—had an additional reason to believe that the new organization they had created would be more successful than the one on the ruins of which it was created.

THE FIRST GENERAL ASSEMBLY

Of course this was only a minor factor in their pride. They took pride in the charter, in the provisions for the prevention of wars and for collective action by the U.N. against the aggressor nation; they took pride in those parts of the charter which dealt with international co-operation in the pursuit of the peaceful tasks of humanity; their hearts were overflowing with hope and their minds with convictions, that here an order for a better world had been born.

James F. Byrnes, the United States secretary of state defined this state of near elation in a few

View of a meeting of the U.N. Security Council on the Iranian question.

United Nations mediator for Palestine, Count Folke Bernadotte (*second from right*), with his staff at the U.N. Disaster Relief Headquarters.

sentences: "There are principles of law incorporated in the Charter which should be regarded as the law of the lands." And British Prime Minister Clement Attlee elaborated on the humanitarian aspect of the charter. In his welcoming speech, at the first session of the General Assembly, Lord Attlee said: "I am glad that the Charter of the United Nations does not deal only with governments and states or with politics and war, but with the simple elemental needs of human beings whatever be their race, their color, or their creed. In the Charter we reaffirm our faith in fundamental human rights. We see the freedom of the individual in the state as an essential complement to the freedom of the state in the world community of nations. We stress too that social justice and the best possible standards of life for all, are essential factors in promoting and maintaining the

Bernadotte's funeral. The governor general of the Dodecanese, Nicholas Marvis, and the Greek minister of information place their wreaths. Count Bernadotte was assassinated in the Israeli sector of Jerusalem.

Dr. Ralph Bunche, acting U.N. mediator for Palestine, in conference with General A. Lundström (*right*), chief military observer.

peace of the world."

It seemed to be really a kind of a "springtime of nations," a honeymoon of international co-operation. The central hall of Westminster Palace in London, in which the delegates of fifty-one nations assembled for their first General Assembly, sounded a happy clarion to the world:

We the Peoples of the United Nations determined to save succeeding generations from the scourge of war, . . . to reaffirm faith in fundamental human rights, . . . to establish conditions under which justice and respect for the obligations arising from treaties and other sources of international law can be maintained, . . . to promote social progress and better standards of life in larger freedom, . . . have resolved to combine our efforts to accomplish these aims.

Evacuation of El Faluja, the stronghold at which Colonel Nasser was with the Egyptian troops, before the cessation of Israeli-Egyptian hostilities.

These high principles of international co-operation in a world of law, stated in such solemn words in the preamble to the charter were soon put to the test. There was not too much time to indulge in idealistic generalities. The first General Assembly of the United Nations Organization had innumerable problems to solve. The provisions of the charter with its nineteen chapters and one hundred eleven articles called for the establishment of the principal organs of the United Nations, which together with the General Assembly had to assure the implementation of the charter and the proper functioning of the United Nations Organization. These organs—the Security Council, the Economic and Social Council, the Trusteeship

Israeli and Jordanian local commanders hold a joint conference under the auspices of the Mixed Armistice Commission at the Mandelbaum Gate, a no-man's land between the Israeli and Arab sectors of Jerusalem.

Council, the International Court of Justice, and the central administrative instrument, the Secretariat—had to be constituted as soon as possible.

Out of the eleven members of the Security Council only five, China, France, Russia, the United Kingdom, and the United States had the status of permanent members. The other six, nonpermanent members of the Security Council, had to be elected with "due regard being specially paid, in the first instance to the contribution of Members of the United Nations to the mainte-

In the delegates' lounge at Lake Success, surrounded by advisers, some of the delegates to the Security Council have an informal discussion before the meeting on a Syrian-Israeli dispute.

Roadblock, near Jerusalem, which cut the highway between that city and Tel Aviv–Jaffa. The Armistice Line of 1948 was drawn across this territory. The road behind the barrier is mined.

Andrei Vyshinsky, U.N. representative of Russia and president of the Security Council, about to take his seat. This meeting of the council considered placing on the agenda a Lebanese complaint against Israel and an Israeli complaint against Jordan.

A United Nations plane connecting Gaza with the rest of the world.

Building in no-man's land in Jerusalem, where the Mixed Armistice Commissions of the U.N. Truce Supervision Organization in Palestine was meeting.

nance of international peace and security and to the other purposes of the Organization, and also to equitable geographical distribution."

The eighteen members of the Economic and Social Council had to be elected. The Trusteeship Council had to be constituted to include U.N. members administering trust territories, Security Council members not administering trust territories, and "as many other members elected for three-year terms by the General Assembly as may be necessary to ensure that the total number of members of the Trusteeship Council is equally divided between those members of the United Nations which administer trust territories and those which do not." Besides those institutions, the International Court of Justice with its fifteen members, no two of whom could be nationals of the same state, had to be established. In addition, the chief administrative officer of the organization, the secretary general, had to be elected.

These initial tasks were accomplished with speed. Members of the principal organs were

In September, 1955, the Security Council unanimously called on Egypt and Israel to take "all necessary steps" to restore order and tranquillity between them, "to desist from further acts of violence," and to "continue the cease-fire in full force and effect."

Dag Hammarskjöld talks with Major General Burns of Canada, chief of the U.N. Truce Supervision Organization in Palestine, and later the first commander-in-chief of UNEF.

elected, and on January 30, the Security Council, at a private meeting and by a secret ballot, decided to recommend to the assembly the appointment of Trygve Lie as secretary general of the United Nations. On February 1, the United Nations had its first secretary general for a term of five years. These were the easy tasks.

Even before the U.N. had its chief administrative officer appointed, and hardly before the organs had constituted themselves, a grave political problem had to be placed on the agenda. On January 19, 1946, Iran informed the Security Council that Russia's interference in Iran's internal affairs might result in international friction. The Security Council was caught up in this problem for almost half a year. Pending crises and mutual accusations among the Security Council members did not reflect the spirit of co-operation between the permanent members that the originators of the charter had hoped for. Danger to peace and security was emphasized and even threats of use of force were used until a satisfactory solution was achieved.

Shortly afterward, on February 4, 1946, another problem was put before the Security Council: Lebanon and Syria, informed of the presence of British and French troops in their territories,

United Nations medal awarded to those who served with UNEF.

Dmitri Shepilov of Russia and Selwyn Lloyd of Great Britain shake hands before a Security Council meeting on the Suez Canal question.

called for intervention of the council. On this occasion the Soviet delegation used its first veto, thus establishing the precedent of exercising the veto power accorded to permanent members of the Security Council. But the British and French troops did not stay long. By the beginning of April, the withdrawal of these troops was completed.

THE INDONESIAN CONFLICT

On January 21, 1946 the Ukrainian Soviet Socialist Republic charged that military action against the local population in Indonesia by British and Japanese forces threatened international peace and security. For almost four years, the United Nations was kept busy with the Indonesian problem. Military operations by the Dutch forces against Indonesia had continued incessantly. Truce agreements were signed and denounced, the Security Council met in emergency session,

John Foster Dulles, United States Secretary of State, and Mr. Lloyd, are seen at a meeting of the Security Council dealing with Suez.

Christian Pineau, French Foreign Minister, as president of the Security Council calls the meeting to order. At the right is Dragoslav Protitch, U.N. Undersecretary for Political and Security Council Affairs.

calls were made for cessation of hostilities. Finally the Security Council assumed the role of a "midwife" of a new nation, recommending, on January 28, 1949, the establishment of a federal, independent United States of Indonesia, and appointing the United Nations Commission for Indonesia, entrusted with the task of supervising the implementation of the resolution.

But the dispute lingered on. Not until November, 1949, was a settlement reached, when, with the participation of the U.N. Commission for Indonesia, a Charter of Transfer of Sovereignty by the Netherlands to the Republic of the United States of Indonesia was signed, and Indonesia was recognized as an independent state, later to be called the Republic of Indonesia. No doubt, the agreement was a signal victory for the peacemaking facilities of the United Nations. On September 28, 1950, the third largest State of Asia, the Republic of Indonesia, was admitted to the United

Mr. Shepilov addresses the council.

Nations, to become its sixtieth member. It was certainly a proud moment for all U.N. supporters when, on April 6, 1951, the U.N. Commission for Indonesia informed the Security Council that

Delegates frequently hold informal conversations before meetings of the council begin.

Two of the seven foreign ministers who participated in the Security Council debate on the Suez issue are seen here exchanging views. They are Koca Popovic' (*left*) of Yugoslavia, and Paul Henri Spaak (*center*) of Belgium. With them (*back to camera*) is Fernand van Langenhove, Belgium's permanent representative to the U.N.

since no items remained on the agenda it was adjourning sine die.

The Commission and the Security Council did not foresee that their conclusion was somewhat premature, for only three years later, in August,

1954, Indonesia raised the problem of West Irian (West New Guinea) demanding the inclusion of the problem on the agenda of the ninth session of the General Assembly. The demand for the incorporation of this territory into the Republic of Indonesia became a source of permanent friction between Indonesia and the Netherlands. Launched by the Netherlands on the road to independence, in the meantime, West New Guinea remained continously on the agenda of U.N. assemblies, adding another issue to the many problems of the cold war.

THE PALESTINE PROBLEM

In the midst of the Indonesian conflict another problem demanded U.N. attention: Palestine and its future. Great Britain, which administered the Holy Land for almost thirty years as the mandatory power, being entrusted, under the League of Nations Covenant, to advance the country toward self-government with the provision of promoting the rebuilding of the Jewish national homeland in that country, decided to terminate the mandate in view of intensifying attacks and opposition of the Jewish population. On April 2, 1947 the

John Foster Dulles, Dmitri Shepilov, Selwyn Lloyd, and Christian Pineau were among those present at a council meeting on the Suez dispute.

United Kingdom asked for a special session of the General Assembly to examine the Palestine question. At this session, held between April 28 and May 25, a Special Committee on Palestine was established. The eleven members of the committee, representing eleven member states, visited the Middle East and prepared a report containing twelve general recommendations with a majority and minority plan. The majority plan called for a partition of Palestine into an Arab State, a Jewish State, internationalization of Jerusalem and an economic union for all three parts; the minority plan provided for a federal state, with an Arab and a Jewish state with Jerusalem as its capital.

With the adoption on November 29, 1947, of the majority plan of partition of Palestine by a vote of 33 to 13, a stormy chapter in the annals of the Middle East and the United Nations Organization was opened. The plan, accepted by the Jewish Agency, representing the Jewish side met with total rejection by the Arab Higher Committee, supported by all Arab states. Open bloody conflict followed.

The United Nations Palestine Commission established in the resolution of November 29, could never really fulfill its function of supervision of the implementation of the U.N. resolution. In view of the deteriorating military situation, the Security Council adopted a proposal to call a new

Secretary General Dag Hammarskjöld announcing to the press that he received a letter from the Israeli foreign minister expressing Israel's willingness to withdraw forces from the Sinai Peninsula.

Team of U.N. truce observers on Israeli border.

A section of a street in Port Said damaged by bombings.

special session of the assembly, which met in New York from April 16 to May 14, 1948. A truce commission was appointed. On May 14, the post of United Nations Mediator was established and a decision to relieve the Palestine Commission of its responsibilities became a fact. The proclamation of the State of Israel on May 14, the day the British Mandate over Palestine expired, was followed immediately by armed action of the Arab States, Egypt, Iraq, Syria, Lebanon, and Transjordan (later named Jordan after the part of Palestine on the west bank of the Jordan River was incorporated).

The Middle East and the Arab-Israeli relations turned into one of the most explosive problems permanently on the United Nations agenda. The Security Council issued calls for the cessation of hostilities. After a four-week truce became effective on June 11, 1948, the Security Council called for a prolongation of the truce. The provisional government of Israel agreed, but the Arab States refused, and hostilities were renewed. It took a warning of

United Nations Emergency Force patrol preserves tranquillity in the Middle East.

Soldiers of the Norwegian contingent of UNEF patrolling the streets of Port Said.

United Nations observer discusses with Israeli authorities the withdrawal of their forces from a section of the desert.

The vessels *Ausdauer* and *Energie* raise a section of the El Ferdan Bridge, one of the most serious obstacles in the Suez Canal, during salvage work performed by the U.N.

Soldiers of the Yugoslav contingent sleep in the open beside one of their trucks.

the Security Council—that failure to comply with cease-fire orders would be construed as a breach of peace which would require consideration of enforcement measures—to stop the fighting.

The U.N. mediator, Count Bernadotte, who was assassinated in the Israeli sector of Jerusalem, was followed by Dr. Ralph Bunche of the U.N. Secretariat, and a new effort for conciliation started. The third session of the General Assembly adopted on December 11, 1948, a series of resolutions pertaining to the Arab-Israeli conflict: It established a Conciliation Commission composed of representatives of Turkey, France, and the United States to deal with the settlement of all questions;

United Nations Emergency Force advances toward El-Arish after evacuation of the city by Israeli forces. These men are part of a Yugoslav contingent.

a resolution on Arab refugees who fled from Palestine provided that those refugees who wished to return and live in peace with their neighbors should be permitted to do so and that those who did not wish to return have the right for compensation for the properties left behind.

Armistice agreements signed separately with Egypt, Syria, Lebanon, and the Hashemite Kingdom of Jordan, between February and July, 1949 (Iraq remained the only Arab country which did not sign an armistice agreement with Israel), were considered, to a great extent, an accomplishment of the personal diplomatic skill of Dr. Bunche who was later awarded, on this account, the Nobel Prize for Peace. This was a notable distinction, not only for one of the most important civil servants of the international organization, but also for the peacemaking efforts and achievements of the United Nations Organization itself.

The U.N. Truce Supervision Organization (UNTSO), a U.N. organ composed of international observers and headed by a chief of staff, opened the way for a most interesting experiment in the U.N. peacemaking efforts. Although destined for one area of conflict only, the Israeli-Arab borders, the establishment of an organization of military observers, at the place of conflict or possible conflict, proved in later years a major development in the United Nations machinery for pre-

United Nations Emergency Force unit on patrol near El-Arish.

vention of military engagements between warring parties, and was repeated in similar form in other areas.

The high hopes of the days of trucemaking did not materialize. The truce did not become a prelude to peace as provided for in the armistice agreements. Instead, the relations between Israel and her Arab neighbors became a permanent concern of the United Nations organs and, primarily, of the Security Council. Charges and countercharges were voiced by both sides.

Among particularly serious charges was the Israeli accusation against Egypt that she blockaded the Suez Canal against Israeli shipping, and later even goods destined for Israel or coming from Israel, in spite of Security Council resolutions calling for free use of the canal for all nations, including Israel.

The Arabs, on the other hand, complained constantly of Israeli military raids, denying Israel's argument that these raids were only countermeasures aimed at stopping infiltration and sabotage.

The permanence and intensity of the Arab-Israeli conflict is best illustrated by the fact that

United Nations soldier stands guard beside the U.N. flag at a desert bivouac.

Demonstration in front of UNEF headquarters in Gaza. The incident was in contrast to the peaceful, friendly demonstrations which greeted the U.N. forces elsewhere.

in 1953, of the forty-two meetings of the Security Council, twenty-four (and in 1954 twenty-two out of thirty-two) were devoted to what turned into the usual definition on the agenda "the Palestine question."

Visitors to the U.N., newspapermen, and diplomats, used to joke that if there was not a "Palestine question," it would have to be invented for it became an important *raison d'être* for the U.N., and kept its organs busy.

THE SUEZ CRISIS

This rather frivolous approach, in some circles, to the emotion-laden problem had to be completely disavowed after only some eight years of the precarious "peace" between Israel and its Arab neighbors. Arab statements on a "state of war" with Israel, raids and counter raids, commando

attacks even far from the borders, erupted at the end of October, 1956, into a full-scale war between Israel and Egypt. The Israeli army crossed the armistice lines into Egypt and within hours an emergency session of the Security Council was called, upon the demand of the United States representative, Ambassador Henry Cabot Lodge, to consider "the Palestine question: steps for the immediate cessation of the military action of Israel in Egypt." The Egyptian charges of aggression were countered by Israeli assertions of their sovereign right of self-defense against Egyptian commando units, *fedayeen*, which invaded Israeli territory. Article 51 of the charter, providing for self-defense, was invoked.

(Article 51 states: "Nothing in the present Charter shall impair the inherent right of individual or collective self-defense if an armed attack

Soldiers of the Indonesian contingent enjoy after-duty recreation.

Dogs trained to detect mines are used by the contingent from Sweden in patrolling near the armistice demarcation line.

occurs against a Member of the United Nations, until the Security Council has taken measures necessary to maintain international peace and security. Measures taken by Members in the exercise of this right of self-defense shall be immediately reported to the Security Council and shall not in any way affect the authority and responsibility of the Security Council under the present Charter to take at any time such action as it deems necessary in order to maintain or restore international peace and security.")

Days of excitement followed. Meetings lasting almost around the clock; the corridors filled with diplomats and journalists who flocked from all over for the big news; unprecedented pressure for entrance to the visitors' galleries—all these elements contributed greatly to the rise of tension. And when, on October 30, the representatives of Great Britain and France informed the Security Council that Egypt and Israel had been told to withdraw to a distance of ten miles from the Suez Canal, and that otherwise the French and British

Map of Israel, showing existing and proposed borders (January 1, 1961), as well as operations of the United Nations Relief and Works Agency (UNRWA).

More than 5,500 refugee girls of school age in the Gaza strip are wearing school uniforms provided through contributions made by UNEF. Cloth known as "Gaza weave" was woven locally and cut in an UNRWA center.

An UNRWA camp in Gaza.

armies would intervene, there was no longer any doubt that the Security Council would be unable to act. In view of the Anglo-French statement, everybody knew that it would be supported by vetoes. And indeed, the vetoes were casted.

The Anglo-French military intervention was presented as undertaken with the purpose of safe-guarding the Suez Canal and the restoration of peaceful conditions in the Middle East. The device for overcoming the negative votes of permanent members of the Security Council—the call for an emergency special session of the Security Council under the "Uniting for Peace" resolution—had to be invoked. Ironically, it was a communist country, Yugoslavia, at that time an elected member of the Security Council, which introduced the resolution for a measure which six years before had been initiated by the United States to overcome the Russian veto in the Korean war.

The U.N. members, the U.N. staff, the press, all were aware that this was no ordinary crisis. The handling of what became known as the "Suez crisis" will, as one delegate said, "make or break" the United Nations Organization as an instrument for the preservation of peace.

Speed was the rule of the day. No delaying tactics were permitted. Again the debate lasted, without interruption, day and night. The international city on the East River did not sleep; everybody worked. The U.N. Information offices, the guards, the elevator operators, the restaurants, and above all the thirty-eighth floor, that of the secretary general's office, swarmed with assistants, advisers, consultants, and visiting diplomats, who all turned to the secretary general, Dag Hammarskjöld, for instructions and advice. An unceasing flow of documents, reports, communications,

A market in Gaza.

An inhabitant of UNRWA's Nabatieh camp shearing camels.

legal attestations, filled the shelves of the documents desk for diplomats and press alike. The resolutions called for an immediate cease-fire and withdrawal of troops, and in the case of Israel, a withdrawal of her troops behind the armistice lines, from the Ghaza Strip and the Sinai Penin-

Children in Yarmuk camp for refugees, near Damascus.

General view of the Nahr El Bared camp near Tripoli, one of the largest camps in Lebanon, where more than six thousand refugees live in tents.

sula, which was virtually under Israel's control by November 4. The secretary general was requested to observe and report promptly on compliance with the resolutions.

Again the delegates witnessed an unprecedented speed—the task of preparing a plan for an emergency international force was accomplished the very same day on which the resolution was adopted. It was immediately submitted to the assembly which proceeded with a resolution establishing a United Nations command for an International Emergency Force to secure and supervise the cessation of hostilities.

Within less than forty hours the United Nations Emergency Force, to be known as UNEF, became a fact. The United Nations Organization acquired an enforcing arm for its resolutions. Many saw in this decision the implementation of Article 43 of the charter, which, in chapter VII, under the heading "Action With Respect to Threats to the Peace, Breaches of the Peace, and Acts of Aggression" stipulates: "All members of the United Nations, in order to contribute to the maintenance of international peace and security undertake to make available to the Security Council, on its call and in accordance with a special agreement or agreements, armed forces, assistance, and facilities, including rights of passage, necessary for the purpose of maintaining international peace and security."

The representative of Russia, Arkady Sobolev, did not vote for the resolution, explaining that the force was being created in violation of the U.N. Charter, since, according to the charter (chapter VII) only the Security Council is empowered to

set up such a force.

But the UNEF resolution was already moving with utmost urgency toward full implementation. Twenty-four member states offered to participate in the force, but only ten were asked to dispatch their units: Brazil, Canada, Colombia, Denmark, Finland, India, Indonesia, Norway, Sweden, and Yugoslavia. On November 15, the first UNEF unit was on Egyptian soil. The U.N. Truce Supervision Organization, provided the advance party and its chief of staff, General Burns, was appointed commander of UNEF. Again, the Middle East conflicts produced a new form in the U.N.'s instrumentalities for the preservation of peace.

True, this was not a force to impose by armed intervention any U.N. resolution, and it was not intended to take part in military operations

The United Nations Relief and Works Agency cares for vocational training for young refugees.

against one side or the other; rather, it was a force called to assist in the preservation of tranquility in the area through deployment of its units and by patrolling the Gaza Strip, the Eastern border of the Sinai Peninsula, and the region of Scharm-el-Sheikh (controlling the sea approaches to the Gulf of Aqaba and Eilat, which Egypt had effectively blockaded until then to Israeli shipping). Since then the U.N. has been relieved of permanent preoccupation with urgent Arab-Israeli matters, although basically no change in the Mid-

Rations distribution center maintained by UNRWA in Bureij, in the Gaza strip.

Contents of convoy to Mt. Scopus, held by Israel, are examined by personnel of the United Nations Truce Supervision Organization (UNTSO) in presence of both Jordanian and Israeli authorities.

The United Nations Truce Supervision Organization is responsible for the supply of water to the communities of Mount Scopus and Issawiya village, in the Jerusalem area.

View from the headquarters of UNTSO showing New Jerusalem (Israel) to the left and Old Jerusalem with the city wall (Jordan) to the right.

Member of the Ghana police.

Contingent of Moroccan troops at Accra airport in Ghana en route to the Congo.

dle East situation has occurred, and no solution of the problem is in sight.

THE CONGO CRISIS

This pacifying influence of UNEF and its effectiveness played important roles when the Congo crisis of summer, 1960, beset the U.N. As in the organizing phase of UNEF, the U.N. Truce Supervision Organization served as the model and initial pool of personnel. In the same way, on this occasion, ONUC (which derives from the French title, Force de l'Organisation de Nations Unies au Congo), the United Nations military force in the Congo, drew on the experiences and personnel of UNTSO and UNEF alike. Again, the United Nations was called upon to intervene in a most

During a stopover at Kano, Nigeria, soldiers from Mali on their way to the Congo to join the U.N. force go through the mess line.

A Swedish soldier on guard.

explosive situation, which threatened not only disintegration of, and fratricidal war within, a newly independent state, but bore in itself dangers of far-reaching conflicts between the leading nations of the world. A genuine threat to world peace was clearly involved here. But this time, the task was much bigger. The area to be under the U.N. Force's supervision was incomparably more extensive. Multiplying problems of a country undeveloped, and having a minimum of techni-

cally skilled personnel, were looming on the horizon.

The operations in the Congo, lasting over a year, turned into the focal point of the United Nations operations and consumed much of its energy. Aspects pertaining to every phase of human endeavor became the direct responsibility of the international organization. It was placed in the very center of the stormy world situation, and it turned into a forum for some of the most heated exchanges of the cold war.

But the reward for the wisdom and patience of the United Nations, the secretary general, and the advisory committees on the Congo (composed of the member states whose contingents constituted the United Nations force in the Congo), was yet to come. Harassed by strong criticism of U.N. members, weakened by the withdrawal of certain contingents from the force, compelled to act in a country on the permanent verge of civil war—especially after the death of the first prime minister, Patrice Lumumba, the secession of the Katanga Province, and the establishment of a separate government in Stanleyville under Antoine Gizenga (who served as deputy prime minister under Lu-

Deployment of units of the U.N. force as of August 19, 1960.

Congolese women dance to thank the U.N. patrol for settling an incident in the Stanleyville market.

Camp for victims of tribal fighting in the Congo.

mumba)—the United Nations authorities in the Congo continued to work toward national reconciliation between the Congolese forces which threatened the political unity of the country.

With the beginning of the second year of the United Nations' operations in the Congo a decisive change in the Congo occurred. The Congolese Parliament met under United Nations protection, and a new government of Congolese national unity was unanimously elected.

In his letter, dated August 10, 1961, the new prime minister of the Congo, Cyrille Adoula, wrote to the U.N. secretary general: "I take pleasure in informing you that the Congolese Parliament which met at Lovanium under United Nations protection has ended the Congolese constitutional crisis by unanimously placing its confidence in a government of national unity and political reconciliation over which I have the honor to preside." And in his speech to the Parliament, in which the new prime minister outlined the program of the government, he did not fail to stress the role the United Nations played in the Congo. "We must not fail," said Mr. Adoula, "to mention the remarkable assistance which the United Nations mobilized to help us. As the chief of the state [Joseph Kasavubu] emphasized in

Food packages unloaded from U.N. plane by Tunisian troops on the U.N. force.

his speech to the combined chambers of parliament, the United Nations deserves our gratitude. . . . Although it is not a very equitable judge or a very sure prop, the United Nations is nevertheless a life-preserver for all newly created countries and a source of hope for all."

The U.N. political assistance to the Congo was fully matched by the growing extent of U.N. technical assistance. A review of the first year of the U.N. Civilian Operations Program in the Congo, published in August, 1961, states that it has grown in twelve months into a coherent, wide-ranging undertaking—"a civilian technical assistance operation with no parallel elsewhere." In the words of a United Nations document, the report, concerning the year ended June 30, 1961, describes in detail how "an international staff of some 750 working in hospitals and airports, in post offices and

Ghana police on duty in Leopoldville.

farm schools, in city buildings and jungle huts, played an important part in staving off the social and economic chaos that at one time seemed a very present threat in the Congo."

This progress toward consolidation, which gave rise to plans for reduction in the numbers and scope of activities of the U.N. force, was dramatically reversed only about a month after the Congolese prime minister notified the U.N. secretary general that the Congolese constitutional crisis had ended. The separate government in Stanleyville was dissolved, even though the question of the separate army units remained somewhat unclear. Secessionist Katanga, under President Moise Tshombe, refused to recognize the authority of the Central Government.

In this situation the U.N. authorities decided to act. Invoking resolutions of the Security Council, especially the resolution of February 21, 1961,

A soldier of the Irish contingent in the Congo on guard duty at company headquarters in Albertville (August, 1960).

Soldiers from various nations stand guard in Leopoldville.

Members of the commission investigating the death of Patrice Lumumba. Left to right: Ayité d'Almeida (Togo), Justice U Aung Khine (Burma), Salvador Martinez de Alva (Mexico), and Ato Teschome Hailemariam (Ethiopia).

which empowered the U.N. forces in the Congo to "use force if necessary," the United Nations troops in the capital of Katanga, Elisabethville, made an early-morning attack, on September 13, on three key points in the city held by Katanga forces. The ensuing battle in Elisabethville and other Katanga localities lasted for eight days. The U.N. forces did not succeed in their task. The white officers whom the attack was supposed to remove from the Katanga army stayed on. Efforts for a cease-fire started, and were supplemented shortly by the efforts of Secretary General Hammarskjöld who was at that time in Leopoldville, capital of the Congo, on the invitation of the Congo Central Government.

After many communications between Mr.

After the North Korean forces crossed the thirty-eighth parallel, United Nations troops took action to combat the aggression. Here United States Marines move forward.

Warren Austin, United States representative to the Security Council, confers with Trygve Lie, then U.N. secretary general, prior to a meeting of the council on the Korean question.

Tshombe and Mr. Hammarskjöld about the place to be set for their meeting, Ndola, in Northern Rhodesia, was chosen. It was near to the airport of Ndola that disaster struck. Mr. Hammarskjöld and twelve other persons were killed when their plane crashed in flames. Three days later, on Sept. 21, a cease-fire agreement between U.N. troops and the Katanga *gendarmerie* came into force.

The main problems remained unsolved, bearing grave dangers and threatening unpredictable developments. The Katanga secession remained in effect and the Central Government started to concentrate troops to end the secession by force.

United Nations authorities set, on September 28, a new deadline for the expulsion of about one hundred white soldiers serving in the Katanga army, thus following up a previous ultimatum, of August 28, in which the U.N. ordered the expulsion of five hundred white officers believed to be serving in the Katanga army at that time.

On July 30, 1951, a public meeting of the U.N. Commission on Korea was held in a large hall in the provisional capital of the Republic of Korea, Taegu. A large audience heard each individual member of the U.N. commission reaffirm his country's determination to support the U.N. in Korea.

Troops of the U.N. in night combat at the front line.

The vacuum created in the Secretariat after the death of Mr. Hammarskjöld, the U.N. troops' involvement in direct combat, and the preparations of the Central Government to put down the Katanga secession by force, threatened everything which the U.N. achieved in the Congo in over a year of strenuous efforts. This extreme test could well influence the U.N.'s role in the Congo as well as the active standing of the international organization as an instrument for the preservation of peace and order in the world.

There has been an important change in thinking regarding U.N. intervention, however, since the initial request of the Congolese government for United Nations military assistance. The request was made on July 12, 1960, and the following day, Mr. Hammarskjöld stated: "The action of the U.N. Force would be based on the principles that had been arrived at as a result of previous experience in this field. The United Nations Force would not be authorized to act beyond self-defense; it would not be allowed to take any action which would make it a party to internal conflicts; it would include units from African

A burial service for three American soldiers is held in a United Nations military cemetery near Pusan.

Australian troops of the U.N. Army in Korea cross a pontoon bridge over the Taedong River as soldiers of the United States Engineers reinforce it.

A hot meal is a welcome sight to these men of the 1st U.S. Army Corps behind the front line.

states, and the use of troops from any of the permanent members of the Council would be excluded." The developments in the Congo and the growing preoccupation of the U.N. with the situation in the Congo almost completely absorbed the secretary general's attention during his last year of office. During that time, Mr. Hammarskjöld

evolved a completely new conception of U.N. enforcement policies, a conception which must have been at the root of the decision to employ U.N. troops in a military initiative. This conception is clearly presented in the secretary general's introduction to his annual report. Speaking about executive arrangements as provided in the charter, Mr. Hammarskjöld quoted articles 24, 29, and 40. These articles call for effective action for the maintenance of peace and security, the establishment of subsidiary organs for the performance of these duties and the right to use, for the purposes of the charter and under certain conditions, armed forces which are made available to the Council. They also specify the right, under article 48, to request from governments of member nations action on the Council's behalf, as well as the right to request the secretary general to "perform such . . . functions as are entrusted to him by the Council." And to make the meaning of these statements clear, Mr. Hammarskjöld adds: "In fact therefore, the executive functions and their form have been left largely to practice, and it is in the field of the

Men of the U.S. 24th Infantry Division return to the rear after days of fighting.

practices of the organization that cases may be found in the light of which the organization may develop its possibilities for diplomatic, political or military intervention of an executive nature in the field."

The Congo military intervention was certainly the result of this reasoning. As it developed, it put the U.N. to a most serious test, which again gave rise to the saying, the counterpart of which was often heard in the U.N. corridors during the Suez crisis: "The Congo crisis will either make or break U.N. effectiveness."

THE KOREAN TEST

But the feeling of crisis which prevailed so many times in the U.N. since the beginning of the Congo operation, comes into somewhat different perspective when the Korean crisis and its repercussions are recalled.

This Far Eastern peninsula became a United Nations concern as early as 1943, when at the Cairo Conference the leaders of the United States, Great Britain, and China pledged that Korea would be independent after the defeat of Japan. The occupation of Korea by U.S. and Russian troops south and north of the thirty-eighth parallel, respectively, opened an era of strife which led to armed conflict and has not reached a stage

of peaceful and final solution since then. After 1947 the problem of Korea became a matter of continuing concern for the United Nations. A Temporary U.N. Commission on Korea, composed of nine member states, set up to facilitate the establishment of a national government of Korea chosen in elections, could not perform its mandate in view of the Russian refusal of permission to enter North Korea. A South Korean government based on elections was instituted, with the purpose of unification of the country as its first national task.

June 25, 1950 brought a special form of unifica-

Mustang pilots of the R.A.A.F. Fighter Squadron study a target map at their base in Korea.

Montage used in the booklet *United Action in Korea* showing how, in response to a Security Council call for help against the North Korean invaders, the United States and sixteen other nations sent land, sea, and air forces as their contribution to the world's first collective security action.

tion effort: North Korean military forces crossed the thirty-eighth parallel. The Security Council convened the same day on the basis of information, given to Secretary General Trygve Lie by the United States delegation and the U.N. Commission on Korea, that an act of aggression had been committed. By a vote of 9 to 0, with one abstention (Yugoslavia), the Security Council determined that the armed attack was a breach of peace and called for an immediate cessation of hostilities, withdrawal of North Korean forces to the thirty-eighth parallel, and for the assistance of member states in carrying out the resolution.

A second resolution followed on June 27, 1950. It noted that the North Korean authorities had neither ceased hostilities nor withdrawn their armed forces, and recommended that members of the U.N. give such assistance to the Republic of South Korea as might be necessary to repel the armed attack and restore international peace and security in the area. On the same day an announcement of the United States government made it

clear that the United States was responding to the Security Council call and ordering its forces to give support to the forces of South Korea. On July 7, the council, with 7 votes to 0, and with 3 abstentions (Egypt, India, and Yugoslavia) requested all member states to provide military forces in pursuance of the council's resolutions and to make these forces available to a unified command under the United States.

The first international combatant army, fighting for the implementation of a Security Council resolution aimed at the restoration of international peace and security as provided in the U.N. Charter, became a fact. Sixteen nations provided fighting units to the international army. Military contingents of Australia, Belgium, Canada, Colombia, Ethiopia, France, Greece, Luxemburg, the Netherlands, New Zealand, the Philippines, Thailand, Turkey, the Union of South Africa, the United Kingdom, and the United States were unified under one command. Forty-one member states chose various other forms of assistance for the

Resolution recommending that members of the United Nations furnish such assistance to the Republic of Korea as may be necessary to repel the armed attack and to restore international peace and security in the area.

fighting forces—assistance which ranged from the sending of medical units, to small contributions of medical supplies for the international military effort.

Tides of war brought good and bad news to the U.N. Korean command. On November 6, military units of the People's Republic of China entered the conflict. This time U.N. organs could not act as smoothly as a few months earlier. The representative of Russia, who boycotted the meetings of the Security Council after January 13, 1950, as a protest against a representative of the People's Republic of China not being seated on the Security Council, took his seat again on August 1, 1950.

There was a special reason for this Russian change of attitude in addition to the unpleasant lesson of a military action by the United Nations

Syngman Rhee, president of the Republic of Korea, waves a welcome to troops of Ethiopia arriving to join the U.N. forces in Korea.

War orphans amidst the rubble of Inchon.

decided upon in the absence of the Russian representative, and therefore also the absence of his veto. This additional reason was the fact that according to the system of monthly rotations in the presidency of the council, the Russian representative had to assume the presidency of the council in August. Fourteen long meetings of the Security Council in that month proved what power the president of the Security Council holds if he knows how to use the procedural authority he wields. Even without a formal veto, Soviet ambassador Jacob Malik proved easily that with the Russians' return to the conference table, the Security Council could not do much in the way of a follow-up of its previous resolutions on Korea.

In this critical tie-up, a revolutionary measure was undertaken to overcome the Russian veto. On November 3, 1950 the General Assembly adopted a resolution headed "Uniting for Peace" proposed by Secretary of State Dean Acheson. According to this resolution, whenever the Security Council is unable to function because of a lack of unanimity among the permanent members of the council, a special emergency General Assembly may be convoked on twenty-four hours' notice and make "ap-

propriate recommendations to members for collective measures."

All these measures did not assure a final solution of the Korean problem. Even after the assembly adopted, on February 1, 1951, a resolution which found that the government of the Chinese People's Republic failed to accept the United Nations proposals to end hostilities, and had engaged in aggression in Korea, no basic change in the situation followed. Armistice negotiations between the military commanders, which began on July 10, 1951, were not concluded until July 27, 1953. After the armistice, Korea remained a permanent item on the agenda of the United Nations, as one of the international problems deeply immersed in the cold war. There were innumerable attempts at a solution of the problem, but none were successful. Korea remained divided, with the southern part, stationing the United Nations forces, entrusted with the preservation of the cease-fire. The thirty-eighth parallel again was the dividing line between the communist-held North and noncommunist South.

Although this "Uniting for Peace" measure considerably increased the efficacy of the General Assembly, and although it was utilized time and again, not all disputes handled by the U.N. made recourse to it necessary. The dispute over nationalization of the Anglo-Iranian Oil Company in 1951 was considered at six meetings of the Security Council, and the matter was also referred to the International Court of Justice. The nationali-

An old man salvaging bricks and bits of wood which will be used in the rebuilding of his family's wrecked home.

War orphans found in the ruins of Seoul are taken care of by U.N. welfare officer on the staff of the Unified Command.

North Korean prisoners of war.

An almost endless column of refugees crosses the provisional bridge over the Han River.

Refugees on long winter march to safety.

Refugees fleeing Chinese and North Korean troops are directed to secondary routes in order to leave main highways open to military movements.

zation of the Suez Canal Company on July 26, 1956 was brought to the attention of the Security Council. Charges and countercharges were put forward. Threat to international peace and security was invoked. The "open diplomacy" method of airing the complaints at open sessions of the Security Council was supplemented by secret meetings of the Security Council. Later, these meetings turned into the "old fashioned" secret diplomacy. The office of the secretary general served as meeting place of the foreign ministers of the interested powers, and Mr. Hammarskjöld himself lent his vast experience and diplomatic skill to this exercise in using the U.N. Headquarters as a convenient meeting place for diplomats.

The fact that Egypt set forth in the United Nations its Declaration on the Suez Canal and the arrangements on its operation, did not change the opinion of those parties which saw in the Egyptian seizure of the Canal a threat to international peace and security. The ensuing military campaign, which so much engaged the U.N. and proved its influence on world affairs, remains an important chapter in the continuing international concern regarding the Suez Canal problem.

THE SITUATION IN HUNGARY

The influence of the U.N. was much less evident in another international crisis which enveloped it simultaneously with the Suez crisis. The request of France, the United Kingdom and the United States, on October 27, 1956, to consider the situation in Hungary, caused, as Hungary stated, by foreign military intervention, repressing

violently the rights of the Hungarian people, was discussed at several meetings of the Security Council. When a resolution was introduced on November 3 calling upon the U.S.S.R. to withdraw its troops, nine votes were in favor, one abstained and one was against. The latter was Russia's veto.

The Uniting for Peace resolution had to be invoked. And although the General Assembly in its emergency session adopted a resolution calling upon Russia to withdraw, without delay, all of its forces from Hungary, no action followed. None of the resolutions concerning Hungary were implemented. U.N. observers were refused admission to Hungary, and even the U.N. secretary general, Mr. Hammarskjöld, could not visit Hungary. The United Nations members' delegations were not adamant at this development. Many did not conceal their worry at the fact that it was only France, Great Britain and Israel which had thus

A Korean Air Force pilot in the cockpit of his F-51 Mustang prior to taking off for mission over North Korean territory.

far complied with the U.N. resolutions and accepted its moral authority, while Russia refused co-operation openly, completely disregarding the U.N. resolutions and recommendations. The "Problem of Hungary," a new item on the agenda of the General Assembly, joined the growing list of "problems" which became an ingredient of cold war conflicts.

It is interesting to note that at the second part of the U.N. Fifteenth General Assembly, opened in March, 1961, Russia openly proposed to the United States delegation to bargain the withholding of the debate on the Hungarian question for

Chinese Communist and North Korean delegates pose for photographers prior to a preliminary armistice conference.

Russia's willingness not to press for a debate on the U-2 incident, the case of a United States high altitude reconnaissance plane, which was shot down in the heart of Russia in May, 1960.

THE KASHMIR DISPUTE

This Hungarian problem could certainly not compete in duration with many other problems on the U.N. agenda. There is the Kashmir question which occupied the U.N. authorities beginning January 1, 1948, when India first reported to the Security Council that tribesmen and others had been invading the State of Yammu and Kashmir and that fighting was taking place. The princedom, under the scheme of partition and the Indian Independence Act of 1947, became free to accede to either India or Pakistan.

After the invasion had begun, the ruler of the state requested accession to India. The Indian government made it clear that the final fate of the state "should be settled by a reference to the people." Pakistan presented the invasion as an act of self-determination by the Moslem tribes and declared the accession to India illegal. The Security Council, having to deal with a pending threat of war, recommended cessation of fighting and established a United Nations Commission for India and Pakistan (UNCIP), entrusted with the creation of conditions for a free and impartial plebiscite. This organ became a new element in the United Nations peace effort. Observers from various nations were appointed to report on compliance with the cease-fire agreement, which was reached in the meantime. A plebiscite administrator was nominated in 1949, but nothing happened to lead to a final solution of the dispute.

The problem has been smoldering since then, with occasional flare-ups, sometimes on the border lines, but, fortunately, more often in the debates in the United Nations organs. Here some "firsts" were achieved: One of the reports of the United Nations representative in the area produced twelve

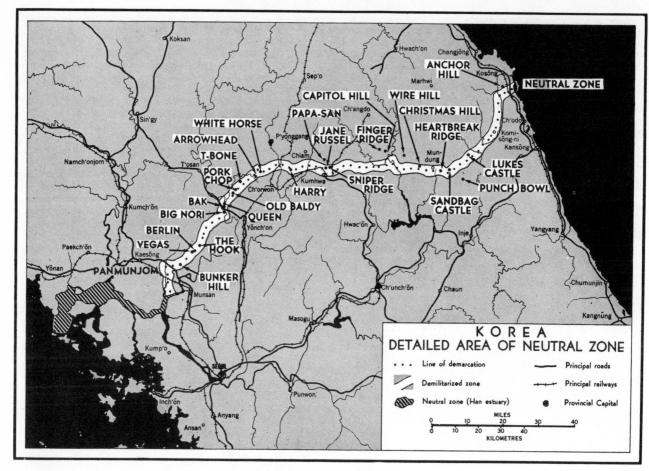

Armistice line in Korea.

Piles of scrap such as these at the Inchon docks are still to be seen throughout Korea.

A shoeshine school for Seoul boys, started in 1952 by Pvt. Kvon Ung Pal, a young Korean transferred from a combat unit to help round up beggar boys. Help for the school came from the U.N. Women's Guild in the form of $10,000 worth of UNESCO gift coupons.

Hungarian refugees in a reception center.

draft proposals for a temporary accommodation between India and Pakistan; and India's representative, at one of the Kashmir debates at the U.N. Security Council, the minister of defense of India, V. K. Krishna Menon, delivered the longest speech in the U.N. annals. The speech lasted over seven hours, during which Mr. Menon fainted of exhaustion but resumed his presentation to bring to an end his arguments against the implementation of the plebiscite solution.

THE QUESTION OF CHINESE REPRESENTATION

Of much more far-reaching consequence for world peace was the question of China, which was submitted in September, 1949, to the General Assembly by the government of China. Phrased "Threats to the political independence and territorial integrity of China and to the peace of the Far East, resulting from Soviet violations of the Sino-Soviet Treaty of Friendship and Alliance of August 14, 1945, and from Soviet violations of the

Charter of the United Nations," it was in fact one of the last acts of the government of China in its fight against the taking over of China by the victorious communist armies. The subsequent resolutions of the United Nations did not change the developments in China. But the problems which emerged from that area affected not only the political climate in the United Nations, but presented a most sensitive organizational problem to the international organization.

The fact that China was a charter member of the U.N. and was one of the first "big four" (later "big five" with the inclusion of France, which came in after aiding in the Allied invasion of Europe), which became permanent members of the Security Council, complicated the situation. The establishment, on the island of Formosa, of a Chinese government under one of the signatories of the Cairo Declaration, General Chiang Kai-shek, created a problem overshadowing many of the permanent U.N. problems. The condemnation of the People's

Urgent session of the Security Council, on October 28, 1956, debates the situation in Hungary.

Republic of China by the U.N. organs as the aggressor during the Korean war, became one of the chief arguments against the admission of the People's Republic of China to the United Nations. The permanent seat in the Security Council, held by the representative of Nationalist China, was contested by Russia and the other communist governments. A growing number of U.N. members, mostly African and Asian states, followed suit.

The debate on Chinese representation became a standard feature at the meetings of the United Nations organs. The ceremonial opening of each session of the General Assembly had its standard procedure, and all attenting these sessions became accustomed to hearing the chief delegate of Russia raise the question as a point of order, to be disposed of by a procedural motion of the representative of the United States to postpone to the next session the consideration of the item to exclude the National Government of China, or to seat the representatives of the Central People's Government of the People's Republic of China. The Credentials Committee afforded similar treatment for the many proposals on this subject, the fate of which was not changed when, starting in

Hungarian refugees cross into Austria.

Three Hungarian women and a child reach Einstadt camp in Austria with all the belongings they could carry.

1956, at the eleventh General Assembly session, India proposed that the item "Question of representation of China in the United Nations" be placed on the agenda.

At the sixteenth session of the General Assembly, the consideration of the problem of Chinese representation in the United Nations took a new turn. The United States abandoned its policy of opposing the discussion of this problem, and supported the proposal of New Zealand to include in the agenda of the session the item headed "Question of the Representation of China in the United Nations." But Russia was not satisfied, and, at her request, an additional item was included, entitled "Restoration of the lawful rights of the

Members of the United Nations Commission on India and Pakistan (UNCIP) are welcomed by Chaudri Ghulam Abbas (*right*), leader of pro-Pakistani Azad Kashmir movement, an organized political and military body which actively opposed the pro-Indian administration of Sheikh Abdullah.

People's Republic of China in the United Nations."

THE PERMANENT PRESSURE OF CRISES

The problem created by the change of government in Czechoslovakia in February, 1948, resulting in communist control, was submitted to the Security Council, but no action was taken. Earlier, in 1946, the Greek question had appeared on the agenda. At the beginning it consisted in a Russian complaint that presence of British troops in Greece constituted interference in Greek internal affairs and was likely to endanger peace and security. The withdrawal of the British troops stationed in Greece by agreement with the Greek government contributed to an early termination of this debate on Greece.

Economic subcommission of UNCIP visits Sopore. Villagers converge on the newly arrived cars.

It was opened again soon after the Greek government complained of the interference of Albania, Bulgaria, and Yugoslavia in her internal affairs by supporting the communist guerillas. A United Nations Special Committee on the Balkans (UNSCOB) was entrusted with the task of settling the dispute, which in time included a most sensitive and unusual problem: the repatriation of tens of thousands of Greek children removed from Greece by the communist guerillas. The United Nations Special Committee on the Balkans was to become one of the few special committees of the U.N. to have its task fulfilled. It was declared discontinued by a General Assembly resolution of December 7, 1951.

Also concerning the Balkans was the Corfu Channel question, brought before the Security Council when the United Kingdom complained

Liaquat Ali Khan (*left*), prime minister of Pakistan, and Pandit Jawaharlal Nehru (*right*), with Sir Owen Dixon, U.N. mediator on Kashmir, at a meeting held at the Government House, New Delhi (July, 1950).

A 1,555–yard-long scroll bearing one million signatures under a Kashmir liberation pledge, is presented to Secretary General Trygve Lie (*right*) by Inamullah Khan, secretary of the World Moslem Conference.

Sir Mohammed Zafrullah Khan, minister of foreign affairs of Pakistan, and Sir Bengel Rau, permanent representative of India to the U.N., converse before a meeting of the Security Council.

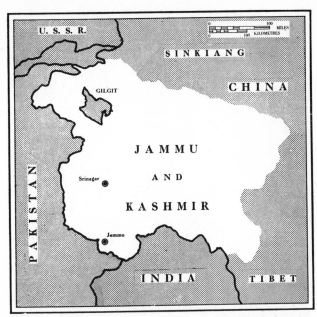

Map of Kashmir. Claimed by both India and Pakistan, this country was one of the early trouble spots the U.N. had to deal with.

United Nations military observer asks directions while going to the cease-fire line to investigate an incident.

Observer shaves at his station in Kashmir.

that Albania had caused damage to British warships and injury to naval personnel by mines planted, allegedly, by Albania in the channel. This case was notable in that the council recommended that Britain and Albania refer their dispute to the International Court of Justice.

The status of the Free Territory of Trieste was considered by the Security Council, and although a solution was found in direct negotiations between the parties concerned, the Memorandum of Understanding signed by Italy, the United Kingdom, the United States, and Yugoslavia was transmitted in October, 1954, to the Security Council. Thus the authority of the international institution was fully preserved.

When the Russian blockade of West Berlin in 1948 turned into a major international crisis, the problem was submitted to the Security Council. Insiders of political developments of those days remember well that negotiations between Russia and the Western powers for an agreement on the Berlin problem began with an informal contact at the U.N. between the Russian representative Jacob Malik and Dr. Philip Jessup of the United States. The United Nations lounge assumed a highly important diplomatic role by giving the opportunity for a preliminary exchange of views without the fanfare of formal diplomatic negotiations.

A somewhat similar situation developed at the sixteenth session of the General Assembly at which

Secretary of State Dean Rusk and Russian Foreign Minister Andrei Gromyko participated. The presence of both at the U.N. session made informal talks on the Berlin crisis possible, again without the obligations entailed by a formal conference and diplomatic negotiations.

But this time the U.N.'s concern with the Berlin crisis was not limited to service as a "brokerage" institution for contacts between the principal interested parties. The seriousness of the crisis, which brought the world to the brink of an atomic holocaust, imposed on the U.N. the most earnest interest in the solution of the crisis. Although the agenda of the sixteenth session of the General Assembly did not include an item on Berlin, this crisis, and not the ninety-one other items on the agenda, were primarily on the minds of the delegates.

The secretary general in his annual report stated bluntly that the United Nations "cannot be considered an outside party on an issue such as the Berlin question, a party which has no right to make its voice heard should a situation develop which would threaten those very interests which the United Nations is to safeguard and for the defense of which it was intended to provide all member nations with an instrument and a forum."

The powers involved in this Berlin crisis fully recognized the secretary general's contention and dealt thoroughly with it in the speeches of their representatives. President Kennedy and Andrei Gromyko made it clear that the Berlin crisis is and should be of concern to the U.N. and that in case direct negotiations did not result in a solution, the U.N. forum should be used as the last resort to save the peace.

Major Emelio Altieri of Uruguay rides horse along the cease-fire line.

Meeting of Indian and Pakistani officers on the cease-fire line is attended by U.N. military observers.

But this involvement of the U.N. in the Berlin crisis was not limited to intentions of using its forum for negotiations or direct intercession between the opposing parties. Among the plans for a solution of the crisis, for the preservation of what Western powers call their freedom, a direct role for the U.N. was envisaged. Stationing of U.N. troops, transferring of some U.N. agencies to Berlin, and even the transfer of the U.N. Headquarters itself or some other form of U.N. involvement and supervision in the solution of the crisis was discussed in the chancelleries. These suggestions put the U.N., as it should be, in the very center of deliberations for a peaceful solution of the crisis.

Many other explosive situations have been dealt with at meetings of the United Nations' main organs—the General Assembly and the Security Council. Tunis and Morocco in their struggle for independence, the case of the Algerian rebels demanding independence, the Lebanese complaint against the United Arab Republic's interference in its internal affairs through smuggling of arms

Inhabitants of small village in Pakistan talk with observer.

United Nations observer group on its way to investigate a violation of the cease-fire agreement.

and combatants to assist the forces which revolted against the government, the Iraqi situation which arose after the violent liquidation of the monarchy, the Jordanian complaint against the U.A.R.'s interference in her internal affairs—all were dealt with at the United Nations and in all some kind of solution was found and the extension of conflict avoided.

The early and late summer of 1958 saw feverish activity at the United Nations, when it was seized with problems of the Middle East. The United States and Great Britain were directly involved in the efforts for the preservation of the status quo in Lebanon and Jordan, after they had been called upon to defend the governments of these countries.

An Emergency Special Session of the General Assembly, the third, was convened on August 8. A United Nations direct instrument for the preservation of peace was established: the United Nations Observation Group in Lebanon (UNOGIL). The observation group, constituted of three members, had at its disposal a team of military observers which in time rose in number to two hundred. It terminated its operations completely

A group of personnel of the United Nations Special Committee on the Balkans (UNSCOB) looks toward the Albanian frontier from Amouda Heights in Central Macedonia.

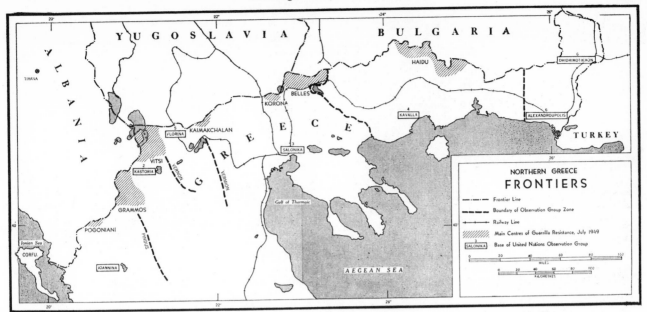

United Nations map shows northern Greek frontiers as of August, 1949.

on December 9, 1958, after a draft resolution of ten Arab states for the solution of the problem was unanimously adopted by the Emergency General Assembly.

The question of Cyprus, Laos, inflammatory propaganda, discrimination against nonwhites in South Africa, the capture of Eichmann by Israelis in Argentina were also of concern to the United Nations. A new form of United Nations intervention in conflicts came into being—the "United Nations presence," a device initiated by the U.N. secretary general which hoped by the sheer presence of a U.N. representative to strengthen peace and tranquility and deter all those who were bent on disturbing the existing situation.

The Western Hemisphere was no exception in this picture of world strife. On June 19, 1954, Guatemala requested a meeting of the Security Council to prevent disruption of peace and international security in Central America and to put a stop to the aggression against Guatemala. A draft resolution to refer the problem to the regional organization—the Organization of American States —was blocked by a Russian veto, but on July 9, the minister for External Affairs of Guatemala, representing the new government, notified the president of the Security Council that peace and order had been restored.

Officers of UNSCOB on balcony of Observer Group Headquarters at Kavalla in northern Greece.

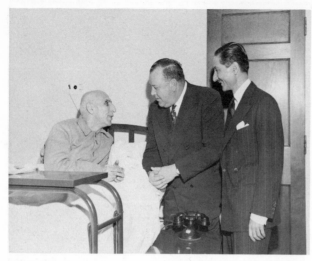

Secretary General Trygve Lie pays a visit to Dr. Mohammed Mossadegh, prime minister of Iran. Lie is accompanied by Ambassador Nasrollah Entezam of Iran, president of the fifth session of the General Assembly.

The question of Cuba came before the United Nations organs frequently. The United States was accused of aiding external aggression against Cuba, of preparations for an invasion, invasion, and of economic war against Cuba. Since 1960 the United Nations has heard seemingly incessant Cuban complaints against the United States, with some of the most viperous discussions and unprecedentedly violent language used.

In the late summer of 1961, the Security Council was especially concerned with two crises, which were considered a threat to international peace and security. Kuwait, a sheikdom on the Persian

Gulf, which attained independence after having been for years a British protectorate, called for a Security Council meeting to consider its complaint that Iraq threatened to annex it. Iraq, in turn, complained at the presence of British troops in the area.

Also considered by the council, a short time later, was the Tunisian complaint of "French ag-

Meeting of the council, under the presidency of T. F. Tsiang of China, considers the request of fifteen states for an investigation of the situation in Morocco.

gression in Bizerte." A meeting was held in urgency in view of the exchange of hostilities in the area, which caused hundreds of Tunisian casualties and some French casualties as well. A resolution of the council calling for a cease-fire and later the secretary general's visit to the area did not

Dr. Mossadegh and Ambassador Ernest Z. Gross, deputy representative of the United States to the United Nations, shake hands before the Security Council meeting on the Anglo-Iranian oil dispute.

Dr. Viqar Ahmed Hamdani (left), converses with Andrei Vyshinsky (right), permanent representative of Russia to the U.N., before the meeting of the Security Council, which discussed placing the Moroccan issue on its agenda.

Sir Senerat Gunewardene (*left*) of Ceylon, chairman of the African-Asian group, and Dr. Djalal Abdoh (*center*) of Iran, exchange views with Hervé Alphand, representative of France, before a Security Council meeting which was to consider a request of thirteen African and Asian countries for discussion of the Algerian issue.

A friendly exchange of views is held prior to a Security Council meeting called to consider Thailand's request for the dispatch of U.N. observers to the Indo-China area. From left: Sir Pierson Dixon, permanent U.N. representative of Britain; Pote Sarasin, Thailand's ambassador to Washington; and Henry Cabot Lodge, United States representative to the U.N.

solve the problem, for Tunisia continued to demand liquidation of the French naval base at Bizerte.

On Tunisian demand, and with the concurrence of a majority of the members of the U.N.,

a third special session of the General Assembly was convened on August 21, 1961 in accordance with rules 8(a) and 9 of the General Assembly's rules of procedure. (Rule 8 states that special sessions of the assembly "shall be held within fifteen days of the receipt by the secretary general of a

Members of the U.N. observer group in Lebanon, at Chtaura station, from which forty-seven observers from twelve countries operate.

request for such a session from the Security Council, or of a request from a majority of the members of the United Nations, or of the concurrence of a majority of the members provided in rule 9." Rule 9 provides that "any member of the United Nations may request the secretary general to summon a special session. The secretary general shall immediately inform the other members of the United Nations of the request and inquire whether they concur in it. If within thirty days of

Night meeting of the Security Council was held in order to continue the debate on the situation in Lebanon and the Jordanian complaint against the United Arab Republic.

Following the rejection of three draft resolutions on the situation in Lebanon, both the United States and Russia called for an emergency General Assembly session.

the date of the communication of the secretary general a majority of the members concur in the request, a special session of the General Assembly shall be summoned in accordance with rule 8.")

Air incidents involving the United States and Russia, with the U–2 incident as the most outstanding case, have been brought before the U.N. These discussions, with charges of espionage and counterespionage aired to the fullest extent, heralded the growing intensity of the cold war and turned the United Nations into one of the most sensitive seismographs of cold war fluctuation. In this respect, the United Nations has presented a true picture of the world situation. Its role as a clearing house and arbitration and conciliation forum for international disputes became even

Senior U.N. military observers meet in a conference hall in Beirut.

United Nations helicopter pilots engage in a discussion before taking off to patrol Lebanese borders to be on the lookout for illegal infiltration of men and arms into Lebanon.

more important than in times of relative tranquility.

Although the U.N. quite frequently reflects conflict, there is no doubt that in reflecting the realities of the world, it is a greater asset for the pres-

Four U.N. observers in Lebanon stop for a chat during their daily rounds.

ervation of peace than it would be if it were living in a world of abstract ideals on international cooperation, as conceived by the U.N. founders. Unfortunately these ideals were shattered in their first confrontation with political reality, even before the ink could have dried on the signatures affixed to the United Nations Charter, which turned it into a binding international document.

Map shows area of operations of the observation groups deployed in Lebanon.

Mrs. Golda Meir, foreign minister of Israel, and Dr. Mario Amadeo, permanent representative of Argentina to the U.N., present their cases at the Security Council meeting which dealt with the abduction of Eichmann from Argentina.

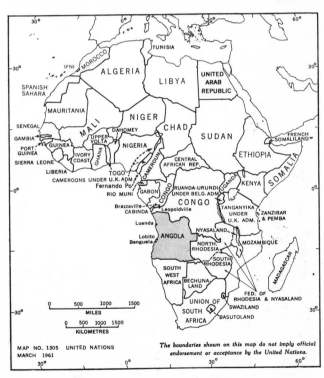

Angola, situated on the southwest coast of Africa, covers an area of 481,226 square miles.

Dr. Raúl Roa, foreign minister of Cuba, addresses the First (Political and Security) Committee of the General Assembly, debating a Cuban complaint against the United States.

One could paraphrase the saying "nothing human is strange to me": Nothing which prevails in international relations, with their conflicts and moments of accord, was strange to the United Nations. For in its years as a diplomatic forum, many international problems have been solved there—disputes have been resolved in agreement, threats of war eliminated, conflicts which could not have been resolved frozen in a status of no war and no peace, fires of war extinguished, expansion of war prevented, and hopes for permanent solutions held out for a future time.

PRINCIPAL U.N. ORGANS IN ACTION

September 20, 1960—the fifteenth session of the General Assembly is about to commence. Thousands of spectators crowd the approaches to the United Nations Building. Thousands of journalists from all over the world flock to the floor of the press section in the U.N. Secretariat Building. Credentials are checked and rechecked. Special security measures require special entry cards, and the U.N. guards at the entrances are entitled to check and, if necessary, search any incoming person's belongings.

Various cards are distributed—some allowing admittance to the Assembly Hall in the press section, and some to the halls of the three councils, where the proceedings of the assembly can be watched on the screen of an internal television circuit. And the corridors adjoining the press section—those long spacious corridors leading to the main halls of the U.N. Building—are crowded with typewriters, television sets, desks, tables, and chairs; and rushing to-and-fro among them, men and women with writing pads in hands dash in and out of dozens of telephone booths installed especially for the session.

The U.N. Office of Public Information meets the need to strengthen United Nations information services to member states, without impairing the over-all central direction of the U.N. information program. Facilities at headquarters "for the representatives of media of mass communication," are provided in accordance with resolution 1905 (XIV) of December 5, 1959, on public information activities of the United Nations.

And among them, especially in those sections of the building which face the entrances, hundreds of photographers, television cameramen, and radio operators struggle for "strategic" positions.

There was reason enough for this commotion and excitement. Only a few hours before, not far from the United Nations building on the East River, a liner, "Baltica," had anchored. On board was the leader of the communist world, accompanied by heads of states of the communist bloc. The "little assembly," the communist assembly, which heralded its coming demonstratively many weeks in advance, was about to enter the General Assembly Building.

Police sirens notified their arrival, and everywhere people peered through windows, cameras clicked, bulbs exploded. In minutes the big show would start—the "greatest diplomatic show on earth" would commence.

View of the General Assembly.

Exterior of Central Hall, Westminster, site of the first session of the U.N. General Assembly, which opened on January 10, 1946.

Three women of Britain's Women's Voluntary Services, who were appointed hostesses for the London session.

Quite a show it was: presidents, prime ministers, foreign ministers, not to mention ambassadors and diplomatic officials of all ranks, were gathered in the great General Assembly Hall. The provisional agenda for the session had already been drawn up, according to the assembly's rules of procedure, by the U.N. secretary general (at least sixty days) before the opening of the session. Thus it was already known to the assembled, since it had been communicated to them well in advance, after being issued on July 22, 1960. Any delegation which had a special request to include an additional item on the agenda had already had the opportunity to do so at least thirty days before the opening of the regular session. A list of twelve supplementary items had been issued on August 24, thus increasing the original list of seventy-three items of the agenda to eigthy-five.

A GENERAL ASSEMBLY IS CALLED TO ORDER

It was a few minutes after 3 P.M. when the

Last Meeting of the U.N. Tenth Anniversary Session, in San Francisco, exactly ten years after the charter was signed.

Boy scouts raise flags of sixty member nations of the U.N. at the Tenth Anniversary Session. Opera House where the charter was signed on June 26, 1945, is on the left. Domed building is the San Francisco City Hall, and the Veterans Building is on the right.

gavel was banged on the black marble desk of the presiding officer of the U.N. Assembly. The rules of procedure of the assembly state that the "chairman of the delegation from which the President of the previous session was elected presides until the Assembly elects a President for the new session."

The delegates were sure that this time they would not be witness to the painful humiliation of a fellow delegate, as was the case only a year before, when the president of the Thirteenth General Assembly, Charles Malik of Lebanon, was no longer a member of his delegation at the opening of the Fourteenth General Assembly, and not he, but the prime minister of Lebanon, who headed the Lebanese delegation, was accorded the honor

Representatives of the Republic of the Congo. Left to right: René Gauze, adviser; Emmanuel Dadet; and Stephan Tchichelle, vice president of the Council of Ministers. This was the opening of the fifteenth session of the General Assembly, in which thirteen new African members were admitted to the U.N.

Queen Elizabeth visits the United Nations. Escorting her on the ceremonial staircase at U.N. Headquarters is Sir Leslie Munro. Behind her is Prince Philip and Dag Hammarskjöld.

of opening the fourteenth regular session of the General Assembly.

This time it was Dr. Victor Andrés Belaúnde of Peru, the president of the fourteenth session who opened the fifteenth session of the General Assembly. His fine Spanish oratory was not confined to mere pleasantries. Dr. Belaúnde used the occasion, as had many in this high office before him, to expound very clear views on the "state of the world." Whoever listened to this speech, which was a careful presentation of the stormy international situation, could easily grasp the profoundness of the international crisis then current. One had only to recall what this crisis meant for

K. T. Mazurov (*left*), chairman of the Council of Ministers of Byelorussian SSR and head of the Byelorussian delegation; and **K. V. Kiselev**, minister for Foreign Affairs. An unprecedented number of high government officials participated in the fifteenth session of the assembly.

The representatives of Albania seated at the desk are **Mehmet Shehu** (*right*), prime minister and chairman of the delegation; and **Behar Shtylla**, minister for Foreign Affairs.

the United Nations in view of the expectations of its founders and their appraisal of the chances for the survival of the U.N. What a far cry the situation was from the one envisaged by Secretary of State Stettinius when submitting the U.N. Charter to the Senate for ratification. At that time he said,

I submit that these five nations, possessing most of the world's power to break or preserve peace must agree and act together if peace is to be maintained,

just as they have had to agree and act together to make possible an United Nations victory in this war. . . . What the Charter does is to place special and binding obligations upon the great nations to use, in unity—together for peace, not separately for war—the power that is already in their hands.

No doubt these were the thoughts of most of

The United States Delegation: Secretary of State Christian A. Herter (*left*), and **James J. Wadsworth**, permanent representative.

the delegates when, according to rule 64 of the rules of procedure of the assembly, the President invited them "to observe one minute of silence dedicated to prayer or meditation." And when the minute of silence was over, a committee of nine members was appointed by the assembly, on the

Delegates of the Republic of Dahomey. Left to right: **François Aplogan, Louis Ignacio-Pinto,** and **Désiré Vieyra** take their seats shortly after Dahomey was admitted to U.N. membership.

President of Ghana Kwame Nkrumah (*left*) at an assembly meeting.

Delegates listen attentively to a speaker at a plenary meeting of the General Assembly.

proposal of the president, "to examine the credentials of representatives." This was the picture at the opening of the Fifteenth General Assembly, but it did not differ basically from the openings of earlier sessions.

Whoever thinks that the phrase "Parliament of Nations" is rather exaggerated has to attend one such opening session of the General Assembly. A simple majority in a secret ballot decides who is

to become president of the forthcoming assembly. There are no nominations. The candidates start running for the office well in advance, sometimes even a year. It is done somewhat in the form of "throwing one's hat into the ring" by announcing publicly the desire to become president of the next assembly.

President of the United States Dwight D. Eisenhower addresses the fifteenth session of the assembly.

Canadian delegation: Prime Minister John G. Diefenbaker (*left*), and Howard C. Green, secretary of External Affairs.

At the fifteenth session, the outcome of the balloting was known with near certainty in advance. When the balloting box was placed up on the left side of the presidential desk and two delegates were nominated to attend the voting procedure at the box, the names of member states were called alphabetically by the executive assistant to the secretary general. One by one the heads of

Prime Minister Jawaharlal Nehru of India, and Minister of Defense V. K. Krishna Menon.

Prime Minister Robert Menzies of Australia (*right*) as head of the Australian delegation.

delegations rose from their seats and walked down the aisle to the podium to deposit their ballot with the name of their candidate on it. Some walked sternly and others, gaily; some with heavy step, and some with light. (The walk back to his seat is often used by a delegate as an occasion for exchange of greetings with friends and acquaintances from other lands, and is often turned into a demonstration of political affinity. Chairman

Khrushchev's embraces with the Cuban prime minister, Fidel Castro, was a crass demonstration of this custom.)

When the balloting was over and the results were announced, a thunder of applause greeted the new president. It is a touching moment when the outgoing president hands over to his newly elected colleague the symbol of his presidential power—the gavel.

But after this act, the "Parliament of Nations" is still not fully constituted. There remains the election of thirteen vice-presidents. The increase from the original seven vice-presidents to thirteen decided upon at the Twelfth General Assembly in 1957, was one of the few organizational measures on which agreement could have been reached to adapt the setup of the U.N. organs to the increase of membership. It was certainly indicative of the

British Prime Minister Harold Macmillan addresses a plenary meeting of the fifteenth session of the assembly.

President Sékou Touré of Guinea addresses a plenary meeting of the assembly.

Premier Nikita S. Khrushchev of Russia addresses plenary meeting.

changing realities in the U.N. that an annex to the resolution about the increase of the number of vice-presidents specified that the thirteen vice-presidents had to be elected according to the following pattern: (1) four representatives from Asian and African states, (2) one representative from an Eastern European state, (3) two representatives from Latin American states, (4) two representatives from Western European or other states, (5) and five representatives from the permanent members of the Security Council. There is an important difference between the election of the president and the thirteen vice-presidents: The president is elected personally whereas for the posts of vice-president, member countries are elected and the heads of their delegations serve as vice-presidents.

In addition, the seven Main Committees of the assembly have to be constituted: the First Committee (Political and Security); the Second Committee (Economic and Financial); the Third (Social, Humanitarian and Cultural); the Fourth (Trusteeship and Information from Nonself-governing Territories); the Fifth (Administrative and Budgetary); and the Sixth (Legal); and, finally, the Special Political Committee. All one

Exchanging views before a plenary meeting of the assembly are (*left to right*) Adam Rapacki, minister for Foreign Affairs of Poland; János Kadar, minister of State of Hungary; Dr. Endre Sik, foreign minister of Hungary; Karoly Erledyi of Hungary; and Wladyslaw Gomulka, first secretary of the Central Committee of the Polish United Workers Party and chairman of his country's delegation.

Prime Minister Nehru returns to his seat following an address.

simple majority, are they submitted as recommendations to the assembly, where a majority of two thirds is necessary to adopt resolutions on important questions. Another important organ of the General Assembly should not be overlooked—the General Committee, composed of the president of the assembly, the thirteen vice-presidents and the seven chairmen of the Main Committees. The General Committee considers the provisional

Senator Nuhu Bamalli (*left*), foreign minister of Nigeria, exchanges views with Oddmund Hoel, member of the Norwegian parliament.

hundred member nations are represented on each of the Main Committees, to which are referred items falling within their fields of competence. And again, in parliamentary fashion, chairmen, vice-chairmen and *rapporteurs* of the Main Committees are elected on the basis of equitable geographical distribution, experience, and personal competence. The many items on the agenda come before the appropriate committees, and only after resolutions in the committees are adopted by a

agenda, makes recommendations to the assembly on the closing date of the session, and deals with other formal matters; but it does not decide any political question.

THE GENERAL DEBATE

When the assembly is constituted and the

Prime Minister of Nigeria Alhaji Sir Abubakar Balewa replies to welcoming statements after Nigeria became the ninety-ninth member of the United Nations.

Representatives of the Republic of the Niger listen to a debate. In the front row (*left to right*), Noma Kaka, Sabo Boukary, and M. A. Katkore.

Opening of a new session of the General Assembly. Representatives observe the customary minute of silent meditation and prayer.

agenda adopted, the general debate can commence. At this Fifteenth General Assembly, with so many heads of governments attending, there was a special abundance of speechmaking. Usually nobody tries to keep his speech within the limits of the agenda. It is a typical, parliamentary general debate, where all international problems are touched upon "in general." It was Chairman Khrushchev's privilege, acting as head of the Russian delegation and performing all the duties of a delegation chairman, to make an innovation: He made the proceedings of the General Assembly come even closer than before to a regular parliamentary session—remarks from the floor, heckling of the speakers, and once even a demonstration, which could hardly be described as "parliamentary". This was the incident in which Chairman Khrushchev removed his shoe and pounded it on his desk as a sign of disapproval of what was said from the speaker's rostrum by Great Britain's prime minister, Harold Macmillan. And it was again Chairman Khrushchev who had to be called to order by the President of the Fifteenth General Assembly, Frederick Boland of Ireland, and it was he who so angered the president, that, banging on the desk, he broke the gavel. This occurrence later prompted one of the delegates from the new African states to start his speech with a remark which was also in parliamentary tradition: "Mr.

The presidential rostrum at a plenary meeting of the General Assembly. From left: Secretary General Dag Hammarskjöld, Assembly President Frederick H. Boland, and Executive Assistant Andrew W. Cordier.

United Nations delegates exchange views informally prior to a meeting of the assembly.

President of the fifteenth session of the General Assembly Frederick H. Boland opens the sixteenth session inviting members to observe a minute of silence in tribute to the memory of the late Secretary General Dag Hammarskjöld, whose empty chair is seen at left.

Full view of the Security Council chamber.

Andrei Vyshinsky (*left*) and Henri Hoppenot of France converse before a meeting.

Dr. Eelco N. van Kleffens (*second from left*), president of the General Assembly, congratulates the representatives of three countries newly elected to the Security Council. Left to right, they are Dr. Victor Belaúnde, Peru; Nasrollah Entezam, Iran; and Fernand van Langenhove, Belgium.

An unprecedented melee occurred during a Security Council meeting called after the assassination of Patrice Lumumba, first prime minister of the Congo. United Nations guards intervened to restore order.

President, it is a pity that you have broken only the hammer, you should have broken the sickle as well."

Although not so stormy and not always attended by such distinguished leaders of their countries as President Dwight D. Eisenhower, Chairman Nikita Khrushchev, Prime Minister Harold Macmillan, Prime Minister Jawaharlal Nehru, Indonesian

Members of the United Kingdom and United States at the ten-power disarmament conference which opened at the Palais des Nations in Geneva on March 15, 1960.

President Sukarno, President of Yugoslavia Tito, President of the United Arab Republic Gamal Abdel Nasser, President of Ghana Kwame Nkrumah, President of Guinea Sekoú Touré, and ruling personalities of the people's republics in Eastern Europe, all the assemblies followed the same procedural pattern and many of them were attended by distinguished diplomatic personalities.

In this highest forum of the United Nations, most important pronouncements of policies have been made. President Eisenhower delivered at the General Assembly, on December 8, 1953, a speech about peaceful uses of atomic energy, the conclusions of which were unanimously endorsed a year later by the General Assembly. This endorsement in turn gave birth, on July 29, 1957, to a new intergovernmental agency, the International Atomic Energy Agency (IAEA). The proposal for total and complete disarmament was made at the Fourteenth General Assembly in person by Chairman Khrushchev. For sixteen years, the General Assembly has served as the sounding-board for

Members of the Czechoslovak delegation to the disarmament conference.

major pronouncements on international policy, and four special emergency sessions have dealt with such major political problems as the Suez and Hungary crises in 1956, and the Lebanon and Congo crises in 1958 and 1960, respectively. In addition, special sessions of the General Assembly have dealt with the problem of Palestine, in 1947 and 1948, and, in August, 1961, with the French-Tunisian conflict over Bizerte.

THE GENERAL ASSEMBLY'S COMPETENCES

From the very beginnings of the United Na-

United Nations Disarmament Commission Chairman Luis Padilla Nervo of Mexico (*left*), greets M. Silviu Brucan of Romania.

tions Organization, the General Assembly, in which all member states are represented and have one vote, irrespective of their territory, population, or resources, assumed its principal role. It was empowered to decide upon the admission of new members, upon suspension of rights of members and of privileges of membership, and upon the expulsion of members, and it served as co-ordinator for the whole organization. The non-permanent members of the Security Council are elected by the assembly as are all elective members of other U.N.'s principal organs. All matters within the scope of the charter could be discussed

at the General Assembly. The Security Council, the Economic and Social Council, the Trusteeship Council, and the secretary general have had to submit annual reports to the assembly. The budget of the U.N. and the contributions to it of member states are subject to the decisions of the assembly.

All facets of international life are within the scope of the assembly: consideration of general principles of co-operation in the maintenance of international peace and security; disarmament; regulation of armaments; making recommendations to the Security Council; recommending measures for peaceful adjustment of any situation which it considers likely to endanger international peace and security, with the exception of situations already under consideration by the Security Council; initiation of studies and making of recommendations for the promotion of international co-operation in the political field, as well as in the economic, social, cultural, educational and health fields.

Ambassador Omar Loutfi of the United Arab Republic addresses a meeting of the commission. At right is Mr. V. A. Kuznetsov of Russia.

MEASURES FOR MEETING EMERGENCIES

The role of the General Assembly, as defined in chapter IV of the charter, was greatly expanded five years after the charter's adoption and ratification. The veto devised to assure unanimity of the great powers in matters of danger to international security and peace, basically within the competence of the Security Council, threatened not only to immobilize the central enforcing agency of the international organization, but even threatened complete destruction of the usefulness of the

Dr. Nervo presides over a meeting of the commission.

Partial view of the U.N. Disarmament Commission in session.

U.N. as an instrument for the preservation of peace.

To meet this challenge to U.N. effectiveness, a revolutionary measure was introduced by the United States delegation and adopted by the General Assembly in November, 1950. This was a time of serious international crisis. The U.N. was already engaged in a deadly contest with aggression in Korea—a serious challenge to its ability to function and fulfill its role as provided for in the charter. The Uniting for Peace resolution sought to overcome the shortcomings of the charter. The fifteen-days waiting period for special sessions was eliminated, and, instead, it was stipulated that in time of emergency, the General Assembly could be called into special session in twenty-four hours by a decision of any seven members of the Security Council, or by a simple majority of the members of the United Nations. In addition, a new commission was set up—the Peace Observation

The First (Political and Security) Committee of the General Assembly at a meeting which dealt with the question of disarmament.

Adlai E. Stevenson of the United States talks with Andrei Gromyko of Russia.

President John F. Kennedy addresses the sixteenth session of the General Assembly (September, 1961).

Commission. Its fourteen members included representatives of the five major powers. Wherever trouble arose, observers were to be sent to assure, by their presence, that peace was maintained.

The resolution was not, however, limited to peace observation alone. United Nations member states were asked to maintain, within their military forces, units trained and ready for duty with the United Nations, whenever and wherever need arose. The far-reaching implications of this resolution have not yet been realized, but there is no doubt that it harbors elements of a potential standing United Nations army. This provision certainly must be seen as a kind of supplementary device to overcome the stalemate which prevented and prevents the implementation of article 43 of the charter.

Unfortunately the services of this Peace Observation Commission were not utilized as often as they could and should have been. Indicative of this state of affairs is the fact that between February 24, 1959 and March 3, 1961, no meeting of this commission was held. And when, on March

3, 1961, the meeting of the commission was called to re-elect Professor Enrique Rodriguez Fabregat of Uruguay as its chairman (a post he has held since 1954), as well as the Vice-Chairman Said Hasan of Pakistan, and Karel Kurka of Czechoslovakia as *Rapporteur,* the election of officers for the calendar years 1961 and 1962 was the only order of business for the meeting.

Not much more fortunate was another provision of the Uniting for Peace resolution calling for the establishment of the Collective Measures Committee, which has to plan details of the United Nations setup for the preservation of peace and security. Proceeding most cautiously, the committee compiled lists of various types of embargos that might be applied against states considered as menacing international peace and order. The committee also concerns itself with regional military organizations like NATO; it is called upon to take all measures which could create the feeling of readiness of the international organization to meet any emergency, and thus it serves as a special kind of deterrent against ag-

Andrew W. Cordier, undersecretary for General Assembly Affairs.

gression—a deterrent on an international scale to a potential aggressor.

THE SECURITY COUNCIL

These special measures, devised to assure the efficiency of the peace preserving machinery of the United Nations, did not, of course, change the basic position of the Security Council as the main instrument of collective security, of prevention of war and resistance to aggression. Article 24 of the charter, which confers on the Security Council "primary responsibility for the maintenance of international peace and security" has been put to the test many times. The horseshoe table, around which the eleven members of the Security Council rotate their seats with the assumption of the presidency of the council at the beginning of each month by another member state, has been the place of many an action which has made not only headlines in the world press

Dr. Ralph Bunche, undersecretary of the United Nations.

G. P. Arkadev, undersecretary for Political and Security Council Affairs.

Chakrawarthi V. Narasimhan, undersecretary for Special Political Affairs. On August 1, 1961, he became chef de cabinet.

but has also inscribed important chapters in the history of nations in the last sixteen years. Sessions which sometimes last all night long, such as those dealing with crises in all corners of the world—in the Middle East, in Korea, in Hungary, in Africa—can be called to order on the shortest possible notice, because the members of the Security Council are permanently at the headquarters, and the Security Council is permanently in session.

Diplomatic courtesy has never been discarded. Even at the height of a crisis, when members of the council are engaged in bitter argumentation related to acts threatening international peace, every member considers it his duty to welcome the incoming president in flattering phrases preceded by some words of praise for the outgoing president. Some diplomats have called this round of pleasantries "the cooling off period" in heated debates.

Another cooling off period is the time taken for the translation of speeches into the two working languages, English and French, in the case of the speaker delivering his remarks in some other official language, Russian, Spanish, or Chinese. Members of the Security Council sometimes have their patience put to a strong test when one of the members delivers a long oration in a non-working official language, and compels the members of the Security Council to sit, sometimes for an hour or more, and listen to a translation of a speech they had already heard translated over the earphones during its delivery, and which they had had a chance to read in the released copy of the speech. The late Andrei Vyshinsky, forceful representative of Soviet Russia, once remained almost alone in the council chamber to listen till late in the evening to the translation of his very long speech—an exercise in patience the other members of the council could not match.

Conflicting oratory, often sprinkled with the harshest words, demonstrated at the very beginning of the Security Council's functioning the truth that the basic tenet for the full effectiveness of the United Nations Organization—the unity of the five big powers—was a matter of the past. The military unity, about which Senator Vandenberg said, at the Senate debate on ratification of the charter, that "the United Nations must never, for any cause, permit this military unity to fall apart" —fell apart in fact even before the U.N. Charter became a binding document with its ratification on October 24, 1945.

The first Soviet veto, cast on February 16, 1946, on a resolution concerning the withdrawal of British and French troops from Syria and Lebanon, was only an overt sign of an existing state of

Dr. Victor Chi-Tsai Hoo, undersecretary in charge of the Department of Conference Services.

affairs. Since then, the ninety-five vetoes the Soviet Union cast within the fifteen years of the U.N.'s existence (compared to France's four, United Kingdom's two, and China's one) were additional proofs of the intensification of the conflict between the noncommunist and communist worlds.

Of course the charter had a built-in confirmation of the indispensability of the veto. During the negotiations on the final wording of the charter,

Secretary General Dag Hammarskjöld presents a sterling silver platter as a farewell gift to Undersecretary Ilya S. Tchernychev of Russia upon his resignation (July, 1957).

Phillips de Seynes, undersecretary for Economic and Social Affairs.

Dr. Hernane Tavares de Sa, undersecretary for the office of Public Information.

the four great powers (France was later admitted as the fifth) instituted the great-power veto as justified by the "major responsibility to be borne by them in maintaining international peace, which they could hardly be expected to undertake to carry out under conditions not agreed upon by themselves." Article 27 (3) of the charter spells out clearly this intention, making decisions on substantive matters dependent upon an affirmative vote of seven members of the eleven-member Security Council, as long as these seven members include the five permanent members of the Security Council. The fact that on procedural matters a normal majority of seven votes sufficed, but that on substantive matters, great power unanimity was

Professor Ahmed S. Bokhari, undersecretary in charge of the office of Public Information preceding Dr. De Sa.

required did, at the outset, demand further clarification. A statement by China, Great Britain, the United States and the Soviet Union (later endorsed by France) at San Francisco on June 7, 1945, defined in clear terms what was the understanding of these powers on the veto. According to this statement, matters not liable to a veto would be decisions on rules of procedure—time and place of meetings, establishment of such bodies and agencies as the council may deem necessary, and invitations to U.N. members to participate in discussions affecting their interest. But the veto

But even with this double veto the composition of the Security Council remained of primary importance for the great powers. The election of the nonpermanent members for the two-year period, with due respect for geographical distribution and the contribution of the candidate-state to the maintenance of international peace and security, became a direct function of the intensity of the world conflicts. In the sixteen years of the U.N.'s existence, only seldom was due respect paid to these provisions. Geographical distribution was not always decisive in the selection of nonpermanent members of the council, and considered even less was their "contribution to the maintenance of international peace and security and the other pur-

Dr. Dragoslav Protitch, undersecretary for the Department of Trusteeship and Information from Nonself-Governing Territories.

had to be upheld in case of a dispute on whether a matter was procedural or not.

A veto in this case, labeled the "double veto," was used by the Soviet Union in 1946 when the council majority proposed to keep on its agenda the case of Spain with the provision that this would not prejudice the assembly's right to take it up. In 1947, this veto was used to block a decision by the council to consider a Greek border dispute; and in 1948, against a proposal by the council majority to set up a subcommittee to hear evidence on the communist coup in Czechoslovakia.

Voting at the Fifteenth General Assembly to fill a vacant seat in the Economic and Social Council.

poses of the organization." In electing the nonpermanent council members, the General Assembly has often—more in recent years than earlier—given a classical performance in parliamentary bargaining tactics, while at the same time exemplifying the intensity of the cold war.

At the Fourteenth General Assembly, in the case of Poland and Turkey, the election of nonpermanent members dragged on for weeks. It was postponed and taken up again, reaching sometimes as many as fifty-two ballots, which yet remained inconclusive. The solution was found only after a compromise was reached, and the two-year term

View of a meeting of the Economic and Social Council in its chamber at the United Nations Headquarters.

The Economic Commission for Asia and the Far East (ECAFE) held a conference in Rangoon, Burma (January, 1952). Shown here are the flags of the United Nations in front of the city hall in Rangoon.

After the opening meeting of the seventh session of ECAFE at Lahore, Pakistan, a garden party was given for the delegates by the prime minister of Pakistan in the famous Shalimar Gardens.

Liaquat Ali Khan (*center*), prime minister of Pakistan, with the delegates of India and Russia (*left*) at the garden party in Lahore.

General view of the opening meeting of the eleventh session of ECAFE, held in 1955 at the Sankei Building in Tokyo.

split into two one-year periods, obliging the elected state, Poland, to relinquish the position after a year, clearing it for the other candidate, Turkey. A similar situation prevailed when Yugoslavia was elected on the thirty-sixth ballot.

DISARMAMENT

In this general atmosphere of a split world, the

Among the delegates present at the ECAFE session in Tokyo were Dr. Soerodjo Ranoekoesoemo of Indonesia and Mr. Harbans Singh of India.

most vital problem of international relations—disarmament—had to be dealt with. It should be stressed that disarmament was not of prime concern to the originators of the United Nations Organizations. Collective security was considered of much greater importance than disarmament.

Again, as with many other matters that arose in the formulation of the U.N. Charter, the experience of the League of Nations seemed to haunt the world leaders. The fact that limitation of armaments was placed as a primary aim of the League—that stipulations concerning it were included in the very first article of the League's covenant, and acceptance of its rulings turned into a condition of admission to membership in the League—seemed to be a sufficient warning to the great powers not to see in disarmament the panacea for world peace. For they had an example before their eyes: disarmament stipulations did not prevent the scourge of World War II. A new approach was necessary: Collective security had to be the remedy. The idea of the "four policemen" (later the five policemen), the prevailing military power

Delegates to the fourteenth session of ECAFE, held in 1958 in Kuala Lumpur, Malaya.

securing the peace of the world, was built into the articles of the charter.

Based on the assumption of lasting military unity of the great powers, the charter made the first references to "principles governing disarmament and the regulation of armaments" not at the beginning of the charter but in article 11, and this only as part of general principles of co-operation in the maintenance of international peace and security. To make clear that regulation of armaments was considered not only a political goal for the preservation of peace, article 26 stated that "in order to promote the establishment and maintenance of international peace and security with the least diversion for armaments of the world's human and economic resources," the Security Council should formulate plans for this purpose. Article 47 of the charter provided for the establishment of a "Military Staff Committee to advise

The first session of the U.N. Economic Commission for Africa (ECA) was opened in 1952 in the parliament building in Addis Ababa, Ethiopia. Emperor Haile Selassie of Ethiopia delivered the opening address.

View of the parliament building in Addis Ababa.

Local university students acted as guides for the commission at its opening meeting. The commission was set up to provide a forum for review of the economic needs of the African peoples.

The United Nations Economic Commission for Africa opened its second session in Tangier. Some delegates and U.N. officials stand outside the building where the session was held.

and assist the Security Council on all questions relating to the Security Council's military requirements for the maintenance of international peace and security, the employment and command of forces placed at its disposal. . . ." In this article, "regulation of armaments and possible disarmament" were again placed at the very end, and disarmament mentioned only with the reservation "possible."

The considerations which governed this approach to disarmament problems were soon to be decisively influenced by two major developments: (1) the utilization of atomic power in warfare and, later, (2) the disintegration of the military unity of the world powers. Secretary of State Dulles commented on the first development as follows: "As one who was at San Francisco in the spring of 1945, I can say with confidence, that had the delegates at San Francisco known we were entering the age of atomic warfare, they would have seen to it that the charter dealt more positively with the problems thus raised."

But the problems arose—problems transcending any that statesmen could have visualized when they were engaged in formulating the aims of the international organization. The urgency of disarmament—of atomic disarmament—grew with the growing awareness of the dangers inherent in atomic arms, the use of which could threaten not only world peace, but the existence of the world itself.

The great powers grasped well what atomic weapons meant for the future of the world. On the proposal of France, the United Kingdom, the United States and the Soviet Union, an Atomic Energy Commission was appointed, as resolved in the first resolution of the First General Assembly. Composed of members of the Security Council and Canada, the commission assembled for its first session in June, 1946. The Security Council horseshoe table had already been devised, although it was not yet in its permanent location, but in the

View of the Regional Conference of European Nongovernmental Organizations held in Geneva (September, 1953).

U.N. temporary quarters in New York. Bernard Baruch presented, on behalf of the United States, a plan for regulation and control of atomic weapons. It was a most far-reaching plan: An International Atomic Development Authority had to be established and be accorded the exclusive rights to control the world's production of atomic energy, atomic research—all activities in any way related to atomic energy, from the mining of uranium to the final process of refining and chemical separation.

Under this plan no state would have been permitted to produce atomic weapons, and violations

of such agreements would be punishable by a Security Council decision without any state having the right of veto. It took five days of consultation among Russia's highest echelons before Russia's representative, Andrei A. Gromyko gave the answer: "The plan is thoroughly vicious and unacceptable." Russia demanded freedom of research and production of nuclear fuel, rejected any talk about the abolition of the veto, and suggested the prohibition of atomic weapons, with controls reduced to only nominal dimensions.

The effort to put the atomic weapons, all achievements of the atomic revolution, as attained by the United States, under a supernational authority was shattered. The United States proposal to put its world monopoly in production of fissionable materials and their military use under non-American supervision, was rejected. The Russian opposition to the Baruch plan was, no doubt, dictated by one objective: to wrest the atomic weapon monopoly from the United States. The explosion of an atomic device by Russia, announced at the Fourth General Assembly, and the appearance of the hydrogen bomb in 1952, complicated even more the problem of atomic disarmament. Intercontinental guided missiles with atomic warheads increased the arsenal of potential

Formal opening of the 1955–56 briefing sessions for nongovernmental organizations, observers, and consultants. Ahmed S. Bokhari, undersecretary for Public Information, addresses the group on "The Agenda of the Tenth Session of the General Assembly."

Delegates from 174 nongovernmental organizations at a conference to discuss ways of informing the peoples of the world about the U.N. and of interpreting the U.N.'s activities to them.

destruction. Outer-space feats entered into the world of politics with Russia putting her "Sputnik" into space, in 1957, to be followed soon after by the United States' "Explorer."

During this entire period innumerable conferences, meetings, and consultations were held, and committees and subcommittees were appointed, all with a single purpose—to promote the idea of disarmament. The United Nations forum, primarily the General Assembly, was often used as the sounding board of disarmament plans. On October 24, 1950, President Harry S. Truman proposed, at a plenary meeting of the assembly, the co-ordination of the efforts of the Atomic Energy Commission and the Commission for Conventional Armaments, established by the Security Council in 1947. Many other suggestions of regulations to be adopted in disarmament efforts were submitted in the course of the years. The initiative alternated between Russia and the United States, with the other major powers either submitting disarmament plans of their own or supporting plans of others.

In January, 1952, a new attempt was made to move ahead with the disarmament negotiations. The General Assembly established a Disarmament

Commission which took over the functions of the Atomic Energy Commission and the Commission for Conventional Armaments. The aims of this commission seemed adapted to the political realities, but as it turned out, even these aims were in contrast with the political situation. The commission had to find a way to make feasible a balanced reduction of armed forces and all armaments, the elimination of weapons of mass destruction, effective international control of atomic energy, and

A group representing the International Council of Women exchanges views before a meeting of the International Conference of Women, held at U.N. Headquarters.

Conference on migration and refugee problems. Representatives of specialized agencies are participating.

prohibition of atomic weapons.

The membership of the Disarmament Commission was to be identical with the membership of the Security Council plus Canada, when that country was not serving as an elected member of the Security Council. After five years, in 1957, the General Assembly adopted a resolution calling for an increase of the membership of the commission by fourteen. Together with the eleven members of the Security Council the commission grew to twenty-five members. A year later, a resolution was adopted to have all member states of the United Nations participate in the Disarmament Commission.

At the fourteenth session of the General Assembly, on September 18, 1959, Premier Khrushchev, winding up his official visit to the United States in a time when the air was filled with the "spirit of Camp David" (that is, the spirit of the supposedly friendly talks held with President Eisenhower at this site), submitted his plan for "complete and general disarmament." A world without armies, without navies, without air forces, without general staffs and war ministries, without military establishments, and with only small arms for internal security, was pictured in Khrushchev's speech. A British disarmament plan presented at the same session by the British Foreign Secretary, Selwyn Lloyd, followed. It proposed a three-stage disarmament process which would eliminate weapons of mass destruction and bring the armed forces to "levels which will rule out the possibility of aggressive war." And the United States Ambassador to the U.N., Henry Cabot Lodge, expressed United States' unreserved support of the greatest possible amount of controlled disarmament, but

with the proviso that "adequate and timely inspection and control must be built into the system."

This trend at the fourteenth session towards more international understanding was preceded by another accommodation between the great powers. On September 7, 1959, representatives of France, Great Britain, the Soviet Union, and the United States jointly informed the secretary general that the four powers agreed to establish a new ten-member disarmament committee based on the recognition of the Russian claim of equality of representation between the socialist and nonsocialist states. Bulgaria, Canada, Czechoslovakia, Italy, Poland, and Romania were added to the four great powers. This was an outer–United Nations body. Its establishment could have been considered both a snub to the United Nations' prestige and to all other states which had a vital interest in disarma-

General view of the opening meeting of the conference on nongovernmental organizations on eradication of prejudice and discrimination. Dr. Brock Chisholm, president of the conference, is in the center.

ment. To dispel misunderstandings in this respect the four powers hastened to state: "Disarmament matters are of world-wide interest and concern. Accordingly, ultimate responsibility rests with the United Nations. The setting up of the disarmament committee in no way diminishes or encroaches upon the United Nations responsibilities in this field. In setting up this committee, the special responsibility, resting on the great powers to find a basis for agreement, is taken into account."

General view of the two-day conference of nongovernmental organizations, held in May, 1960.

The U.N. authority was fully recognized. Reports on the developments in the Ten-Member Committee were to be submitted to the U.N. Disarmament Commission. It was certainly welcome news to the U.N. Disarmament Commission.

And it was a logical decision to have the Ten-Member Disarmament Committee endorsed unanimously by the U.N. Disarmament Commission. The Ten-Member Committee convened in Geneva, in the same city where the three-power conference on the cessation of nuclear testing was taking place. Although formally detached from each other, the workings of the two international conferences remained closely related. An agreement on cessation of nuclear tests would facilitate reaching an agreement on general disarmament. And it seemed for some time that an agreement on the cessation of nuclear testing was close. After the decisions of the three nuclear powers—the

The chamber of the Trusteeship Council.

United States, the Soviet Union, and the United Kingdom—to discontinue testing, a detailed agreement was almost reached on all matters, including inspection. But a sudden change in the Russian position, which occurred in spring, 1961, put prospects for agreement in doubt. After agreeing to an inspection system, the Russian delegation surprised the United States and Britain with a demand that inspection be entrusted to a three-person council, one representing the noncommunist bloc, one the communist bloc, and one the neutrals, with each having the right of veto. The Russian argument against French nuclear testing, which disregarded the nonwritten agreement on temporary cessation of testing, was only of secondary importance. Representatives of Great Britain and the United States made it clear that in their opinion a veto in the inspection council is identical with no inspection whatsoever, and it would render immaterial and purposeless the labor of months and years of negotiations. The disarmament discussions harbored at their roots the dilemma as to which should come first—disarmament or inspection. With the League of Nations, the problem of the sequence as to whether security or disarmament should come first constituted the central obstacle in the disarmament negotiations. In the fifties, a similar problem as to the sequence of inspection and disarmament in the procedure to achieve a disarmed world became the chief obstacle to turning the disarmament dream into reality. And in both cases the core of the problem was anchored in the lack of mutual confidence, at pres-

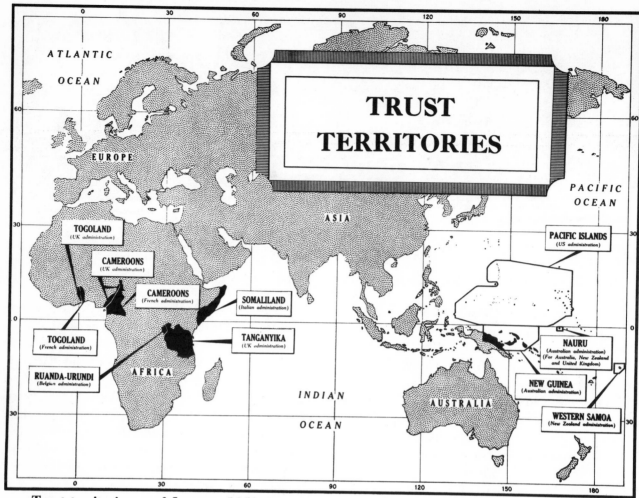

Trust territories as of January, 1952. Since then, many territories have achieved independence.

On September 27, 1961, Sierra Leone became the one hundredth member of the United Nations. At desk (*left*) is Sir Milton A. S. Margai, heading his country's delegation.

Prior to the resumption of the fifteenth session of the General Assembly, these delegates and visitors exchanged views in a lounge at U.N. Headquarters. Left to right, they are Prince Taleb Ibn Ali of Oman, Dr. Mohamed Fathalla El-Khatib of Yemen, Sulaiman Ibn Hemyiar of Oman, and Alhaji Muhammed Ngileruma of Nigeria.

Renewed negotiations between representatives of the United States and Russia, conducted during the summer of 1961, produced a joint declaration of these two countries regarding the question of disarmament. On September 20, the United States and Russian delegations submitted for the consideration of to the sixteenth session of the General Assembly a "Joint Statement of Agreed Principles for Disarmament Negotiations."

This agreement was reached at a time when the negotiations in Geneva on the cessation of nuclear explosions had already been discontinued. Russia had resumed nuclear explosions in the atmosphere on September 1, 1961—a step which the United States declared a compelling factor in its decision to resume atomic tests some two weeks later. These tests were conducted underground to "avoid the hazards of fallout."

It was against this background of events that President Kennedy, on September 25, presented to the General Assembly the United States declaration of "Freedom from War." The plan for "general and complete disarmament in a peaceful world" envisaged six steps which would lead to a complete and general disarmament: (a) signing immediately, without waiting for general and complete disarmament, a treaty banning testing of nuclear devices; (b) stopping the production of fissionable materials for use in weapons or for their transfer to any nation that now lacks such weapons; (c) prohibiting the transfer of control over nuclear weapons to nations that do not already have them; (d) keeping nuclear weapons from seeding new battlegrounds in outer space; (e) de-

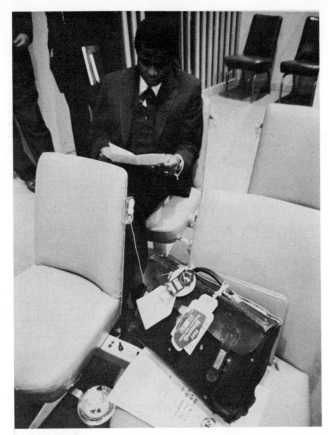

Zuberi Mtemvu of the Tanganyika African National Congress prepares to address the Fourth (Trusteeship) Committee.

ent manifested in the fear of surprise attack, which certainly cannot be alleviated by pronouncements of victory by one bloc in the world conflict, over the other.

It seems that in the last forty years, the leading powers of the world have refrained from acknowledging openly the basic truth that the sequence of security and disarmament, or inspection and disarmament, in their disarmament negotiations should be supplemented by an additional most important factor which must precede any disarmament agreement. That factor is mutual confidence.

In the aftermath of the collapse of the summit meeting of May, 1960, one more attempt was made to keep disarmament talks going. At the second part of the fifteenth session of the General Assembly, which started March, 1961, an agreement was reached between the United States ambassador to the U.N. and the Russian delegation not to discuss disarmament problems at the fifteenth session, and thus to enable the new administration in the United States to evolve a new disarmament policy.

U Tin Maung of Burma, who became president of the Trusteeship Council in 1961.

Pupils enjoy the swimming pool at the junior school of Usumbra, capital of Ruanda Urundi, a trust territory administered by Belgium.

Maize being processed at an agricultural training school in Tanganyika.

stroying, gradually, existing nuclear weapons, and converting their material to peaceful use; and (f) halting the unlimited testing and production of strategic nuclear delivery vehicles, and gradually destroying them as well.

This disarmament program provides for effective verification to insure that "retained armed forces and armaments do not exceed agreed levels at any stage." This inspection problem was in fact the most objectionable detail for Russia, which has continually insisted that inspection will lead to spying. The Russian representatives have never explained why they do not consider this spying danger mutual, in that inspection arrangements would be mutual.

The United States plan contained an important innovation: it envisaged the establishment of an international disarmament organization under the United Nations which would afford full influence on disarmament matters to all U.N. member nations, great or small. The new plan was a depar-

Samoan women casting their votes in a plebiscite.

ture from the past United States positions. In the past the United States had always wanted one agreed phase of disarmament to be carried out before another was discussed. The new plan envisaged negotiations on a broad basis and settling of any question on which agreement could be reached. Notwithstanding this general plan for disarmament, the United States delegation introduced for inclusion on the agenda of the General Assembly an item dealing with nuclear weapons

NORTHERN CAMEROONS TRUST TERRITORY PLEBISCITE

TO YOU WHO LIVE IN THE NORTHERN CAMEROONS TRUST TERRITORY AND WHO REGISTERED AS VOTERS THIS YEAR

Come early on Saturday the 7th of November and decide whether you want your country to become part of the Northern Region next year OR whether you want to leave consideration of this matter to some other time in the future.

This is what we want you to do:

Come here with your registration cards early on Saturday the 7th of November.

The Polling Officer will check your name against the list of those registered to vote.

He will give you a ballot paper & tell you to go into the polling booth ALONE.

If you want your country to join Northern Nigeria next year put the ballot paper in the WHITE box. If you want to postpone consideration put it into the ORANGE COLOURED box.

You cannot vote twice.
You cannot vote on behalf of anyone who is ill.
You cannot vote on behalf of anyone who has died.
You cannot vote on behalf of anyone else.
You cannot enter the polling station after 5 p.m.
You can only vote where you were registered.

THIS HAS NOTHING TO DO WITH THE FEDERAL ELECTION

Preparation under U.N. supervision for a plebiscite in the trust territory of Northern Cameroon.

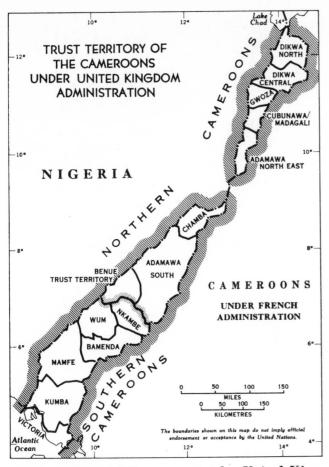

TRUST TERRITORY OF
THE CAMEROONS
UNDER UNITED KINGDOM
ADMINISTRATION

The boundaries shown on this map do not imply official
endorsement or acceptance by the United Nations.

Trust territory of Cameroons under United Kingdom administration.

tests. The title of the item, which was included in the agenda against Russian opposition, reads "The Urgent Need for a Treaty to Ban Nuclear Weapons Tests Under Effective International Control."

The Russian representative, Foreign Minister Gromyko, who spoke after President Kennedy, suggested an eight-point program "to free international relations from the burden of the cold war." The Russian plan suggested (a) the freezing of all military budgets; (b) renunciation of atomic weapons; (c) banning of war propaganda; (d) signing of an East-West nonaggression pact; (e) withdrawing of all foreign-based troops; (f) banning production of nuclear weapons; (g) establishment of "atom-free" zones; and (h) reducing of surprise attack dangers.

Of course the Russian proposals were only an addition to their standing proposals on general and complete disarmament. All the delegations to the General Assembly saw these disarmament proposals in the context of the international situation, which all appraised as one presenting a threat to world peace surpassing any which the world had to face in the many crises since World War II.

THE SECRETARIAT

The tripartite approach to the administration of

Meeting of the Trusteeship Council. Four petitioners (*table, center*) from the French Cameroons were given a hearing by the council.

The Fourth (Trusteeship) Committee of the General Assembly listens to petitioners.

international institutions and to the implementation of international agreements, which Soviet Russia introduced into the Geneva talks of nuclear testing, seems to have heralded a decisive turn in Russian policies toward the institutions of international co-operation.

When Chairman Khrushchev proposed, at the fifteenth session of the General Assembly in 1960 to change the structure of the one-man chief administrative office of the United Nations by having the functions of the secretary general be performed

Somali girl listens intently to a speaker during a political meeting prior to the establishment of the state of Somalia.

United Nations visiting mission to the trust territories in West Africa was greeted by the prime minister of the Gold Coast (later Ghana) Kwame Nkrumah (center).

Visitors at the leper camp at Yendi in the former trust territory of Togo.

by a three-man body, one representing the non-communist world, one the communist world and one the neutrals, there were many who considered this proposal only a step aimed at a demonstration

United Nations poster entitled "The Trusteeship Problem," issued by the U.N. Department of Public Information.

of dissatisfaction with Secretary General Dag Hammarskjöld's conduct of the United Nations operations in the Congo. But subsequent statements of representatives of the Soviet Union on this matter led to the conclusion that the Russian demand was no demonstration—it was a pronouncement of a policy which the Soviet Union intended to pursue continually. The extension of the veto principle into all areas of international co-operation seemed to be the prevailing Russian policy.

In view of this new Russian policy, the attacks against the late U.N. secretary general by Russia assumed special meaning and special importance. There was another time when the Soviet Union went all out against the secretary general, but that attack was not followed by a demand for basic changes in the organizational setup of the Secretariat, and the scope of competence of the secretary general. The first secretary general of the United Nations, Trygve Lie, whose regular, five-year term of office expired on February 1, 1951 and was extended for an additional three years on November 1, 1950, tendered his resignation before a plenary meeting of the General Assembly on November 10, 1952, before his second term of office expired. The step was a direct result of the Russian demand for his resignation, accompanied by a complete rupture of relations with the secretary general and an official nonrecognition policy toward Mr. Lie. The Korean war and the United Nations role in it had turned Russia against the secretary general.

The resignation of Trygve Lie put on the assembly's agenda a new item: "Appointment of the Secretary General of the United Nations." The Security Council met six times in private between March 11 and 31, 1953, to consider candidates to be recommended to the General Assembly. A secret ballot, on March 31, approved the French proposal to appoint Mr. Hammarskjöld of Sweden to the post of secretary general. On April 7, by secret ballot, the General Assembly adopted the council's recommendation. Three days later Mr. Hammarskjöld was installed by the General Assembly to his office, and the United Nations gained a new chief administrator, who was to lead this organization in times of stress, of conflict perhaps even more grave than those which had beset the U.N.

under the secretaryship of Trygve Lie.

The new secretary general faced the challenge of his office with unprecedented resourcefulness, devotion, skill and diplomatic ability. The thirty-eighth floor of the Secretariat Building was very soon turned into a center of unceasing activity. There were no specific working hours. Every hour, when necessary, became a working hour. The campaign of fraternizing with the thousands of U.N. staff members was soon recognized as being not merely a gesture of good will, and as not stemming merely from a belief in getting down to the "grass roots." "If you want to lead, you have to know the people you want to influence and inspire." This seemed to be the maxim of the new secretary general. Article 101 which empowers the secretary general to appoint the staff of the U.N. secretariat burdened the secretary general with unusual responsibility, but it strengthened his standing with the multi-thousand and multi-nation administrative apparatus for whom he was to be the "hiring and firing" superior alike.

This administrative power, which makes the office of the secretary general vulnerable by demands of member states for what they consider an appropriate share in staffing the Secretariat, especially its higher echelons, is supplemented by much more important functions, as provided in the charter. The chief administrative officer of the United Nations is accorded, in article 99, a highly political authority, which by its very nature must be controversial. This article entitles the secretary general to draw the attention of the Security Council to any matter which in his opinion "may threaten the maintenance of international peace and security." This authority, on which the signatories of the charter agreed, was supplemented in the Charter by some additional provisions which were intended to assure the neutrality of the chief executive officer of the United Nations in all decisions he might be called upon to make. Under article 101 "the Secretary General and the Staff shall not seek or receive instructions from any Government or from any other authority, external to the organization. They shall refrain from any action which might reflect on their position as international officials responsible only to the organization." The preservation of this aloofness and neutrality toward foreign influences is obliging not only for the secretary general and the U.N. staff, it

obliges also each member nation "to respect the exclusively international character of the responsibilities of the Secretary General and the Staff and not to seek to influence them in the discharge of their responsibilities."

As these articles were written nobody foresaw that after fifteen years of their application they would be turned into a crucial legal, political, administrative, and organizational problem of the United Nations. Although the fifteenth session of the General Assembly was an important one for many reasons, the most important occurrence of that session is related to these very articles of the charter. The basic idea of an independent, international civil service incorporated in these articles came under the concentrated fire of Russia's Premier Khrushchev. Denying the possibility of a truly independent and neutral international civil service, Premier Khrushchev demanded a basic change in the tenets of the U.N. functioning system. He demanded that the one chief administrative and executive officer of the international organization, the secretary general, be replaced by three secretary generals, each holding equal power, and each therefore able to block any administrative or executive action of the United Nations. Under this proposal, such action could be performed only under condition of unanimity of the three secretary generals, each representing, as Russia defined it, "socialist countries, states which are members of Western powers' military blocs, and neutralist countries."

This new concept of the office of the secretary general was rejected by the overwhelming majority of the United Nations. In fact only the "socialist countries" stood for it, whereas the Western powers and almost all neutralist countries disapproved of it. Such a change in the composition and basic idea of the secretary general's office, they argued, would be tantamount to paralyzing the entire organization and disenabling it to perform any duty, since it would then be permanently subject to the veto of one of the secretary generals. Although some of the neutral countries tried to search for a compromise in the form of a single secretary general with three deputy secretary generals to participate in policy-making decisions, they too remained in a minority and did not change the basic approach of Russia and the non-communist countries on this matter. Mr. Hammar-

International Court of Justice, meeting in secret session.

skjöld himself, against whom this attack was directed, was not reluctant to express his views on the matter. In an address at Oxford University on May 30, 1961, on the theme "The International Civil Servant in Law and in Fact," he contested the assertion of Mr. Khrushchev that there can be no such thing as an impartial civil servant, and stated:

In fact it [Khrushchev's assertion] challenges basic tenets in the philosophy of both the League of Nations and the United Nations, as one of the essential points on which these experiments in international co-operation represent an advance beyond traditional "conference diplomacy" is the introduction, on the international arena, of joint permanent organs, employing a neutral civil service, and the use of such organs for executive purposes on behalf of all the members of the organizations. Were it to be considered that the experience shows that this radical innovation in international life rests on a false assumption, because "no man can be neutral," then we would be thrown back to 1919, and a searching reappraisal would become necessary.

This was one of Mr. Hammarskjöld's replies to Russian demands concerning the reorganization

of the secretary general's office. It was preceded by a demand for Mr. Hammarskjöld's resignation and by Russia's official announcement that as of February, 1961, it would no longer recognize him as a U.N. official, and would sever any contacts and relations with him as principal administrative officer of the organization.

It is clear that this kind of relationship between the head of the U.N. Secretariat and a permanent member of the Security Council did not contribute to the strengthening of the organization, although it was Mr. Hammarskjöld's contention, as he stated at one of his press conferences, that nobody "should fear it influences either the direction or the spirit in which action is undertaken," that is, by the secretary general in the performance of his duties. To those who remember many of the resolutions of the Security Council, which have entrusted the secretary general with strictly political missions, exceeding even the most liberal interpretation of the character of his office, this Russian change of attitude must appear of radical importance. The system of passing the political "buck" to the secretary general, concerning international problems under U.N. consideration, compelled Mr. Hammarskjöld to warn, early in 1960, that there is a limit to what nations can expect of his office. Members of the United Nations, he warned, cannot dodge their responsibilities.

The source of the controversy about the status and organizational form of the secretary general's

Sir Hartley Shawcross (*center*) presenting the British case at a hearing on the Corfu Channel incident.

office is embedded in a resolution of the Security Council, made at the beginning of the Congo crisis. The resolution gave Mr. Hammarskjöld, with Russia's at first unreserved concurrence, most extensive powers to handle the Congo crisis, including the full authority for organizing a force to secure peaceful conditions in the newly independent republic. It is interesting to recall that a somewhat similar attack on the competences and character of the secretary general's office was directed about a quarter of a century before, at the time of the League of Nations, when Italy and Germany demanded, in 1932, that political affairs within the Secretariat be conducted by a committee of high officials.

Mr. Hammarskjöld's political initiatives, which his office was granted in the charter, were also employed by the first secretary general of the U.N., Trygve Lie. In 1950, Mr. Lie circulated a ten-point document—a program for achieving peace through the United Nations within twenty years. The program, one of many proposals of Mr. Lie, which included recommendations for the solution of the China representation problem, was dealt with by the General Assembly and received the full consideration of a political initiative.

Political initiatives are only part of the secretary general's prerogatives. The secretary general's office is responsible for the composition and organization of the entire Secretariat of the United Nations. Assisting the secretary general's office in performing its duties are the Office of Legal Affairs, the Office of the Controller, the Office of Personnel, two undersecretaries for Special Political Affairs, the Department of Political and Security Council Affairs, the Department of Economic and Social Affairs, the Department of Trusteeship and Information from Nonself-Governing Territories, the Offices of Public Information, of Conference Services, of General Services, and for Public Administration.

THE ECONOMIC AND SOCIAL COUNCIL

In this wide scope of activities, it is also the secretary general's duty to supervise an area of activity of the U.N. which was accorded in the charter a place of no lesser importance in the preservation of international co-operation than that of maintaining peace and security. This activity is directly related to the part of the charter's preamble which enjoins the U.N. to "reaffirm faith in fundamental human rights, in the dignity and worth of the human person, in the equal rights of men and women and of nations large and small . . . ," and to "promote social progress and better standards of life in larger freedom."

These purposes of the charter's preamble have been strengthened and underscored in chapter I, article 1, of the charter, under the heading "Purposes and Principles." According to this passage, the United Nations is intended "to achieve international co-operation in solving international problems of an economic, social, cultural, or humanitarian character, and in promoting and encouraging respect for human rights and for fundamental freedom for all, without distinction as to race, sex, language, or religion . . . and to be a center for harmonizing the actions of nations in the attainment of these common ends."

Although all the U.N. organs were entrusted with the task of striving for the implementation of these high principles, the organizers of the United Nations arrived at the conclusion that a special organ to deal with these problems permanently and centrally would assure a much greater degree of implementation than having these tasks dealt with by the other organs of the United Nations. As early as August, 1941, when the Atlantic charter was formulated, "the fullest collaboration between all nations in the economic field with the objective of securing, for all, improved labor standards, economic advancement and social security" was considered as one of the main aims to be achieved after the conclusion of a victorious war against the Axis powers. It was therefore clear that the Economic and Social Council (ECOSOC) had to rank after the General Assembly and the Security Council as the third most important organ of the United Nations.

The eighteen members of the council, elected for a three-year period and eligible for re-election immediately at the end of one term of office, are among the most busy people at the United Nations Headquarters. Meeting as required (but always at least twice a year), in accordance with its rules, which include a provision for "the convening of meetings on the request of a majority of its members," the Economic and Social Council could well be called the permanent guardian and instrument of the U.N. in the field of international cooperation for general progress of humanity toward higher standards of living, greater productivity, extension of educational facilities, and assurance of equality without distinction of race, color, sex, nationality, or religion.

The philosopher's saying, "Nothing human is alien to me," is thus applicable to the activities of the Economic and Social Council. And because human problems are innumerable, so also are the questions which are dealt with by ECOSOC. When all the other organs of the United Nations have a reprieve from their strenuous work, it is the Economic and Social Council which affords the visitor to the U.N. Headquarters an opportunity to witness a meeting of a U.N. organ.

Unfortunately the hall of this council only seldom sees packed galleries. There are usually no sensational developments there. No immediate crises and no quick solutions are to be found. But the sober problems for improving the human lot are always crowding the council president's desk, as the long and learned reports of various commissions, which the council is empowered to establish, tower before the eyes of the council members. The balanced economic and social development of a given country or group of countries, the

ratio of growth of production as compared with the increase of world population, violation of human rights and fundamental freedoms, and thousands of other, related problems, are always on the agenda. The majority of those present and voting, which is sufficient for the adoption of resolutions, recommendations, and opinions, is much easier to reach than in any other organ of the United Nations. The experience of the fifteenth session of the General Assembly, when thirteen ballots proved inconclusive since neither Belgium nor India, as candidates for the sixth elected seat, received the two-thirds majority necessary for the election of an Economic and Social Council member, was rather exceptional in the history of this council and the election of its members.

There was something even more conspicuous in this election. Announcing an agreement reached to end the deadlock, the President of the Fifteenth General Assembly Frederick H. Boland stated that "the Western group is prepared to agree that Belgium and India decide not to press their candidatures at this session of the assembly and another European candidate is elected now, then the Western European group will be prepared to support two candidates from among the members of the Asian-African group at next autumn's election for seats now occupied by Afghanistan and Spain." The statement came of course after an agreement had been reached between the interested groups, and the vacancy was filled on the twenty-first ballot, with Italy receiving 81 votes, 18 votes over the required two-thirds majority of 63 votes.

This hard contest for a seat on the Economic and Social Council signaled a growing interest in the council and a growing awareness of its importance, as it manifested the unpleasant truth about the deep divisions plaguing the United Nations, where bloc was often set against bloc, and where the dividing line between groups considering a question was not always based on the merits of the issue under consideration, but on many other factors—"cold war" calculations being not the least of them.

The temporary deadlock, described above, is fortunately not the rule in the Economic and Social Council. At the ECOSOC table, one could observe perfect harmony between all its members in their strivings toward the basic aims of the coun-

A hearing on the Anglo-Iranian oil dispute (June, 1952). At the court session (*from left*), Ambassador Nasrollah Entezam, Iranian Prime Minister Mohammed Mossadegh, and Iranian Minister to the Netherlands Hossein Nauab.

cil. Giving information and assistance to the Security Council and performing services with the approval of the General Assembly are some of the innumerable tasks the council fulfills on its own, in the area of its competence.

The universality of these obligations and their direct relation to local conditions and needs all over the world has found expression in the council's history of mobility which it adopted in the early days of its existence. Although basically and naturally located at the U.N. Headquarters, its sessions were and are being held, one could say, "around the globe." The eleventh session of the council was held at Geneva, July-August, 1950; the twelfth session at Santiago, Chile, February-March, 1951; and the 1961 summer session again at Geneva. These organizational measures for the council's mobility have recently been extended into the field of structural composition of the council. The Fifteenth General Assembly adopted a resolution calling on the secretary general to report to the Sixteenth General Assembly on the steps taken for the decentralization of the economic and social activities of the organization. In fact this resolution was completely in line with the already existing tendencies in the activities of the Economic and Social Council, which has its functions decentralized through separate economic commissions for Asia, for Africa, for Latin America, and for Europe. As conceived by the U.N. authorities, this division of functions was aimed not at a re-

gional separatism, but, on the contrary, at the intensification of the effectiveness of the council's activities, with due concern for and use of local conditions and personnel drawn from the people on the spot.

The Economic Commission for Europe (ECE), established in March, 1947, paved the way toward decentralization. It was followed by the Economic Commission for Asia and the Far East (ECAFE), established March, 1947; the Economic Commission for Latin America (ECLA), established in February, 1948; and the last in this order, the Economic Commission for Africa (ECA), established April, 1958, as one of the many signs of the growing role of the African continent on the world scene, and within the United Nations workings especially. In his annual report on the activities of the U.N. covering the period from June 16, 1957 to June 15, 1958, the secretary general gave the following appraisal of this development in the activities of the Economic and Social Council:

The expansion of the regional commission's system is clearly related to a trend that has made itself felt in our work. Within the framework of the policies of the United Nations, the commissions provide a means whereby regional groupings of members may jointly develop their own policies and take practical action for economic development, complementing the work of the global organs that deal with these subjects. By promoting concerted intergovernmental action and a continuous exchange of experience on common problems, the commissions have rendered services that have become increasingly appreciated by the participating governments and have reinforced the technical assistance that the organization has been able to lend to underdeveloped countries.

This trend toward decentralization could be considered a natural process, seeds of which can be found in those articles of the charter which deal with the Economic and Social Council. In fact, article 57 of the charter turned the council into a kind of "parent organization" for many international bodies, some of them of longer standing than the United Nations itself. The International Labor Organization, established in 1919; the Universal Postal Union, established in 1875; and other international organizations, defined as "specialized agencies," some of them established at later dates, all have been brought into relationship

The judges of the International Court, photographed between hearings in a case brought before the court by the government of Portugal against the government of India concerning right of passage over Indian territory.

with the United Nations—the Economic and Social Council serving as the sole "agent" of the U.N. for these relations.

Article 57 of the charter makes this relationship clear: "The various specialized agencies, established by intergovernmental agreement and having wide international responsibilities, as defined in their instruments, in economic, social, cultural, educational, health, and related fields, shall be brought into relationship with the United Nations."

But the founders of the United Nations were not satisfied with this statement of basic principles about the mutual relationship between the U.N. and the specialized agencies alone. A few additional complementary articles served as guiding outlines of this co-operation, which turned the specialized agencies in fact, if not constitutionally (that is, if not from the formal, legal point of view), into subsidiary agencies of the council. They participate, without vote, in the proceedings of the Economic and Social Council and their activities are reported to the council.

NONGOVERNMENTAL ORGANIZATIONS

In this general framework of a broadening scope of activities and of diversified instruments for performing the mission of the U.N., with which the council is entrusted by the charter, there is a provision which, it could be said, symbolizes best the intention of the founders of the United Nations. This intention was that it become an instrument with which not only states and political leaders are concerned and in permanent contact, but also an institution to which people the world over, men and women associated with each other within various organizations, could have a direct relationship, independently of the their national, official representations at the United Nations.

Article 71 of the charter implements this democratic principle, empowering the Economic and Social Council to "make suitable arrangements for consultation with nongovernmental organizations which are concerned with matters within its competence." There is no doubt that this provision was to a certain extent influenced by the fact that at the Conference on International Organization, at which the U.N. charter was drafted, representatives of forty-two national organizations in the United States assigned as consultants to the United States delegation pressed for such a provision. Their contribution was recorded on a plaque which hangs on the wall of the conference room in the Fairmont Hotel in San Francisco. The plaque, dated April 25–June 26, 1945, reads: "In this room met the consultants of forty-two national organizations assigned to the United States Delegation to the Conference on International Organization in which the United Nations Charter was drafted. Their contribution is particularly reflected in the Charter provisions for human rights and United Nations consultation with private organizations."

Whoever ventures to visit the United Nations Headquarters will easily discover that this provision did not remain a dead letter. Located on the third floor are the spacious offices of the nongovernmental organizations—one of the busiest spots at the U.N. With women the central force in the day-to-day activities, the office serves as a liaison center between the hundreds of organizations, which have made co-operation with the U.N. one of the important elements of their program.

Divided into categories A and B—those of the A category having a basic interest in most activities of the council the world over, and those in

Opening session of the court.

category B specifically concerned with only a few of the fields of activity of the council—these organizations may propose items for inclusion in the agenda, may send observers to public meetings of the council and its commissions, may submit written documents for circulation as documents of U.N. bodies, and may present their views orally.

Many of the organizations have their "permanent representatives" at the United Nations, and some of them have become part and parcel of the U.N. "landscape," in the corridors, in the lounges of the delegates, and in conference halls. At meetings at which they are allowed to participate, they often take the floor; their names and views appear in the official documents of the council, and when attending such a meeting one can hardly discern which representative speaks with the authority of a state behind him, and which is expressing only the views of one of the nongovernmental organizations.

This activity of private individuals, which is, no doubt, reported to the members of the organizations, is often supplemented by direct contact of members of these organizations with the United Nations. Seminars, organized visits, lectures, model Economic and Social Council meetings bring, during the year, many thousands of members of these organizations in direct contact with the U.N., serving the double purpose of acquainting the public with the U.N. and giving the U.N. the atmosphere of mass contact with people. Thus the international institution is elevated from the isolation of

diplomatic encounters between professional diplomats, toward the ideals of democratization, and through it, toward higher standards of open diplomacy.

THE TRUSTEESHIP COUNCIL

This effort to make the people feel that they are interwoven as closely as possible into the activities of the United Nations and its organs was carried even further within the framework of the Trusteeship Council. The small table which faces the large horseshoe of the council table in the Trusteeship Council hall symbolizes vividly these intentions of the U.N. founders. At the Economic and Social Council, the people can speak up only through the intermediary of organizations they belong to, whereas at this small table in the Trusteeship Council, even a single individual has the right to take his seat. There he is permitted to present his grievances against anybody whom he considers as doing harm to his interests, or he may bring before the council any wishes he deems appropriate. The U.N. Charter provides for such a direct contact in article 87(b), which states that the Trusteeship Council may "accept petitions and examine them in consultation with the administering authority."

This right of petition was and is being used to the utmost. In the first five years of operation, the Trusteeship Council received and considered more than 700 petitions, and at the twenty-seventh session of the council, which opened on June 1, 1961,

235 petitions and communications were received from persons and groups concerning conditions in various trust territories. The council's Standing Committee on Petitions examines these petitions in advance, before they are submitted to the council, and the members of this committee as well as the council itself, often have the benefit of direct contact with the authors of the petitions, who venture to travel as far as from the Gold Coast of Africa, or from the Pacific Islands to set foot in the U.N. Headquarters. Here they are rewarded by a feeling of contact with the highest authority in the world. And here they can make their appeals and expect justice to be meted out.

Colorful robes of a native tribe in Africa, gold-embroidered tunics in the classic style of Roman attire, a genuine floating coat of a giant seven foot man from the Marshall Islands, a black-bearded Arab from Oman in a snow-white garb, with his head covered with a genuine "keffiyah"—all of these and many others in their national dresses appear at the U.N. Trusteeship Council in their struggle for better living conditions, for self rule, or for independence. Here a permanent demonstration is being given of how the national authority of a state submits to international supervision and accepts the implications of exposure of its conduct and the conduct of the affairs of the trust territory to international scrutiny.

Some far-reaching decisions pertaining to the birth of new states, and to their boundaries, have been influenced by this direct contact with local populations acting within the right of petition. The state of Ghana, which was created after British Togoland and the Gold Coast were united, serves as a classic example of this point. Ghana is a most dynamic political entity on the African continent, whose influence has become conspicuous not only in Africa, but in the councils of international politics as well. There is the case of Joseph Henry Allasani, the head of the Togoland delegation and one-time schoolteacher turned political leader, who pleaded with the Trusteeship Council in March, 1954, to have his native Northern Togoland joined with the Gold Coast. As he spoke before the council, he kept in mind that somewhere, 6,000 miles away in his native land, people of his Dagomba, Gonja, and Mamprusi tribes were attentively waiting for the news about the accomplishments of their envoy. Mr. Allasani spoke in a very simple, yet most convincing manner:

It makes me very sad when I think of what it cost my people to send us here. It costs about £700 [about $2,000] for each of us and the tribes—people have defrayed all our expenses. Collections have been made for weeks past to raise the fund to pay for this trip to New York. Even the school children have contributed their pennies. It is a great hardship for Togolanders, some of whom don't earn more than £3 or £4 [$8.40 to $11.20] a year. But they feel it is worth it. To them it is a matter affecting their whole lives—to make their voices heard before the United Nations. This money would help my people buy many things they need—hospital equipment and drugs, radio sets and schoolbooks—but they feel any sacrifice is worth-while in order to send us to New York to present their case to the United Nations.

For those peoples, for those tribes, the United Nations is not an abstract idea, not an instrument of international politics with which only diplomats have to be concerned. To them, the U.N. is the authority which is assisting them by implementing the provisions of the charter, which enjoins the U.N. "to further international peace and security, to promote the political, economic, social and educational advancement of the inhabitants and their progressive development toward self-government or independence as may be appropriate in the particular circumstances of each territory, . . . to encourage respect for human rights and for fundamental freedoms for all without distinction as to race, sex, language, or religion."

The administering powers may be called upon to implement these high principles, not only due to the obligations they assumed in the charter, but also as a result of special trusteeship agreements they signed when they assumed responsibility for these territories. The territories were either held previously under the system of mandates of the League of Nations, were those which were detached from enemy states as a result of the Second World War, or else were those voluntarily placed under the system by states responsible for their administration.

And indeed the Trusteeship Council became, early in the U.N.'s history, one of the examples of U.N. efficiency and the strict observation of the charter.

In this chapter of noble achievements, the Trusteeship Council supervised, assisted, and accelerated the attainment of independence of growing numbers of states. It is certainly a tribute to the powers administering trust territories and to the Trusteeship Council alike, that after fifteen years of the U.N.'s existence, President of the Council U Tin Maung of Burma, at the twenty-seventh session of the council, could have stated in his opening remarks that the council will complete its noble mission when all trust territories obtain their independence—an end which, he said, is "in sight."

The march toward this goal started in 1957 when the former British Togoland in West Africa emerged from trusteeship. It was united with the Gold Coast as a result of a plebiscite held under U.N. supervision, and became part of the independent state of Ghana. Of the ten territories covered by trusteeship agreements, seven territories in Africa were under British, French, Belgian, and Italian administration; two territories in the Western Pacific were under Australian and New Zealand administration; and the trust territory of the Pacific Islands was under United States administration. Next to achieve the trusteeship goals after Togoland were two territories in West Africa administered by France: the former French Cameroons and French Togoland, which gained independence as Republics of Cameroon and Togo, respectively, on January 1 and April 27, 1960. Somaliland in East Africa, a former Italian colony, administered by Italy, united with British Somaliland and achieved independence as Somalia on July 1, 1960.

Three additional trust territories—Tanganyika, British Cameroons, and Western Samoa—were on the agenda of the U.N. General Assembly at its fifteenth session. At this session some of the final steps were taken for the attainment of independence by the three trust territories: Tanganyika's independence was slated for December, 1961; the British Cameroons, as a result of a plebiscite supervised by the U.N., was to join its northern part with Nigeria and its southern part with the Republic of Cameroon, on June 1 and October 1, 1961, respectively; and Western Samoa voted on May 9, 1961, under U.N. supervision, for the approval of its constitution and for independence to commence on January 1, 1962.

By this latter date there will remain only the trusteeships of Ruanda-Urundi (Belgium), New Guinea (Australia), Nauru (jointly administered by Australia, New Zealand, and the United Kingdom), and the trust territory of the Pacific Islands —the Marshalls, Carolines, and Marianas (United States). This last territory, was the only one designated as "strategic," and was therefore put under the supervision of the Security Council, which exercises the functions of the U.N. with the assistance of the Trusteeship Council in political, economic, social, and educational matters.

To have this march toward independence accelerated, a whole international machinery for

Photographed at the bench during an opening session are fifteen judges of the court and the ad hoc judges designated by the governments which presented the case to be heard.

supervising the administration of the trust territories was conceived. Annual reports, visiting missions, petitions, and a questionnaire containing 247 detailed questions, has turned the United Nations into a virtual partner in the administration of these territories. The Trusteeship Council composed of (1) member countries administering trust territories, (2) permanent members of the Security Council which do not administer trust territories, and (3) as many other members, elected for a three-year term by the General Assembly, as may be necessary to assure equality in numbers between administering and nonadministering members, operates under the authority of the General Assembly, which recommends and advises ways and means of making the trust the U.N. has taken over on behalf of peoples in these territories justified and worth-while.

This category of "trust" finds its expression also in the permanent communication between the people of the trust territories and the U.N. organs by means of U.N. information centers, which are being set up in the territories. Many of the General Assembly resolutions have dealt with this problem and one of the recent resolutions requested the secretary general to use all media of mass communication to keep the peoples of the trust territories adequately informed of the aims and activities of the United Nations and, in particular, of the international trusteeship system.

In this history of adherence to the U.N. principles and to resolutions of the U.N. organs, a permanent discord became a part of every session of the U.N., and of deliberations of many of the U.N. organs. The Union of South Africa, which administers a former German colony which became a League of Nations mandate after World War I—the territory of South-West Africa—refuses consistently to heed the provisions of the charter pertaining to former mandate territories. None of the provisions pertaining to the trust territories is considered by South Africa to be binding. Since the very inception of the U.N., the Union of South Africa has refused to co-operate with the Trusteeship Council, and year after year the problem of South-West Africa is subjected to U.N. debates, remonstrations, resolutions. Many thousands of pages of U.N. documents and innumerable hours of U.N. meetings have been devoted to this issue. Even the International Court of Justice was called upon to act on this question. The court's finding, that the Union of South Africa has at least to adhere to the provisions of the Mandate Commission under the League's covenant, has yet to be implemented.

NONSELF-GOVERNING TERRITORIES

But having disposed of the territories of former realms of the defeated powers in World Wars I and II, the charter (and afterward, on the basis of it, the U.N. itself) had to deal with another, similar problem—the problem of dependent territories which were part of the colonial system of European empires. The final wording of Chapter XI of the charter, in which the problem of these territories is dealt with, was a result of many consultations and many an irritation among the United Nations and Allied powers before the war was over.

The fate of these territories early became a part of deliberations between the major powers—primarily, of course, between the United States and the greatest imperial power of those days, the United Kingdom. Britain's Prime Minister Churchill was not especially pleased by some of the public declarations of the United States leaders on this matter. President Roosevelt's declaration, made in May, 1942, in a conversation with the Russian foreign minister, Molotov, that "the white nations could not hope to hold these areas as colonies in the long run," was supplemented by a declaration of the Undersecretary of State, Sumner Welles, who was even more explicit in his address on Memorial Day of the same year:

If this war is in fact a war for liberation of peoples, it must assure the sovereign equality of people throughout the world as in the world of the Americas. Our victory must bring in its train the liberation of all peoples. Discrimination between peoples because of their race, creed or color must be abolished. The age of imperialism is ended. The principles of the Atlantic Charter must be guaranteed to the world as a whole in all oceans and in all continents.

And Secretary of State Cordell Hull wrote in late summer, 1942: "We have always believed that all peoples without distinction of race, color, or religion who are prepared and willing to accept the responsibilities of liberty are entitled to its enjoyment." Hull promised that the United States would "use the full measure of [its] influence to support attainment of freedom by all peoples who by their acts show themselves worthy of it and ready for it."

Churchill and his government were not pleased with these tendencies in defining the aims of the war. In a cable to President Roosevelt, Churchill reminded him not to be too hasty with statements of this kind, and added, "Atlantic Charter application to Asia and Africa requires much thought."

When the stage of drafting declarations arrived, every word counted. The definition of "independence" was very much contested between the United States and its allies. At the first Quebec conference, August, 1943, Anthony Eden, Great Britain's foreign secretary, made it clear that the word "independence" troubled him very much. In a conversation with Harry Hopkins, Eden referred to a suggestion by Roosevelt that Britain might give up Hong Kong as a gesture of good will and dryly remarked that he had not heard the President suggest any similar gesture by the United States. So it was only natural that Great Britain objected to the 1943 "Draft Declaration on National Independence" and that on Britain's insistence the word "independence" was dropped in favor of "self-government." Later, both controversial terms were dropped and instead the title for this declaration became "Draft Declaration Regarding the Administration of Dependent Territories," still later to become the "Declaration Regarding Nonself-Governing Territories" in the U.N. Charter.

This history explains why chapter XI of the charter does not once mention the term "independence." Article 73 of this chapter enjoins the U.N. "to promote to the utmost, within the system of international peace and security . . . the well-being of the inhabitants of these territories and to ensure, with due respect for the culture of the peoples concerned, their political, economic, social and educational advancement . . . to develop self-government, to take due account of the political aspirations of the peoples, and to assist them in the progressive development of their free political institutions"; and article 74 obliges, that in respect to these territories the policy of U.N. members "must be based on the general principles of good neighborliness, due account being taken of the interests and well-being of the rest of the world, in social, economic and commercial matters."

So in fact no limitations were imposed by the charter on the U.N. members regarding the nonself-governing territories. But in spite of that, a provision was included to preserve a certain degree of authority for the international organization in respect to these territories. Article 73(e) obliges the administering U.N. members "to transmit regularly to the secretary general, for information purposes, subject to such limitations as security and constitutional considerations may require, statistical and other information of a technical nature relating to economic, social, and educational conditions in the territories for which they are respectively responsible."

The "Committee on Information from Nonself-

Governing Territories" became, therefore, the central U.N. organ for supervising the implementation of these provisions. Composed of eight administering members and an equal number of nonadministering members, the committee engaged itself, through the years of its existence, not only in receiving information, but in instituting studies of various aspects of life in these territories, in making recommendations, and in giving advice and counsel. At its twelfth session, for instance (April 24—May 26, 1961), the committee considered a special study on social advancement in dependent territories and arrived at a series of conclusions—among them one which states that "the social and economic advancement of all territories depends in large measure on the development of an adequately paid, integrated, stabilized and efficient labor force."

View of the Peace Palace in The Hague, headquarters of the International Court of Justice.

As with many other resolutions of its kind, this resolution was of course based not only on results of special studies. The information which the administering states submit is the main source material for any conclusion the committee arrives at. In 1960 information was transmitted from fifty-one dependent territories. Of these, forty-one were administered by the United Kingdom, three by New Zealand, three by the United States, one by the Netherlands, and one jointly by France and the United Kingdom. Of the U.N. members administering nonself-governing territories, only Portugal and Spain have not transmitted written information to the committee. At the twelfth session of the committee, Spain participated cooperatively for the first time, and its representative made an oral statement providing the committee with detailed information on political, economic, social, and educational conditions in the nonself-governing territories under its administration. The Portuguese refusal to participate in the committee's activities was subjected to expression of regret, to protestations, and to proposals to have the secretary general prepare background papers, containing statistical and other information relating to economic, social, and educational conditions prevailing in the territories under its administration. In 1960 and 1961 this problem of territories administered by Portugal became a major concern of the principal U.N. organs. Security Council meetings and resolutions dealing with the situation in Angola, in Western Africa, far exceeded the provisions of Chapter XI of the charter, and were deeply immersed in the political struggles between the communist and noncommunist blocs. The noncommitted (primarily the Asian and African) U.N. members played a most important role in these encounters. The Portuguese contention was that Angola is part of Portuguese national sovereign territory and therefore any steps taken by the U.N. on Angola are a violation of the charter's provision, which exclude the internal affairs of states, which are United Nations members, from the competence and interference of U.N. organs.

At the fifteenth session of the General Assembly the entire legal fabric of charter provisions concerning the nonself-governing territories underwent a radical change. On December 14, 1960, a resolution was adopted under the title "Declaration on the Granting of Independence to Colonial Countries and Peoples," paragraph 5 of which states: "Immediate steps shall be taken, in Trust and Nonself-Governing Territories or all other territories, which have not yet attained independence, to transfer all powers to the peoples of those territories, without any conditions or reservations, in accordance with their freely expressed will and desire, without any distinction as to race, creed or color, in order to enable them to enjoy complete independence and freedom."

Although the resolution was intended largely to give special stress to prevailing tendencies in world affairs, it was nevertheless a kind of revolutionary measure, not only as far as conditions in many parts of the world were concerned, but also in relation to the provisions of the U.N. Charter. The

Members of the British delegation to present British arguments on the Anglo-Iranian oil dispute.

highest international body, by a vote of 89 for and 9 abstaining (Australia, Belgium, the Dominican Republic, France, Portugal, Spain, the Union of South Africa, the United Kingdom, and the United States, with Dahomey absent), advised the world community that an end to all forms of national dependence had to come about. The implications of this resolution could not yet have been fully realized, but there is little doubt that its wording as well as its basic principles will be used not only against those U.N. members who formally hold dependencies, but also as an argument in disputes against seemingly well-established state entities, with multinational or multiracial component nations within their boundaries.

THE INTERNATIONAL COURT OF JUSTICE

The interpretation of this resolution, which is rightly considered to be the last word in the process of liberating dependent nations, will certainly require frequently the legal opinions of authentic interpretators. Thus, the International Court of Justice will be brought into play, for it is the organ whose establishment was to provide a legal instrument, not only for settling of international disputes, but also for giving legal opinions on matters of interpretation of international documents, as well as advisory opinions at the request of the General Assembly, the Security Council or any other organ or specialized agency of the United Nations.

This fifteen-member judicial body, with its seat at the Hague, Netherlands, replaced the Permanent Court of International Justice instituted with the establishment of the League of Nations. Elected independently by the Security Council and the General Assembly for a term of nine years, the members of the court may be re-elected, but two judges could not be of the same nationality. Although only two languages, English and French, are the official languages, the parties presenting their cases before the court are permitted to use any language they desire. Functioning under a special statute of the international court, the court is permanently in session. "Only states may be parties in cases before the court," and the court is open "to the States parties of the Statute," that is, to all member states of the United Nations. (Non-member states of the U.N. could also be parties to the statute of the court.)

These provisions did not assure automatic intercession of the court in international disputes. States were not obliged to submit their disputes to the court. Unlike the justice of national states, international justice remained optional. States which were parties to the statute could at any time declare that they recognized as compulsory, in relation to any other state accepting the same obligation, the jurisdiction of the court in all legal disputes concerning (1) the interpretation of a treaty, (2) any question of international law, (3) the existence of any fact which, if established, would constitute a breach of an international obligation and (4) the nature or extent of the reparation to be made for the breach of an international obligation.

By the end of 1958, thirty-eight states (Australia, Belgium, Cambodia, Canada, China, Colombia, Denmark, the Dominican Republic, El Salvador, Finland, France, Haiti, Honduras, Israel, Japan, Liberia, Lichtenstein, Luxemburg, Mexico, the Netherlands, New Zealand, Nicaragua, Norway, Pakistan, Panama, Paraguay, the Philippines, Portugal, Sudan, Sweden, Switzerland, Thailand, Turkey, the Union of South Africa, the United Arab Republic, the United Kingdom, the United States, and Uruguay) had accepted or renewed their acceptance of the compulsory jurisdiction of the court. But some of the states, while accepting reciprocally the compulsory jurisdiction in legal disputes, reserved to themselves the right to determine what issues are domestic and therefore not subject to the competence of the court. Regarding this reservation, the U.N. charter provides, in article 94, that "each member of the U.N. under-

take to comply with the decision of the International Court of Justice in any case to which it is a party"; and further, "If any party to a case fails to perform the obligations incumbent upon it under a judgment rendered by the court, the other party may have recourse to the Security Council, which may, if it deems necessary, make recommendations or decide upon measures to be taken to give effect to the judgment."

Unfortunately, of all the instruments of international co-operation, the court has been used the least. But even in the prevailing atmosphere of reluctance to submit disputes to the court—a reluctance often influenced by the slow judicial processes of the court—the International Court of Justice was called upon many times to settle international disputes. Besides the Corfu Channel case, in which Great Britain accused Albania of damaging with mines its naval craft passing through the channel, and the Anglo-Iranian dispute over oil concessions, other cases found adjudication and legal solution before the court.

There was the case of contested sovereignty over the islets and rocks of the Minquiers and Ecrehos groups, located between the British Channel island of Jersey and the coast of France, in which the court ruled that the United Kingdom was entitled to sovereignty over these islands. It was an excellent exercise in historical knowledge, with both sides using every possible historical, political, and geographical argument. The contest employed the finest authorities of England and France in these fields, who kept the court busy for two years until it finally arrived at its decision.

There was the case of Italy against France, the United Kingdom and the United States, which involved the problem of gold removed from Rome in 1943 by Germany and recovered by the victorious Allies. The gold had to be returned by the three Western powers. Thus Italy got consideration of her claim.

And there were many cases in which the court could not act, because one of the parties notified the court that it regarded the institution of court proceedings unacceptable, and this in turn caused the court to have the case removed from the list. Such was the case regarding a United States application of October, 1952, requesting the court to find that Russia was liable for damage caused in the sum of $1,620,295 after a United States aircraft

The International Court of Justice listens to Dr. Ivan Kerno (*left center*), assistant secretary general of the United Nations Department of Legal Affairs, deliver a statement at the opening of hearings on the interpretation of the peace treaties with Bulgaria, Hungary, and Romania.

was allegedly shot down by two Russian aircraft; a similar fate befell another United States application, against Czechoslovakia, caused by an aerial incident. Time and again the jurisdiction of the court was rescinded by parties (nations) which somewhat preferred their cases aired either through diplomatic channels or left in abeyance until political conditions changed or times became more favorable either for mutual accommodation or for a court ruling.

The court was much more successful in providing advisory opinions at the request of United Nations organs. In this respect a most important opinion could be mentioned, related to the problem of admitting new nations to membership in the United Nations. For many years the blocking of admission of new members was not only an irritating element in relations between U.N. member nations, but was also a principal obstacle to United Nations universality. The use of the veto power in the Security Council became a decisive device in preventing new members from being admitted. Could this obstacle be overcome by according the highest U.N. authority, the General Assembly, where no veto prevails, the power to decide? A request for an advisory opinion on this question was submitted to the court by the fourth session of the General Assembly, in 1949, and the opinion was given, a year later, upholding existing practice. The court ruled that the assembly cannot admit a new member by its own

decision, since, according to the charter, the admission of a state to membership is to be effected by the General Assembly upon the prior recommendation of the Security Council.

What is the basis of the court decisions? What kind of law had been decided upon in the statute of the court to mete out international justice? The answers to these questions lie within international conventions, international customs, general principles of law recognized by civilized nations, and judicial decisions and teachings of highly qualified publicists. These are the sources of law on which the court is supposed to base its findings. The development of international law supplies an ever-growing codification of legal principles on which nations base their relationships. The International Law Commission, established by the General Assembly on November 21, 1947, has been busy ever since in working out a series of international rules. The Law on the Sea, Diplomatic Intercourse and Immunities, a draft Declaration on Rights and Duties of States, Nationality Law (which includes statelessness)—these are some of the accomplishments of the commission.

Among these efforts at codification of international law it is worth-while to mention a resolution of the General Assembly, adopted at its 1946 session, which affirmed the principles of international law recognized in the U.N. Charter and in the judgment of the International Military Tribunal, which was established for the prosecution and punishment of major German war criminals. A code of offenses against the peace and security of mankind was formulated by the International Law Commission, and for years it was subject to discussion by the General Assembly. But the draft of the code could not be acted upon as, according to U.N. members, the code raised questions related to the definition of aggression—a question on which unanimity was more elusive than in any other international problem.

As has been the case with all the other organs of the United Nations, the frequency with which the International Court of Justice has been called upon for solution of international problems, and its influence on the evolvement of a world community of law, have remained tightly knit with the general international situation — its phases of heightened tensions and its passing periods of relaxation.

UNITED CARE FOR THE FAMILY OF MEN

When news dispatches from the tiny kingdom of Laos alerted the world to a possible international military conflagration, when fourteen nations assembled in Geneva, Switzerland, to strive for a solution of this explosive problem in Southeast Asia, and when a representative of the U.N. secretary general established U.N. presence there, there still remained other items of news to round out the picture of trouble in Laos.

On the shelves of the United Nations documents desk one could have found news of a different character, pertaining to this very same area. This was not alarming news; it did not carry the message of pending dangers, and those reading it did not have a feeling of emergency. Theirs was a completely different reaction—a reaction of expectation, of hope, of an opportunity for a better life to be given to many millions of people.

The Mekong River—the mighty river whose waters flow, to a great extent unused, into the vast stretches of the South China Sea, and which was so often mentioned as the dividing line between the warring forces in the Laotian struggle—entered the annals of international relations in a more hope-

Khone Falls on the Mekong River is surveyed by U.N. team to prepare plans for hydroelectric power development.

ful context as well. The Mekong River Project, a grandiose project of irrigation and land amelioration, kept numerous United Nations experts busy for years, engaging the attention of the Technical Assistance Board, the Food and Agriculture Organization, and the World Health Organization.

The special character of international interest in the Mekong River is certainly one of the best illustrations, not only of the extreme diversity of the problems facing the international community, but also of their so divergent meanings—as divergent as are the meanings of peace and war, and as are strivings for human betterment and armed clashes between opposing political factions.

STATISTICS—A BASIS FOR PLANNING

In this field of efforts toward betterment of the human lot, the United Nations can certainly register one of the finest and proudest chapters of international co-operation. Although some intrusions of political tensions could not be completely eliminated, in general, this has been a field of relative accord. Scores of nations have co-operated fully and experts of all races and national allegiances have pooled their knowledge and experience to assist the less privileged—those who have not yet had the opportunity to reach the standards of technical skill, education, and production which could eliminate, or at least start combating effectively want, disease, and illiteracy.

It is an all-embracing effort. When, in 1960, a livestock disease caused drastic losses in Europe, the Middle East, and Asia, the Food and Agriculture Organization (FAO) assisted in organizing control of the disease and arranged for supplies of vaccine to be flown into the infected areas.

Prices paid abroad for hides from Lybia have risen, thanks to improvements in production techniques made possible by advice from experts sent by the FAO.

Production in Afghanistan rose by 70 per cent

Surveying of the Nam Ngum River, tributary of the Mekong.

after an FAO expert from Haiti advised the local growers how to increase their cotton crop 2.5 times and how to harvest their grain in a much shorter time, thus making possible the cultivation of much more land. He did not introduce modernization of agricultural equipment; no modern Caterpillars or combines had to be purchased and no new technical skills acquired by the farmer. The existing tools, as primitive as they are, were put to work more efficiently and appropriately. A scythe may have replaced a sickle, a hoe may have replaced a mattock, and a seed may have been planted in a manner slightly different than formerly.

Methods of rice-growing in Japan, which yield sometimes more than twice as big a crop as methods used in India, have been brought to the Indian subcontinent, increasing production of the main dish of the populace.

The extension of electric power transmission and distribution systems in the Protectorate of Uganda has been accomplished due to a loan of $8.4 million by the International Bank for Reconstruction and Development.

Action to curtail lead and zinc supplies to a level approximately 2 per cent below the estimated world consumption in 1961 was agreed upon by the International Lead and Zinc Study Group at a session in Mexico City. The existence of substantial stocks of unsold metal created grave problems in countries producing these metals and a reduction was necessary to prevent hardships and even possible upheavals in countries concerned.

A conference to establish educational needs of Africans and to plan programs determining how to supply those needs was held in Addis Ababa, Ethiopia. Existing statistical data compounded by the services of the United Nations Educational, Scientific, and Cultural Organization (UNESCO) revealed that of twenty-five million children in Tropical Africa, which comprises thirty countries, nearly seventeen million children have no education facilities whatsoever.

About fifty-five million children and mothers the world over, in 104 countries and territories have directly benefited in 1960 from the aid of the United Nations Children's Fund.

Ten fellowships from nine countries received appropriations in 1960 for study in the fields of narcotic control, opium identification, and treatment and rehabilitation of drug addicts.

During the period from July 1 to December 31, 1958, more than 130 countries and territories received technical assistance; more than 8,000 experts worked in ninety countries and territories. Sixteen thousand fellowship awards were made in the same period to trainees in the less developed countries, which gave them an opportunity to learn how to run a workshop, a hospital, a school, a factory, or a research institute.

A $100,000 appropriation in 1960 was used for a seminar held in Tokyo, on the role of substantive criminal law in the protection of human rights, and the purposes of legitimate limits of penal sanctions. A seminar on the protection of human rights in criminal procedure was held in Austria, while in Ethiopia, a seminar on the participation of women in public life was held.

A proposal was made for a United Nations conference on the application of science and technology for the benefit of the less developed areas, with special emphasis on (1) the development of the economy of the less developed countries through better utilization of their human, raw material and energy resources, (2) acceleration of industrial development through the use of the latest achievements in science, technology, and engineering, (3) development of agriculture, (4) training of national personnel, and (5) improvement of public health.

A report was presented by the International Civil Aviation Organization describing the

One of the major projects of U.N. Technical Assistance was directed at proper utilization of Mekong River waters.

organized and budgeted by the United Nations Relief and Works Agency for Palestine Refugees (UNRWA). Relief was given to several hundred thousand refugees in Korea through the United Nations Korean Reconstruction Agency (UNKRA).

One could go on endlessly to illustrate the broad scope of U.N. activities. These activities have been carried on either directly, or with the assistance of organizations, agencies, funds, and banks, which the international community has established through the years. In this over-all effort for the betterment of the human lot everywhere, natural and human resources have been explored and co-ordinated from the Middle East to the most remote island in the Pacific.

The United Nations and agencies related to it have supplied the world with vital statistics—basic tools for social and economic planning, and nowadays, a prerequisite of progress and development:

There is, for example, the problem of natural increase, with all its implications of overpopulation and poor nutrition. Every two minutes there

progress of civil aviation in 1960 and discussing the possible development of supersonic aircraft which may be expected to enter airline service in the next decade, and revealing that by the end of 1960, the world's air transport fleet was made up of the following types of aircraft: turbojet, 388; turboprop, 723; piston-engined (4 motors), 1,621; piston-engined (2 motors), 2,286; and jets, only 7.7 per cent of the fleet.

Prophylactic and therapeutic measures were taken against cerebrospinal meningitis in the Sudan and the Republic of Chad, with the assistance of the World Health Organization (WHO).

A contribution of the office of the U.N. High Commissioner for Refugees in Geneva was made to fulfill the Cambodian government's needs for assistance to refugees flocking into that country from neighboring Laos. Some 18,000 refugees, under the mandate of the U.N. High Commissioner for Refugees were taken care of prior to resettlement at the initial expense of $4 million. A vocational training center for Arab refugees was

United Nations poster issued by the Department of Public Information.

are 170 more people in the world; every hour, 5,000 more; every day, 120,000 more. This is the daily net increase arrived at by subtracting the average 150,000 deaths every day throughout the world, from the 270,000 births in the same period. Placed on an annual basis this means 48 million more births than deaths in a world population that is increasing at a rate of 1.7 per cent each year. The world population consisted of 2,905 million people in mid–1959, compared with 2,495 million in 1950 and only 1,810 million in 1920. The annual rate of increase in population is highest in Oceania (2.4 per cent), which is closely followed by America (2.1 per cent), and is the lowest in Europe (0.8 per cent). Asia and Africa are close to the world rate of 1.7 per cent. At the present rate of increase, the world population will double within forty years.

Directly related to these population data are the estimates of life expectancy—a child born somewhere in Scandinavia could expect to live 75 years and a child born on the same date in the Republic of Guinea is expected to live no more than 31 years.

Expenditure on food is another indicator of the standard of living and stage of economic development a country has reached. In Ceylon, for example, this expenditure reached 54 per cent of total income, in Ghana 57 per cent, in Ecuador 49 per cent, and in the Republic of Korea and in Yugoslavia 48 per cent; whereas in countries such as Sweden, Denmark, Norway, Belgium, the United Kingdom, France, the Netherlands and Austria, it amounted to no more than between 27 and 35 per cent. During the course of an average day the typical urban worker in the United States eats 4.45 lbs. of food, including milk and milk products, meats, vegetables, fruits, eggs, cereals, and sugar. A typical urban worker in India consumes in the same span of time 1.24 lbs. of food, and 85 per cent of it is rice.

The list of statistical data goes on, revealing standards of living in various areas and setting the goals for less developed countries to achieve the standards of the developed nations. European and Asian countries are behind North America in the production of most agricultural staples, despite the fact that 70 per cent of the Asians are engaged in agriculture, 45 per cent of the Russians, and 30 per cent of the Europeans, as against 15 per cent of the

North Americans. And here are some details which explain to a great extent the diverse levels of production and efficiencies in various countries: A total of 430 million people in India average 1,890 calories a day, 27.5 million Filipinos average 1,940 calories a day, while 5 million Danes get 3,420 calories a day.

The data also covers such categories as energy, transportation, public finance, trade, housing, medical care and medical personnel, books, and radio and television sets. Regarding the latter, there were, in 1959, 365 million radios in the world, with a half (183 million) in North America (169 million in the United States alone), and 133 million in Europe. There were 86 million television sets, with 53 million in the United States, 10 million in the United Kingdom, 3.6 million in Russia, 3.4 million in Canada, 3.4 million in the

Aqaba, a port in Jordan on the Red Sea, has been developed with U.N. assistance.

Federal Republic of Germany, 3.3 million in Japan, 1.6 million in Italy, and 1.4 million in France.

In the great debate about the rates of increase in real gross product of various countries, the United Nations serves again as the most reliable source of data. The *United Nations Yearbook of National Accounts Statistics* for 1960 reveals that the highest average annual growth rate in the world was achieved for that year by the Federal Republic of Germany (7.5 per cent); the highest in Latin America was achieved by Venezuela (8.3 per cent); in Asia by Japan and the Republic of China (8 per cent each). In Eastern Europe, where the standard used is net material product at constant prices, growth rates exceeded 6 per cent. But at the same time, some other countries had a very moderate growth rate: Ireland less than one per

Ronald M. MacDonnell of Canada, secretary general of the International Civil Aviation Organization (ICAO).

cent; Argentina about one per cent; and Belgium, Denmark, and the United Kingdom about 2.5 per cent. The United States annual growth averaged 2.6 per cent for 1954–1958.

THE U.N. AND THE SPECIALIZED AGENCIES

Facts, figures, analyses, estimates, surveys, reports, pour by the hundreds into U.N. Headquarters every week, every month, every year, piling up an ever-growing library of data which serves many purposes—acceleration of industrial development, raising standards of living, and eradication of wrongs, inefficiencies, diseases, and illiteracy. And all come from the great family of United Nations organizations or from the Intergovernmental Agencies Related to the United Nations, known more generally as the "specialized agencies."

The United Nations Charter provided the basic principle of incorporation of the activities of these institutions into the general efforts of the United Nations Organization. The Economic and Social Council serves as a kind of "parent" organization for these many agencies, which U.N. insiders early christened jokingly with the name "U.N. soup." As was mentioned in the previous chapter, article 57 of the charter states that various specialized

agencies were to be linked to the United Nations. This was to be done in accordance with the provisions of Article 63, which states:

> The Economic and Social Council may enter into agreements with any of the agencies referred to in Article 57, defining the terms on which the Agency concerned shall be brought into relationship with the United Nations. Such agreements shall be subject to approval by the General Assembly. . . . It may co-ordinate the activities of the specialized agencies through consultation with and recommendations to such agencies and through recommendations to the General Assembly and to the Members of the United Nations.

These portions of the charter have become the legal, constitutional basis for co-operation between the U.N. and the specialized agencies.

The agreements with the specialized agencies as mentioned in these articles came into force at quite an early date of the United Nations' existence. Starting with December 14, 1946, when the agreement with the International Labor Organization (ILO) came into force, and ending with the agreement with the Intergovernmental

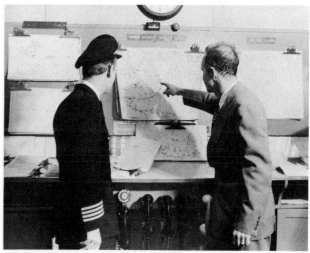

Information on international weather conditions is important to pilots on international flights. This pilot is being briefed on weather conditions prior to a transatlantic run.

Maritime Consultative Organization (IMCO) which came into force January 13, 1959, twelve such agreements have been signed and they regulate the integration of the agencies into the framework of the United Nations Organization. A similar agreement regulates the working relationship between the U.N. and the International Atomic

Syahfuan Gatam (*left*), of Indonesia, a participant in the fourth ICAO Trainee Program, looks at some equipment at the fire station of the Montreal airport.

Energy Agency, which is not a specialized agency, but an autonomous intergovernmental organization, under the aegis of the United Nations, established to promote the peaceful uses of atomic energy.

SPECIALIZED AGENCIES WHICH PRECEDED THE U.N.

The birth of some of these agencies was not a result of the victorious conclusion of World War II or of strict humanitarian considerations. As early as in the days of the Inter-Allied Declaration and the Atlantic Charter, economic and social security, improved labor standards, and economic advancement were considered by the signatories of these documents to be no less important for the preservation of peace than the elaborate arrangements for security and for fighting aggression. A world of content people, free from want, hunger, and disease, was considered as a world less prone to incitements to war.

Even before the final decisions concerning the establishment of an international organization were taken, and before its name was finally decided upon, the foundations of some of these agencies had been laid. The United Nations Conference on Food and Agriculture met in the United States at Hot Springs, Virginia, in May, 1943, with a clear resolve to prepare plans for the solution of food problems, and for the elimination of hunger and want. The International Labor Organization was already a well-established agency of international co-operation, and had been working for many years toward the preservation of the rights of workers, and toward social justice and higher standards of living, when the United Nations Organization came into being. Established by an article in Part XIII of the Treaty of Versailles, it had been since 1919 an autonomous and self-sufficient organization. It outlived the League of Nations with which it was associated, and it had the good fortune to earn at an early date the support of the United States, which joined this organization in 1934 and shielded it from the impact of World War II. Although its basic aims and constitution remained intact, a conference of ILO in May, 1944, in Philadelphia, adopted what became known as the "Philadelphia Charter." Here full co-operation was pledged with other international bodies that would also be working for effective international and national action to achieve general objectives such as full employment, higher living standards, and co-operation between employees and employers.

The United Nations Educational, Scientific and Cultural Organization (UNESCO), originated in a conference of Allied ministers of education held in London, in 1942. It was approved as a permanent agency in February, 1945, and its name was formally agreed upon in November, 1945. This organization is in fact a new edition of the League's

International Civil Aviation Training Center in Mexico, established with the help of ICAO.

Ad hoc commission on prisoners of war met in Geneva in September, 1957.

Committee on Intellectual Co-operation, if not in the scope of its activities, then at least in the general conceptions which governed the thoughts of both sets of founders.

Among the international organizations which preceded the U.N., some rank well back into what could be called the prehistory of attempts at international co-operation. The Universal Postal Union (UPU), for example, started functioning under the name of the International Postal Committee as early as in 1863. The International Telecommunication Union (ITU) was established as The International Telegraph Union in 1865. And the World Meteorological Organization (WMO) started out in 1878 as the International Meteorological Organization.

TECHNICAL ASSISTANCE

Organizations, agencies, funds, banks, have from the beginning of the U.N. assumed the function of assisting countries in need. What became known as the "Point Four Program" of the United States, a form of assistance to underdeveloped countries on a bilateral basis, was assumed by the United Nations in the form of technical assistance plans, which became early in the U.N.'s history an impor-

tant activity of the international organization. Within the competence of the Economic and Social Council, technical assistance first concentrated its efforts upon public administration, and on the promotion of training in that field. For the U.N. considered improved standards of public administration a basic condition of national development. Prior to technical assistance in the field of social welfare, which the U.N. took over from the United Nations Relief and Rehabilitation Administration (UNRRA), the costs of the technical assistance projects were covered by appropriations from the U.N. general budget. Modest in budgetary expense and limited in scope, these were the beginnings of an undertaking which kept on growing with the passage of years. Starting with a budget of $145,000 in 1950 it reached a budget of over $30 million—and even this amount is now considered only a beginning.

Of course many constitutional and organizational changes have been introduced in the framework of the technical assistance program. Many a new name has been introduced, new bodies have been established, new forms set up, but all these changes were centered around one aim: international co-operation in efforts to assure balanced

Bonabes de Rouge (*left*), secretary general of the League of Red Cross Societies, views the Nansen Medal accorded the league for distinguished activities on behalf of refugees.

economic growth, development, conservation and utilization of resources, cultural and social progress, and improvement of standards of health and living in all nations.

THE PROGRAM EXPANDS

With this wide scope of aims before itself, the U.N. must have realized quite soon that what was being done on the basis of early resolutions and with such a limited budget was not sufficient—was not even a drop in the tremendous sea of human needs, which continued to be so outspokenly illustrated in the many publications of the United Nations and the different agencies. An expanded program of technical assistance became imperative.

As early as in 1949, the Economic and Social Council prepared a plan for such a program, which was unanimously approved by the General Assembly on November 16 of that year. To be financed from voluntary contributions by members of the United Nations and by the related agencies—the International Atomic Energy Agency (IAEA), the International Labor Organization (ILO), the Food and Agriculture Organization (FAO), the United Nations Educational, Scientific and Cultural Organization (UNESCO), the International Civil Aviation Organization (ICAO), the World Health Organization (WHO), the International Telecommunication Union (ITU), and the World Meteorological Organization (WMO)—the Expanded Program of Technical Assistance received the tools

which could assure, at least in part, considerable means for a really sizable effort.

The guiding principles of the program have set its goals clearly: "To help underdeveloped countries, to strengthen their national economies through the development of their industries and agriculture, with a view to promoting their economic and political independence in the spirit of the Charter of the United Nations, and to ensure the attainment of higher levels of economic and social welfare for their entire populations."

But soon even this expanded program was not considered sufficient for the growing needs it was designed to meet. The growing urge for an accelerated pace of economic development called for an increasing flow of international public funds. Thus a report on a Special United Nations Fund for Economic Development (SUNFED) was born. Year after year, starting from 1953, this idea of an international development fund returned in various forms to the forums of the United Nations. Initial amounts of from $200 million to $250 million were mentioned. The name, scope, functions, and organizational details of the program were discussed.

At the twelfth session of the General Assembly, in 1957, the United States delegation proposed the establishment of a Special Projects Fund within the Expanded Program of Technical Assistance. There were other proposals as well, until on December 14 of that year, the General Assembly decided to establish a United Nations Special

Dr. Auguste R. Lindt (*center*), United Nations high commissioner for refugees, and Yul Brynner (*right*), the well-known film actor, sign a document confirming Brynner's appointment as special consultant to the refugee commission.

United Nations poster in the "Man Against Want" series.

Fund as an expansion of the existing technical assistance and development operations of the U.N. and the specialized agencies.

In the Expanded Program of Technical Assistance—the special fund, with the co-operation of the specialized agencies—the international community gained a much more potent instrument for assistance to underdeveloped countries than it had ever had before. The originally rather limited finances for this field of activities of the U.N., which had to be drawn from the general budget of the U.N., grew to considerable dimensions.

But besides the financial, practical meaning of these amounts, there was a special aspect of this development which must have generated a general feeling of good will and brotherhood among nations. In the last quarter of each year, members of the U.N. attend a "pledging conference," held at the U.N. Headquarters at the regular annual session of the General Assembly. At this conference, every U.N. member announces its pledge, as a contribution to the financing of this peaceful and brotherly effort. These pledging conferences,

which were introduced immediately after the inception of the expanded program, give some idea of the pace at which states are becoming conscious of their obligations toward their fellow members in the U.N. In 1950, fifty-four member nations pledged a total of $20,036,170; in 1952, sixty-five members pledged $18,797,232; in 1953, sixty-nine members pledged $22,320,725; in 1954, seventy-one members pledged $25,021,556; in 1955, seventy-one members pledged $27,666,707; in 1956, seventy-seven members pledged $28,833,682; in 1957, eighty-four members pledged $30,837,533; and in 1958, eighty-four members pledged $31,307,193; while the cash disbursments in 1961 would amount to about $31.5 million according to the managing director of the United Nations Special Fund, Mr. Paul G. Hoffman. By the end of 1961, total authorizations by the special fund should reach nearly $100 million, Mr. Hoffman states. Mr. Hoffman suggests a target figure of $150 million for total contributions to the special fund and the expanded program. And when pledges to the expanded program and special fund for 1961 were considered, they represented a threefold increase over what had been pledged for the expanded program alone in 1958.

At the tenth pledging conference, held on October 8, 1959, Mr. Hammarskjöld pointed out that "in ten years, more than 8,000 experts of seventy-seven different nationalities have served in the field as advisers and instructors; some 14,000 fellowships have been awarded by the U.N. and its related agencies; altogether 140 countries and territories have received assistance. . . . The program has provided a valuable leaven for economic and social development throughout the world."

Of course in appraising the growth in numbers of governments pledging their contributions, the fact of the growth of the number of U.N. members should be borne in mind as well. But even with this distinction in mind, it is worth-while to stress that many of these new U.N. members are hardly in a position to contribute considerable amounts, and thus the increase in the sums available for the U.N. assistance activities has largely to be credited to the more prosperous nations, which are constantly increasing their share in the budget of these U.N. operations.

This growing sense of responsibility for the welfare of less developed countries is clearly illus-

Hillarn Katende of the Pokomo tribe in Kenya was trained as hospital assistant and is bringing medical help to his fellow tribesmen as the "Bwana Kaditari"—Mr. Doctor.

trated in another development in this field. The share of Africa in all forms of U.N. assistance is constantly growing, so that in 1960 the distribution of project costs by regions showed that Africa was the beneficiary to the extent of 15.4 per cent of this assistance, as compared with Europe, 6 per cent; Latin America, 25.9 per cent; the Middle East 17.9 per cent; and Asia and the Far East 33.3 per cent. Compared to a period only a few years ago, Africa's share has increased many times over.

But there is another important aspect of the assistance program. The recipient country, which receives assistance only at its own request, is obliged to contribute toward the living costs of the experts sent in, and to provide a variety of services related to the activities within the framework of a given project. Based on accession to standard technical assistance agreements, the U.N. program carries with it a most important feature in consideration of the national sensitivity of

recipient countries: the technical assistance is often, for many countries, a two-way operation. Skills of every country are being exploited, and almost no country has the feeling that it is only a recipient and not a giver as well. A chart in a U.N. publication on the Expanded Program of Technical Assistance for the year 1960, visibly demonstrates this interdependence between nations. According to the chart, Argentina had forty-one foreign experts aiding it, but it also had thirty-one of its own experts who were active in other countries. Lebanon had twenty-seven foreign experts and supplied twelve experts; Yugoslavia had forty-one foreign experts and supplied fifteen; Pakistan had sixty-six foreign experts and supplied twelve.

The fact that U.N. assistance is given in almost every field of human activity, and that it is supplied through many specialized agencies, makes this utilization of skills of many nations, many cultures, and many civilizations, not only possible,

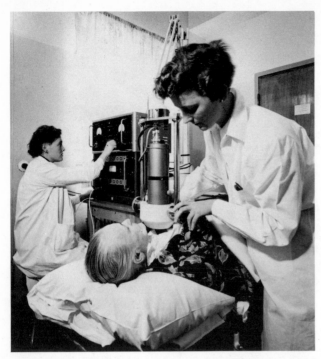

A patient receives an injection of radioactive gold at the Cancer Institute in Oslo, Norway.

The branding of livestock is part of an African program to improve stock control.

but almost imperative. How this assistance is given—through which channels it is brought—is best illustrated in the variety of specialized agencies, funds, and organizations which together constitute the collective instrument of organized mankind for its progress.

Which of these instruments of mutual help is the most important? Is it the Food and Agriculture Organization, or the United Nations Children's Fund, or the United Nations Educational, Scientific and Cultural Organization, or is it the International Bank for Reconstruction and Development? No doubt, a discussion about their relative values should be likened to a fruitless discussion which seeks to determine the most important part

As a preventive measure in the struggle against disease, DDT finds wide application. Here, Indian children receive the disinfectant.

of the human body. So without prejudices as to their degree of importance, all of these instruments will be reviewed.

UNITED NATIONS CHILDREN'S FUND

Among the many United Nations specialized agencies, the United Nations Children's Fund is perhaps the best known, or, one might say, the most "popular." It became a symbol—a symbol of U.N. achievements in international co-operation, of U.N. humanitarian influence and practical activity, of human affinity and brotherhood. Tens of millions are the beneficiaries, and tens of millions are the co-workers and contributors. Children

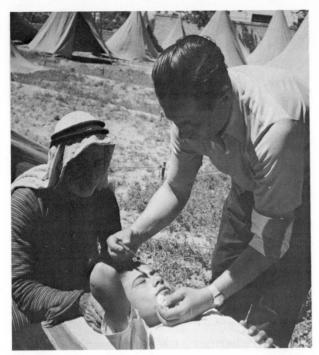

To save them from blindness, the World Health Organization (WHO) treats thousands of youngsters in Arab refugee camps. The menace, trachoma, is a contagious eye disease widespread in the Middle East.

and their families are the recipients, and are contributors as well. Its message reaches every corner of the world, its emissaries bring joy and health everywhere. Established in 1946 as the United Nations International Childern's Emergency Fund, it had its name changed to the present "United Nations Children's Fund" in 1953.

What is this institution doing? It supplies everything which is necessary to help children and mothers keep healthy—medicines, food supplements such as milk and fish liver oil, spray guns, midwife kits, and trucks and automobiles to transport these implements of human well-being. Factories and laboratories are being equipped, new methods of production introduced, standards of living elevated. And when UNICEF formally trespasses upon the domain of the World Health Organization, nobody cares, nobody is angry, no rivalry arises.

The United Nations Children's Fund is the U.N. agency which attracts the most general public assistance. Children in school, parents in parent-teachers associations, workers in offices—all find a way to contribute to the fund. In 1960, ninety-eight governments contributed a total of $21.5 million to UNICEF. Private contributions by the

the U.S. Committee for UNICEF amounted to $1.5 million. Together with income from other sources—one of them the popular sale of greeting cards—the amount which was at the disposal of UNICEF was brought to $25.8 million. Allocations for UNICEF needs in 1960 amounted to $28 million. Due to the system of "local matching" the assisted countries have spent, or have committed themselves to spend, the equivalent of $78 million for child care.

These funds are being put to the best possible use. Not only emergency needs are being considered. Countries are being stimulated to initiate permanent health, nutrition, and welfare services from which not only children benefit, but the entire population as well. Centuries-old diseases are being brought under control and combated effectively. Antimalaria campaigns have helped to reduce this crippling disease considerably, and forty-seven projects to combat it are in operation with UNICEF aid. Antituberculosis campaigns conducted in many countries have helped to almost completely eradicate the danger of this disease throughout entire countries. Leprosy, the horrible disease afflicting about twelve million people the world over is being combated, and millions of those affected are being treated. A total

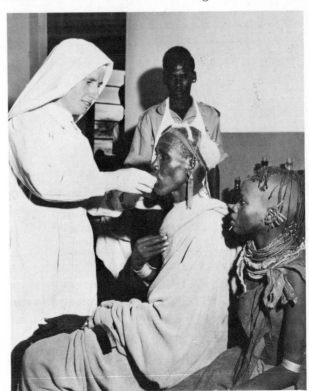

Treatment at a hospital for nomads in Kenya.

Aerial view of the headquarters, in Geneva, of the International Labor Organization.

of 31.4 million people have been treated in anti-yaws campaigns, and in 1961 alone three million additional people have been treated for this disease. (Yaws causes sores and could gradually eat away the flesh; but when caught in time, one fifteen-cent shot of penicillin could remove in a few weeks all traces of the disease.) Nine and one-half million people are being treated for trachoma, a crippling eye disease.

A clinic of the United Nations Educational, Scientific and Cultural Organization (UNESCO) in Maribal Valley, Haiti.

Nutrition problems are being solved with the guidance of UNICEF. Food production is being increased through such means as community and school gardens, the raising of poultry and small animals, fish culture, and food preservation. One hundred million pounds of milk powder is being shipped within the current year for supplementary feeding programs, to be distributed free of cost in forty-eight countries. One thousand six hundred

New headquarters of the Universal Postal Union (UPU) in Bern, Switzerland.

units providing maternal and child health services have been equipped with the help of UNICEF in twenty-six countries and territories. And within this general effort it is again UNICEF which provides aid in emergencies—in earthquakes (as in Chile), cyclones (as in Mauritius and Pakistan), and famine (as in the Congo). In Asia alone UNICEF helps to give undergraduate training to over five thousand nurses and midwives and courses for assistant midwives have trained well over ten thousand.

No wonder that the word UNICEF became a magic slogan the world over and that it carries the

Gerald C. Gross, secretary general of the International Telecommunication Union (ITU).

World Meteorological Organization (WMO) sponsors the launching of automatic weather reporting instruments, in Payerne, Switzerland.

message of the United Nations idea more efficiently than thousands of pages of treatises on international co-operation and human brotherhood.

WORLD HEALTH ORGANIZATION

Closely related and often interwoven with the activities of UNICEF are the functions which WHO performs. One of the largest United Nations specialized agencies, it strives to implement the basic tenet of its constitution "the attainment by all peoples of the highest possible level of health."

As is the case with many other instruments of international co-operation, WHO has its roots in

Preparing for a campaign against locusts in the desert.

the ideological principles of the League of Nations. The League of Nations Health Organization, and the Office International d'Hygiène Publique in Paris, must surely have served as examples, when, at the San Francisco Conference on International Organization in 1945, the creation of a special institution to deal with matters of world health was envisaged. In 1946, representatives of sixty-one countries drafted and signed the constitution of WHO, which came into being officially in 1948, after twenty-six U.N. members had ratified the constitution. But membership in WHO was not restricted to U.N. member nations alone. Every state not a member of the U.N., whose application was approved by the World Health Assembly could become a member of WHO.

The World Health Organization is called upon to combat diseases, to assist governments in strengthening health services, to promote improved standards of teaching and training in the health, medical, and related professions, and to establish international standards in all fields concerned with

New permanent headquarters of WMO formally opened in Geneva in July, 1960.

health. The organization is made up of an assembly, executive board, secretariat, director general, and a staff. Working with a budget which in 1959, for instance, achieved the amount of $14.3 million, WHO draws for its activities considerable amounts from the U.N. Expanded Program of Technical Assistance as well. In 1958, this source supplied $5 million to WHO funds.

Starting with twenty-six members in April, 1948, WHO grew continuously as new members joined in the general effort for improvement of health

Indian model of a radiosonde about to be demonstrated at a WMO-sponsored international comparison of balloon-borne weather instruments.

standards. By 1959, WHO had eighty-five members. In the framework of its activities, combating of specific diseases soon became only a part of its total effort. Health preservation, a system of international health safeguards, an international warning system in case of contaminating diseases, introduction of drugs in uniform strength, an international pharmacopoeia (a book providing formulae for preparing medicines in uniform strength), statistics concerning diseases in various countries—all of these tasks are now being performed by the World Health Organization. It is an agency which has become one of the most potent media of assistance to developing countries on all continents.

Poster publicizes U.N. Technical Assistance.

FOOD AND AGRICULTURE ORGANIZATION

After having provided for minimum health needs of children and mothers, after having safeguarded the populace prior to the outbreak of illnesses, and after having helped to overcome chronic diseases, a most important, related prob-

A mosquito is about to be captured and analyzed in preparation for anti-malaria campaign in Paraguay.

Thirty-seven million boys and girls have been tested and seventeen million vaccinated in an antituberculosis campaign.

lem still remained. One cannot keep people healthy—that is, prevent diseases and overcome them—by the use of medicine alone. One has to nourish them adequately. One has to supply their bodies with a minimum of nutritive elements, which unfortunately many millions of people the world over do not have in sufficient quantities. The Food and Agriculture Organization was set up to see to it that this problem was eradicated as soon as possible—that no human being on earth went to bed hungry, and that no organic deficiencies in human bodies were caused by insufficient nourishment.

As with other specialized agencies, FAO grew in membership yearly from the time of its founding, in October, 1945, as the first of the U.N. specialized agencies. It is devoted to the collection of information on nutrition, agriculture, forestry, fisheries, and dedicates itself to the promotion of national and international actions toward the improvement of all aspects of production, marketing, processing, and distribution of agricultural products. It promotes conservation of natural resources, and is called upon to furnish assistance

on request, primarily through the U.N. Expanded Program of Technical Assistance. The organization is composed of a conference, council, director general, and staff.

Budgeted on a biannual basis, $17 million for 1958–1959, for instance, FAO has written and is writing daily, magnificent chapters in human prog-

Mombasa (Kenya) port equipment acquired with aid from U.N. specialized agencies.

Danny Kaye traveled over one hundred thousand miles for the United Nations Children's Fund (UNICEF) as "ambassador-at-large to the world's children." His film "Assignment Children," which was shot during his first UNICEF trip, has been shown around the world in seventeen languages.

Seal of the United Nations Children's Fund.

ress. Besides its purposes mentioned above, the FAO is concerned daily with such matters as increase of yields, halting of soil erosion, development of land and water resources, plant production and protection, animal production and disease control, and rural welfare. Experts from FAO give advice on these matters to every country which requests it. In 1958, as many as 420 experts acted on behalf of FAO, 280 fellowships were assigned in the same period, and innumerable studies were published and used as guides by dozens of coun-

World Health Organization and UNICEF malaria-control teams at work in India.

Poster issued by the U.N. Department of Information. In one year, UNICEF provided pieces of clothing for two million children.

tries. The tale of FAO accomplishments is told not only by its many publications and by the many hundreds of people who have acted on behalf of FAO, but also by its indelible material signs the world over—forests which have been saved from deterioration or even complete extinction, fields which have become green, barns which are being filled to capacity for the first time in known history, rivers which have had their waters harnessed for the benefit of men, and fisheries which have multiplied their catch. It is a tale of progress, a model of assistance to all who are in need.

INTERNATIONAL MONETARY FUND

Considering economic progress an important prerequisite of international peace, the founders of the United Nations must have reached another conclusion: that monetary stability is also a most important element of political stability, and, with it, of international peace. The history of European financial collapses after World War I, the prehis-

Seal of the World Health Organization.

tory of the ascendance to power of Hitler, which came about on the ruins of the German monetary system and the unlimited devaluation of its currency—all the political repercussions which began from currency troubles—made it appear imperative, at the earliest stages of the preparations for

Dr. C. A. Werner, overseas medical director of Chas. Pfizer & Co., presents a gift of terramycin on behalf of his company to Dr. P. M. Kaul, director of the New York Liaison Office of the World Health Organization.

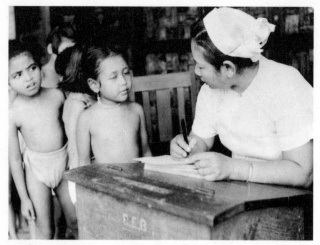

One of the periodic health examinations in Burma with assistance of UNICEF and WHO.

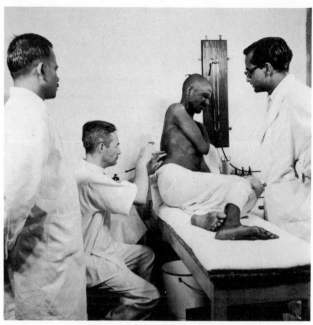

Head of a WHO team examines a patient at a center in Patna, India.

Farmer in Dacca, Pakistan, is vaccinated against tuberculosis.

The midwife from the Mother and Child Sub-Center in Bantva, India, chats with a young mother during one of her house-to-house visits.

Health educator in Egypt (*in white blouse*) instructs village women in Calioub Province about ways to fight bilharziasis, a disease which is responsible for one out of every five deaths in Egypt.

The United Nations Children's Fund provided supplies for house spraying with DDT in Barbados.

Egyptian health workers examine snails, carriers of bilharziasis.

United Nations poster publicizes activities of the World Health Organization.

A U.N. poster pertaining to conservation problems.

Seal of the Food and Agriculture Organization.

Expert of the Food and Agriculture Organization (FAO) shows Israeli farmers parts of a milking machine.

Dr. Jaya Jhaveri at a local primary health center in Saurashtra, India, advises a young mother on child care.

an international organization that this aspect of the life of nations be well taken care of. When the war was still in its full fury, in July, 1944, forty-four nations responded to the call of President Roosevelt and assembled at Bretton Woods, New Hampshire, to draft the articles of agreement for the establishment of the International Monetary Fund. The agreement came into force on December 27, 1945.

The purposes and functions of the fund were defined with brevity and lucidity but its operations are nonetheless interwoven into the most intricate banking and financial operations. To facilitate the expansion of international trade, and thus help to maintain a high level of employment and income, to promote exchange stability, to maintain orderly exchange arrangements, to avoid competitive exchange depreciation, to help in the establish-

ment of a multilateral system of payments, and to strive for the elimination of currency restrictions, and, last but not least, to assist members in need by making the fund's resources available to them under adequate safeguards—these are purposes which, in their implementation through the years, have helped many a country to get on its feet financially, saved many a country from currency disaster, and contributed in many a country to the preservation of economic stability, and, through it, to the prevention of political upheavals.

The sums involved in the fund's operations perhaps serve as the best illustration of its importance and of the scope of its activities. Between March, 1947, and December, 1958, the fund concluded exchange transactions with thirty-seven out of its sixty-eight members. The amounts these countries purchased in United States dollars, pounds sterling,

New FAO headquarters in Rome.

United Nations poster tells of the Food and Agriculture Administration's role in combating agricultural problems.

Seal of the International Monetary Fund.

Deutchemarks, Belgian francs, and Netherlands guilders amounted to $3,223,952,693,040 during this period in exchange for an equivalent in their own currencies.

This potent instrument of international co-operation, then, provides not only the tangible means for economic advancement, but performs many advisory services to member states as well. It also maintains a program of technical assistance which is quite extensive, in fields pertaining to the fund's activities.

INTERNATIONAL BANK FOR RECONSTRUCTION AND DEVELOPMENT

Another aspect of financial activities for the

Per Jacobsson, director of the International Monetary Fund, at an informal meeting with correspondents at U.N. Headquarters.

Seal of the International Bank for Reconstruction and Development.

promotion of economic progress the world over has found its expression in the establishment of the International Bank for Reconstruction and Development. Being in a category similar to the fund, the bank also had its first articles of agreemen drawn by the United Nations Monetary and Financial Conference, which met at Bretton Woods, July, 1944, on the invitation of President Roosevelt.

The inaugural meeting of the board of directors of the bank was held at the same time and place as

the meeting of the board of the fund, in Savannah, Georgia, in March, 1946. Since then, the bank has embarked on a broad program of assistance in the reconstruction and development of its member states. To achieve these purposes the bank facilitates investments of capital, promotes private foreign investments by guarantees, and when private capital is not available, makes loans from its own resources or from funds borrowed by it.

The annual reports on the bank are always a most interesting indication of what is going on in the many countries striving for development, and for improvement of living standards. The reports reveal, for example, that the rehabilitation and modernization of the Pacific Railroad of Mexico was accomplished with a loan of $61 million from the bank; $15.9 million has enabled Colum-

Silting dam under construction at El Durazno, Mexico, built with aid from the international bank.

bia to add 190 miles of railway to its transportation system; $19.1 million has given Ceylon the means to increase its hydroelectric installations; $16.2 million lent to India has helped to build a thermal plant which supplies the bulk of electric power to Bombay; $23 million has assisted Peru to irrigate 125,000 acres of uncultivated land; and $25 million is assisting Israel in the development of the Dead Sea Potash Works.

Recently, a new affiliate of the bank—the International Development Association (IDA)—has been established to finance economic growth in the less developed countries.

Dam construction in the Valle de Bravo near Mexico City, financially assisted by the International Bank for Reconstruction and Development.

The bank also made funds available for the hydro-electric power plant in Ixtapantongo, Mexico.

Bankers approve loan documents which granted Italy assistance in its twelve-year program for the agricultural and industrial development of its southern areas.

Between July 1, 1960 and January 31, 1961 the bank made loans totaling $5.5 billion in fifty-four countries and territories. And all this is not charity. Transactions are based on strict business considerations. The annual report of the bank contains a chapter on earnings, reserves, and repayments. It gives some idea of the bank's operations. The annual report for 1954–1955, the tenth annual report of the bank, shows a net income of $24.7 million compared with $20.3 million in the pre-

ceding year. In addition, loan commissions, representing a charge of one per cent on outstanding balances of all loans, totaled $13 million.

In granting loans for national development projects, it is only natural that the bank be engaged in a vast operation of surveying local conditions, appraising rentability of a given project, its technical feasibility, and even to be engaged in fact-finding about the general economic conditions in a country which applies for a loan. Thus, the bank performs important functions in the general framework of technical assistance and its operations are thereby intricately interwoven into the general fabric of international co-operation.

This automatic steel-rolling mill in France was financed by a loan from the international bank.

The Colense power station in Natal, Union of South Africa, was built with the help of two loans from the international bank.

Diesel locomotives for expansion of transport in Australia were purchased with assistance from the world bank.

INTERNATIONAL FINANCE CORPORATION

Although the International Bank for Reconstruction and Development provides expressly for promotion of private foreign investments, it took the bank ten years to arrive at the conclusion that a special financial institution for this purpose would do much better. And so, on the initiative of the bank, a new financial institution came into being in 1956—the International Finance Corporation (IFC). Concerned with investing in productive private enterprises (in association with private investors and without governmental guar-

antees), and serving as a clearing house for investment opportunities, the International Finance Corporation assisted in the development of private enterprises in Australia, in Brazil, in Chile, in Mexico, and in Pakistan. It added to the economic progress of these countries, served as an example of how to make investments, how to appraise their rentability, and how to assure substantial returns.

Compared with other agencies, IFC is of rather limited scope. It still has to prove that it could justly be ranged with all the other specialized agencies, funds, and organizations.

INTERNATIONAL LABOR ORGANIZATION

Among the many conditions necessary to the promotion of human well-being, attention has to

Seal of the International Finance Corporation.

be paid to a factor which is highly important in the appropriate utilization of human resources, of financial means, and in the proper functioning of the entire society—the labor force. The International Labor Organization, over forty years old, has written into its history important chapters in the efforts of men for the betterment of the lot of all. The slogan "social justice" acquired practical meaning in the framework of the ILO's activities. Freedom of association, an eight-hour workday, protection of wages, holidays with pay, medical care, social security, the right to bargain

Headquarters of the International Bank for Reconstruction and Development, Washington, D. C.

Seal of the International Labor Organization.

collectively, maternity protection—all these conditions of work, which seem natural to us today, became as they presently are due largely to the International Labor Organization and its world-wide influence. Its standards have influenced and still do influence even those countries which are not members of ILO, or are not signatories to one of the "conventions" stipulating the accepted standards of labor conditions.

The "conventions" and "recommendations" of

ILO form together what is being called the International Labor Code. Since the establishment of ILO, it has adopted 115 conventions and 114 recommendations, and the total number of ratifications of these conventions and recommendations reached 2,300 by the middle of 1961. This high figure can easily be understood if one keeps in mind that ILO is one of the specialized agencies membership in which is most sought and wanted. At the forty-fifth session of the International Labor Conference, held in June, 1961, in Geneva, the one hundreth member of ILO was voted into membership: the Islamic Republic of Mauretania. Not being a member of the U.N., it had to be admitted by a two-thirds vote of the government's, employers', and workers' representatives.

These three elements—government, employers, and workers—are the ones participating in the activities of ILO. Of course, by its very character as a body enabling organized co-operation between employers and employees, ILO affirms the unity of

Commemorative ceremony marks the 40th anniversary of the International Labor Organization, at the Palais des Nations, Geneva, 1959.

purpose of both these latter elements in furthering production of goods and raising the standard of living. But this can only be achieved in concurrence with the governments concerned, which have to assure the political and administrative framework of such co-operation.

The far-reaching technical revolution of recent years, caused by automation and prospects of more leisure time, have not caught ILO unprepared. It has also not failed to recognize the importance of basic political changes taking place in a great part

David E. Morse, director general of the International Labor Organization.

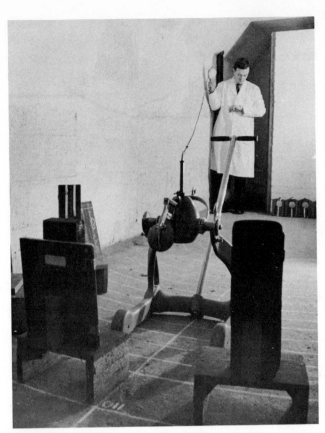

An ILO technician studies protection of workers against radiation.

of the globe, with almost two thirds of the human race involved.

Certainly indicative of ILO purposes and ways of thinking is a voting machine exhibited at ILO's International Labor Exhibition at Turin, Italy. The visitor is invited to vote on any of eight possible improvements in working and living conditions. One may vote for longer paid holidays, the elimination of unemployment, or perhaps a lowering of the retirement age. In introductory remarks to a survey of world labor relations, submitted to the forty-fifth session of the International Labor Conference, David A. Morse, director general of the ILO, remarked: "Strength, spontaneity, and adaptability in labor relations reinforce the whole fabric of society. Weakness opens the way for the arbitrary and the coercive in political as well in industrial affairs. The conference may therefore serve a larger purpose—in furtherance of responsible, democratic growth—by giving renewed stimulus to the improvement of labor relations throughout the world."

In serving these goals, the International Labor Organization is playing a most important role in the march of developing countries toward industrialization and higher standards of living. The fact that in many of those countries, the labor unions are in the very forefront of national political efforts, lends ILO additional influence on one of the most sensitive problems of our day. Working with a budget which reached, for instance in 1959, approximately $8.5 million, ILO is one of the most important instruments of the United Nations Technical Assistance Program. In times when skills and vocational training are of decisive importance, ILO's technical assistance programs are often the very backbone of plans for helping countries in their efforts to lift their standards of production, to further industrialization, and, through these, to raise the standard of living.

THE UNITED NATIONS EDUCATIONAL, SCIENTIFIC AND CULTURAL ORGANIZATION

In this race toward economic advancement, with industrial development and rising standards of living as potent contributions to the stability of the world, and thereby to peace and security, neither government, employers, or employees—the factors instrumental in translating these goals into the language of practical organizational forms—failed to understand that material well-being is not sufficient for men's progress, that men's material progress is to a great extent dependent upon or conditioned by his spiritual standing, his cultural and educational development. The saying, "One idea is worth more than a hundred thousand bayonets," implies that when a world of peace is being organized, culture, education, and science have to

Accelerated Training Center for adults, in Cairo, assisted by ILO.

Apprentices at the North Cairo Refrigerator and Air Conditioning Training Center, organized with ILO assistance.

Safety engineer cautions a sanding machine operator to wear safety glasses. Artificial eye dramatizes his point.

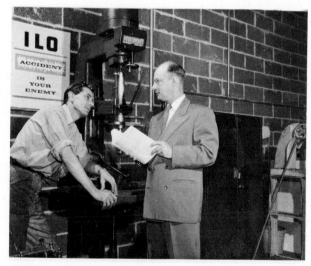

Employer discusses details of the Industrial Safety Code, published by the ILO.

Signs and posters play an important part in the ILO campaign against accidents at work.

Seal of the United Nations Educational, Scientific and Cultural Organization.

become an inseparable part in the means for the attainment of material advancement.

The United Nations founders grasped this truth even more than did the founders of the League of Nations with their Committee on Cultural Co-operation. The United Nations Educational, Scientific and Cultural Organization constitution states its purpose clearly. It is intended to "contribute to peace and security by promotion of collaboration among the nations through education, science, and culture in order to further universal respect for justice, for rule of law, and for the human rights and fundamental freedoms for all."

These goals have been pursued incessantly by UNESCO in the fifteen years of its existence. Education, culture, science—in none of these fields can one miss the influence of UNESCO: The seven hundred million illiterate people in the world soon became a project for UNESCO experts; the first committee of the International Geophysical Year was organized with the help of UNESCO; invaluable treasures of ancient art found in archaeological excavations have been turned into the common property of the world by UNESCO albums; treasures of the worlds of art, literature, and science have been opened to millions by UNESCO's counsel and assistance in opening libraries and in promoting publications; the first extensive survey of the Indian Ocean in an effort to provide new sources of food for a quarter of the world's population will be carried out by UNESCO. Of course there is still no way to judge whether the fifteen

years of UNESCO's existence, of its penetrating, world-wide activities, have fulfilled the noble words of the preamble to UNESCO's constitution. "Wars begin in the minds of men," the preamble reads, "and it is therefore in the minds of men that the defenses of peace must be constructed." But even if these words have not yet been fully implemented—and if they had, it would certainly herald a decisive revolution in human minds and nature, if accomplished within only fifteen years —even without hard facts completely to justify the great hopes vested in this institution, the examples of its positive influences and contributions in the promotion of international standards of education and culture are innumerable.

Arithmetic class in Maribal, Haiti, in a school founded by UNESCO.

New UNESCO buildings in Paris.

Catholic school in Jacmel, Haiti.

A child reads a story to her younger brothers. General literacy is a UNESCO goal.

Staff members stand at the entrance to the office of the Fundamental Education Project at Santiago Nayarit, Mexico.

OTHER SPECIALIZED AGENCIES

The Food and Agriculture Organization, WHO, ILO, UNICEF, UNESCO, and the financial organizations, do not represent the entire "family of the United Nations." Others within this family include the International Civil Aviation Organization (ICAO), which has to insure safe and orderly growth of international civil aviation; the Universal Postal Union (UPU), which is responsible for the daily miracle, now considered natural, that mail—over two billion pieces annually—can be sent to and received from all corners of the world; the International Telecommunication Union

Library of the UNESCO Research Center in Calcutta, India.

(ITU), providing for ever improving and more efficient use of telecommunication, and harmonizing actions of nations in this field; the World Meteorological Organization (WMO), which facilitates international co-operation in the establishment of networks of stations and centers to provide meteorological services and observations, and promotes establishment of systems of weather observation—functions which have a direct bearing on almost every aspect of human activities; and the Intergovernmental Maritime Consultative Organization (IMCO), which formally came into existence in 1959, and is concerned with matters relating to the safety of shipping. In addition, there is the International Trade Organization (ITO), and the General Agreement on Tariffs and Trade (GATT), which strive to assure maximum freedom in commercial intercourse between nations (GATT is an international contract, which incorporates schedules of tariff concessions and sets general rules relating to transit trade, antidumping duties, customs valuation, and quantitative restrictions on imports and exports).

Seal of the International Civil Aviation Organization.

Last, but certainly not least, there is the International Atomic Energy Agency (IAEA), which is intended to implement the idea of a practical application of atomic energy for peaceful purposes, and is concerned with the effects of atomic radiation—purposes suggested by President Eisenhower in a speech—of which the IAEA is a direct result—given before the U.N. General Assembly on December 8, 1953.

All of these agencies together represent a part of U.N. activities and influences which seldom catch headlines, seldom attract public attention by stemming overt crises. But the beneficial activities of these agencies are known to the millions who

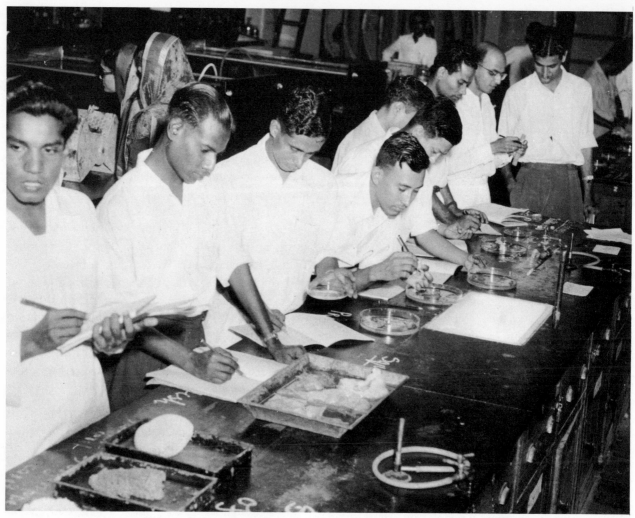

International course in marine biology, organized by UNESCO, in Bombay, India.

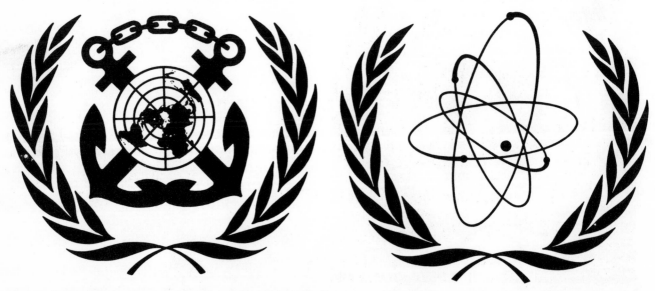

Seals of the International Maritime Consultative Organization (*left*), and the International Atomic Energy Agency.

have witnessed them. Millions have benefited from their accomplishments. This is international co-operation at its best—international co-operation which could not be construed as an instrument of coercion, as might be the case if the benefits came from a single nation. This is co-operation which is international in every detail, in every tenet of its ideology and organizational implementation. The offices of these institutions are dispersed all over the world—in New York, Geneva, Washing-

BUREAU INTERNATIONAL DE L'UNION POSTALE UNIVERSELLE BERNE (SUISSE)

Seal of the Universal Postal Union.

ton, Rome, and Paris. There are regional offices in New Delhi, Cairo, Djakarta, Addis Ababa, and Mexico City. And the personnel engaged in their service are drawn from many nations and are sent to all parts of the world.

These activities amount to a permanent exchange program on a multination basis, training tens of thousands of people to understand and to be faithful to the principles of international co-operation, of mutual assistance, and of mutual responsibility of all men for the welfare of their neighbors.

Seals of the International Telecommunication Union (*top*), and the World Meteorological Organization.

Ambassador Koto Matsudaira (*second from right*) of Japan, depositing documents relating to his government's acceptance of the Convention on the Intergovernmental Maritime Consultative Organization.

First assembly of the Intergovernmental Maritime Consultative Organization (IMCO), held in Church House, Westminster, London.

Wyndham White, executive secretary of the Interim Commission of the International Trade Organization.

FACING THE CHALLENGES OF THE FIFTIES AND SIXTIES

"Each age," it has been said, "is a dream that is dying, or one that is coming to birth." And indeed, the coming to birth of the new age in international co-operation is not a painless process. Many beliefs are being shaken and new ones have yet to be born. Although written before the atomic age, before hundreds of millions started their accelerated march toward independence, before the desire for equal opportunity for all became all-embracing, the United Nations Charter carried in itself not only the spirit necessary to meet the challenges of the coming age, but had included, in its preamble, provisions to that end, as well.

HUMAN RIGHTS

In this search for adaptation to the problems attending growth and progress, a special role is being played by the provisions pertaining to the institution which was defined as "human rights." During the U.N.'s existence, these provisions concerning human rights have assumed many meanings. The growing desire of people in developing countries to share the blessings of freedom, social justice, equality, and improved economic conditions, have been directly related to the conception of human rights. And equally related to this conception has been the sense of responsibility of the more fortunate nations to contribute to the ful-

Veteran diplomats of the United Nations applaud President Eisenhower as he steps to the rostrum to address the opening session of the U.N. commemorative meeting, held at San Francisco in June, 1955, ten years after the charter was adopted.

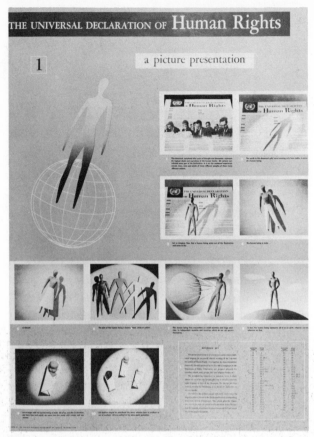

The United Nations Department of Public Information interprets pictorially the Universal Declaration of Human Rights.

The Addis Ababa seminar on human rights was attended by women leaders from thirty-four African nations including (*above*) representatives of Upper Volta and Zanzibar.

Che Halimahton binti Abdul Majid, the first woman elected to the Federal Legislative Council of Malaya.

Begum Shareefah Hamid Ali, of India, and Alice Kandalaft Cosma, of Syria, members of the Commission on the Status of Women.

The delegates to the Buenos Aires session of the Commission on the Status of Women were welcomed by President of Argentina Arturo Frondizi.

Fifteenth session of the U.N. Commission on the Status of Women, Geneva, Switzerland (March, 1961). Fourth from left is Mrs. Tamar Eshel of Israel, chairman.

Delegates Gladys A. Tillett (*left*), and Joan Vickers at the session.

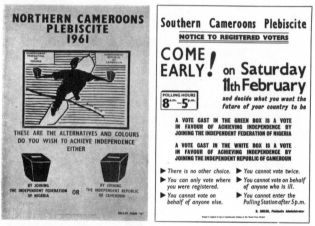

Poster depicts steps in Libya's emergence as an independent nation.

Plebiscite notice to Cameroon voters. The plebiscite was held under U.N. supervision.

fillment of these desires of their fellow men. And it was not long before human rights turned into an instrument of the struggles for freedom by nations yet under foreign rule.

This development by the U.N. of the human rights concept into a potent instrument in meeting the challenges of the fifties and sixties was only partly envisaged by those who framed the charter. The provision of the preamble to the charter calling for a reaffirmation of "faith in fundamental human rights," and of article 1 of the charter establishing among the purposes of the United Nations, "promoting and encouraging respect for human rights and for fundamental freedoms for all without distinction as to race, sex, language and religion," were rather vague. Elaboration and clarification of them was soon required. There was no common standard, accepted by all, as to what "human rights" meant. Fundamental human rights meant different things to different people. People brought up under Western civilization identified human rights with civil rights of the individual—with rights which had their origin in the Magna Charta and "habeas corpus." The newly independent nations of Asia, and later Africa, saw in these rights only one aspect of what society can assure a human being. Social security and freedom from want appeared to them as important as any civil right, or all civil rights together.

These basic, differing conceptions about the meaning of fundamental human rights put special strain on the Commission on Human Rights, which was established at the very beginning of the U.N.'s activities. Article 68 of the charter, which

Representatives of the Republic of Chad listen to the proceedings of the U.N. General Assembly, which admitted their state to membership, together with thirteen other African nations.

called for a commission "for the promotion of human rights," was implemented without delay. In January, 1947, the commission, under the chairmanship of Mrs. Eleanor Roosevelt, held its first meeting. The eighteen-member commission had before itself extensive terms of reference. According to them the commission had to submit to the Economic and Social Council recommendations regarding "(a) an international bill of rights; (b) international declarations or conventions on civil liberties, the status of women, freedom of information, and similar matters; (c) the protection of minorities; (d) prevention of discrimination on grounds of race, sex, language or religion; (e) any other matter concerning human rights not covered by items (a), (b), (c) and (d)." It was only natural that some special aspects of the commission's tasks were entrusted to special bodies. Accordingly, the Subcommission on Prevention of

Discrimination and Protection of Minorities, and a Commission on the Status of Women came into being.

The two-years-long deliberations of the Commission on Human Rights bore fruit. In December, 1948, when the General Assembly met in Paris, in the Palais de Chaillot, The Universal Declaration of Human Rights was adopted without one dissenting vote. Out of 58 member nations represented, 48 voted for, 8 abstained and 2 were absent. The Russian representative, Andrei Vyshinsky, did not spare critical remarks. He argued that people do not have inherent rights, because only governments have rights, by virtue of sovereignty, and only governments may grant these rights or withhold them. But when the vote was taken Mr. Vyshinsky and his delegation, together with other delegations representing Rus-

Congo Premier Patrice Lumumba stands on a table to address troops in Stanleyville. On the ground behind him are Congo President Joseph Kasavubu (*wearing dark suit*)**, and Justice Minister Remy Mwumba** (*third from left*)**.**

sia's allies, the Union of South Africa, and Saudi Arabia, abstained.

Those who framed the declaration and those who adopted it did not hide their inner elation and pride. They called it a "Magna Charta of humanity," and certainly only vaguely anticipated that here they had given humanity a document on which many future developments would rest. The thirty articles of the declaration considered, to a maximum extent, all the prevailing opinions of the time on human rights. They covered civil, political, economic, social, and cultural rights. The president of the U.N. General Assembly at which this declaration was adopted, H. V. Evatt of Australia, spoke about the document as the one to which "millions of people, men, women and children all over the world, many miles from Paris and New York, will turn for help, guidance and inspiration."

And he was right. There is almost no political, social, or cultural problem in which the rights which the declaration proclaims, would not be invoked. In debates on social and economic problems and on peaceful endeavors handled by the Economic and Social Council and by the Trusteeship Council, in stormy debates on political matters in the Security Council and in the assembly, the Universal Declaration of Human Rights serves often as a point of reference—as a justification in the struggle for economic and social progress, or for political advancement.

But the declaration serves as an exemplary document in a context wider than that of the United Nations' activities alone. Many international conventions and agreements, whether drawn under the auspices of the United Nations or not, either include the declaration in full or in part. The peace treaty with Japan, the agreement relating to the Free Territory of Trieste, and the agreement between France and Tunisia, made use of the declaration, and its principles were included as well in many new national constitutions drafted after 1948. December 10, 1948, the date of adoption of the declaration, was proclaimed Human Rights Day by the General Assembly in 1950. It is celebrated every year in most countries.

But the second step, the natural consequence of this declaration—the binding covenants on human rights to which states could accede, thus turning the covenants into binding international obligations—did not follow. Draft covenants on civil, political, economic, social, and cultural rights were prepared by the Commission on Human Rights, but after their submission to the Economic and Social Council, and, through it, to the General Assembly, these covenants did not reach final adoption. They are discussed year after year in the Third Social, Humanitarian and Cultural Committee of the General Assembly. But there were some exceptions which made it possible to assure implementation of certain human rights, not only through pronouncements, but also through firm international obligations, brought about by their being adhered to and ratified by many governments. Examples are the Convention on the Pre-

vention and Punishment of the Crime of Genocide, and conventions on Rights of Women. A direct result of the Nazi-Germany policy of extermination, the genocide convention was an important step toward the prevention of acts which tend to destroy, in whole or in part, a national, ethnic, racial, or religious group. In view of the experiences of World War II, and the legal doubts which the Nürnberg trials of the leaders of Nazi-Germany caused, the convention included a series of provisions for the punishment of those guilty of genocide. The parties to the convention—over sixty states adhered to it—pledged themselves to extradite the guilty, who then had to be punished either by a national tribunal in the country where genocide was committed, or by an international penal tribunal "whether they are constitutionally responsible rulers, public officers, or private individuals." This provision should be considered revolutionary as far as previously existing legal concepts of responsibility are concerned, since it put an end to the argument that orders received from superiors released the perpetrator of the crime from legal responsibility.

It was certainly natural that the problems concerning the status of women found their solution in a series of conventions, for they became a sub-

Premier Lumumba (*third from left*) at the press conference at U.N. Headquarters.

An Ethiopian patrol on a street in Stanleyville.

ject of the continuous concern of a special Commission on the Status of Women. A Convention on Political Rights of Women, adopted by the General Assembly in December, 1952, a Convention and Recommendations on Equal Pay for Equal Work, adopted by the International Labor Organization in 1951, and a Convention on the Nationality of Married Women, adopted by the General Assembly in 1957, did not exhaust the series of problems which crowded the agenda of the Commission on the Status of Women. But the lack of covenants which would turn the Declaration on Human Rights into a binding international agreement handicapped seriously the hopes of instituting a world order in which basic human rights and freedoms would be protected by national legal systems and by international agreements.

The Action Program of 1953, which included a program of reports on the observation of human rights by national governments, to be submitted once in three years, lent certain practical validity to the provisions of the declaration. For their implementation was to be exposed to international scrutiny—by itself a potent factor in inducing compliance with the declaration.

A Ghanian soldier of the U.N. force meets two soldiers of the Swedish contingent.

A member of the Mali unit of the U.N. force on duty on the road leading to the Albertville airport. Sandbags were used to block the road at checkpoints.

"INTERNAL AFFAIRS"

But the meaning of human rights has been stretched far beyond the field of protection of civil, economic, social, and cultural rights.

Peoples struggling for their right to join the family of free nations, especially the struggle of peoples in Asia and, more recently, in Africa, as well as in all other parts of the world, have brought the human rights into the forefront of their political assault against the old order.

With growing frequency the principles of human rights were invoked at United Nations debates. This would occur whenever a group, ethnically or otherwise distinguished, defied the existing political order. In fact, this problem began to have a bearing on the question of United Nations competences, its framework of activities and influence.

In the name of "human rights and fundamental freedoms," one of the basic principles of the United Nations, explicitly expressed in article 2 (7) of the charter, was overriden many times. States such as France, in the discussion over Algeria; Portugal, over Angola; Russia, over the situation in Hungary after the 1956 revolt; and the Union of South Africa, over the conditions of the non-white population, have always based their opposition to U.N. intervention on this article of the charter. It states: "Nothing contained in the charter shall authorize the United Nations to intervene in matters which are essentially within the domestic jurisdiction of any state or shall require the Members to submit such matters to settlement under the present Charter." In fact this was the basic provision demanded by all the charter members of the United Nations as a guarantee for their sovereignty, and as a precaution against any possibility of United Nations intervention in their internal affairs.

With the growing pressure for independence of colonial peoples, this provision came under continuous attack. In fact, it has become the practice in recent years to discard this reservation completely. Neither France, nor Portugal, nor the Union of South Africa have succeeded in shielding what they called internal problems from intervention by various United Nations organs.

This important evolution in the interpretation of the U.N. Charter and its provisions has been

Soldier of the Irish contingent on duty at the Albertville airport.

based pre-eminently on the argument that the right to self-determination is a basic political right, a basic political freedom which has to override all other considerations in the charter. To support this argument, the charter preamble and articles regarding human rights and fundamental freedoms have been invoked. Especially prominent among these is article 55 which states: "With a view to the creation of conditions of stability and well-being which are necessary for peaceful and friendly relations among nations based on respect for the principle of equal rights and self-determination of peoples . . . the United Nations shall promote . . . universal respect for, and observance of, human rights and fundamental freedoms for all, without distinction as to race, sex, language, or religion."

These general tendencies have also found their expression in the fact that the Commission on Human Rights recommended to the General Assembly the establishment of two commissions: one for a survey on the right of peoples and nations to "permanent sovereignty over their natural wealth and resources," and the other to examine situations which allegedly result from denial or in-

Members of the Irish contingent of ONUC aboard a train leaving military base at Kamina en route to Albertville.

adequate realization of self-determination. And for those who are not ready to accept these arguments, member states which side with the policy of U.N. intervention in what the states concerned consider "internal affairs," produce another argument, based on the reservation implied in the final sentence of article 2 (7) which states: "This

The first supreme commander of the U.N. force in the Congo, Major General Carl van Horne (*second from right*), and an advance party arrive at the airport in Elisabethville.

principle [of nonintervention] shall not prejudice the application of enforcement measures under Chapter VII," which is the chapter carrying the title, "Action With Respect to Threats to the Peace, Breaches of the Peace, and Acts of Aggression." Thus, whenever a dispute of this kind arises, in addition to the invocation of the principles of human rights and fundamental freedoms, the situation disputed is called a threat to peace, thus justifying U.N. intervention.

This far-reaching evolution in the doctrine of U.N. competence has added new dimensions to the international organization. It has, to a great extent, although still within a limited sphere, been substituted for the doctrine of state sovereignty on all matters the state proclaims and considers "internal." Unfortunately, this milestone in U.N. evolution and progress, vigorously defended and promoted by the new nations, has yet to become a general nondiscriminatory principle which is binding for all U.N. member states.

OUTVOTING THE MAJOR POWERS

Directly related, although of a different charac-

ter, is the General Assembly's problem of voting and rendering decisions. The march of the U.N. toward universality of representation has been accompanied by a basic change in the balance of political power within the United Nations. With the smaller nations (largely within the Afro-Asian bloc) constituting almost half the United Nations

General van Horne and his staff examine a map in connection with troop deployment.

United Nations soldier watches demonstrators.

membership, none of the big powers can be assured in advance of a majority in a vote taken in the General Assembly on matters of principle, and on important political matters, where, in either case, decisions could be adopted only with a two-thirds majority. Neither could any great power assure itself of one third plus one, to block any resolution it considers contrary to its policy or to its national interest.

This development, which is one of the basic problems of the sixties in the U.N., could be viewed as a wished for reality of the present-day world, as a kind of permanent buffer between the opposing atomic giants—a most positive change in world politics, which gives at last real influence to the many, even if they do not share the interests of the mighty.

But this appraisal of the situation, although possibly true with respect to the principles of the workings of the United Nations, might be fallacious in relation to the real interests of the major powers and their tolerance toward being continually outvoted. Of course, suggestions of voting weighted according to a member state's power, re-

Crowds line up in Leopoldville to await a group of demonstrators. A Ghana police officer is on duty (*foreground*).

A scene in Leopoldville during a demonstration.

sources, and population, are discarded outright, as they would be alien to the entire conception of an international organization in which all member states are equal and have one vote in its main representative body, the General Assembly. But some kind of *modus vivendi,* or some basic agreement in this respect, must be reached if the United Nations is to continue to meet successfully the challenges of our era, laden with changes and deepest revolutions.

Secretary General Dag Hammarskjöld found it necessary to deal with this problem twice within only a few weeks. At his press conference at May 29, 1961, he said:

As regards majority, of course the whole question has arisen because of the fact that we now have majorities here which are partly rather incalculable in relation to big-power politics and therefore may represent a hampering or complicating problem in big-power thinking. I think that we must try to find our way to a new balance where on the one side the big powers give all the respect due to a majority but where, on the other hand, the majorities do recognize that there are problems which simply cannot be solved by voting, but where, what I call the real veto does apply.

A political speaker in Leopoldville.

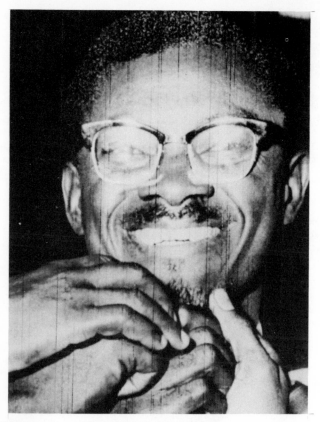

Ministers congratulate Lumumba after vote of confidence of the Chamber of Deputies confirming him in office (June, 1960).

And on June 26, 1961, he elaborated this theme, stating:

I have already, I think, on some occasion indicated the need to have a balance between the recognition of the crucial vote of the major powers, on one side, and the rights and responsibilities of the majority of nations, on the other side. What I see as the future of the United Nations is in the direction of such a balance. The vast majority of members must, so to say, come into their own positively in relation to the permanent members of the Security Council. Their significance, their importance, their responsibilities and their rights, must be fully recognized. But on the other hand, the majority should, of course, look realistically at the world as it stands today and see clearly what is the role and what must be the role of the big powers. . . . I would rather say that I see the future of this organization very much as one of an organ which primarily serves the interests of smaller countries, which otherwise would have no platform in world affairs—these smaller countries however, within the organization, intimately co-operate with the big powers.

THE TREND TOWARD THE GENERAL ASSEMBLY

This understanding of the smaller powers is the more imperative in view of the trend to refer the

Ethiopian troops inspected by Emperor Haile Selassie before departing for the Congo.

Ambassador Rajeshwar Dayal (*left*) of India, briefed by Dr. Ralph Bunche on the eve of his assumption of the post of the secretary general's personal representative in the Congo.

greatest possible number of problems to the General Assembly. Although this trend of transferring the authority of the United Nations Organization, in its most important functions, from the organ in which it was originally vested by the charter—the Security Council—started very early in the history of the U.N., it has assumed in recent years dimensions which suggest that this is more than a passing development. (The record of Security Council meetings is quite interesting in this respect: in 1946, there were eighty-eight such meetings; in 1947, one hundred thirty-seven; in 1948, one hundred sixty-eight; in 1949, sixty-two; in 1950, seventy-three; in 1951, thirty-nine; in 1952, forty-two; in 1953, forty-two; in 1954, thirty-two; in 1955, twenty-three; in 1956, fifty; in 1957, forty-nine; in 1958, thirty-six; in 1959, five; in 1960, seventy.)

The United States, seeking to override the obstacles of the veto at the Security Council, initiated the Uniting for Peace resolution that authorizes the General Assembly, in cases in which the Security Council is paralyzed by a veto, to recommend to member states collective measures in-

Colonel Joseph Mobutu, chief of staff of the Congo Army, addresses a news conference after the army took power.

Lumumba, deposed premier of the Congo, leaves his plane at Leopoldville airport under guard of soldiers loyal to Colonel Mobutu (December, 1960).

cluding the use of armed force for the restoration of peace and security. But Soviet Russia was also partly responsible for the transference of authority from the Security Council to the General Assembly. Russia urged the assembly to adopt extraordinary measures regarding Spain, as it brought before the assembly, the Soviet complaint about "United States aggression against China" and the status of former Italian Colonies. This development was a direct result of the way the veto power at the Security Council was executed. This major problem was also dealt with by the Secretary General: "The real veto problem for which in fact the word 'veto' is a misnomer," he said, "is based on the fact that there are questions which cannot be solved without agreement between the big powers, especially in this case between the predominant military powers. There is the artificial veto problem, that is to say, the attempt by this or that power to make its consent essential for questions which naturally should be solved, let us say, on a majority basis." But this was not, and is not, the only reason for the process of concentrating

U.N. powers within the General Assembly.

The very fact that it is the General Assembly in which the small powers have a say and can influence U.N. decisions is by itself a sufficient reason for the overwhelming majority of member states, which are not members of the Security Council, to lean toward increasing the power and influence of the General Assembly. To a certain extent it is a kind of revolution against the principles of the charter which give the Security Council, and through it, the five permanent members of that organ, decisive powers within the framework of the United Nations Organization.

This problem of the fifties, growing in evidence in the sixties, has been accompanied by another development. Security Council meetings have begun to resemble General Assembly meetings, in that a growing number of states have been admitted to express their opinions at the council's meetings. The liberal interpretation of the provision permitting a state which is not a member of the Security Council but whose interests are involved in a dispute considered by that body, to

On February 17, demonstrators assembled to protest against the death of Lumumba in front of the U.N. Headquarters.

participate in the dispute even if it is not directly a party to it, produced situations where in addition to the Security Council members, up to ten representatives of other states have participated in the council's deliberations. The debates on the Congo at the Security Council serve as a vivid illustration of this situation, in that almost all of the African U.N. members took part in these debates at one stage or another. This is a trend which certainly demands further consideration and thought.

ADJUSTMENT TO A CHANGING WORLD

There is no doubt that the growth of U.N. membership made organizational changes in the composition of U.N. organs imperative. The Security Council is no more representative of the membership of the U.N. than is the Economic and Social Council. Both require adjustments; both require increased membership. The charter did provide

A Congolese looks at the car in which Premier Lumumba, according to Katanga province authorities, made his escape from a farmhouse prison, February 4, 1961. The anti-Lumumba Katanga officials said on February 13 that the former premier and an aide had met death at the hands of tribesmen near the area where the automobile was found, about two hundred miles from Elisabethville.

Aerial view of the Lovanium University buildings where the Congolese parliament met under U.N. security guarantees.

for possible future changes, although nobody thought that the changes would be needed so soon.

Article 108 of the charter states clearly: "Amendments to the present Charter shall come into force for all Members of the United Nations when they have been adopted by a vote of two thirds of the members of the General Assembly and ratified in accordance with their respective constitutional processes by two thirds of the Members of the United Nations, including all the permanent members of the Security Council." Article 109 even provided for a General Conference for the purpose of reviewing the charter and stipulated that in case this conference did not take place before the tenth session of the General Assembly, that assembly should consider a proposal to call such a conference. The article stipulated as follows: "The conference shall be held, if so decided, by a majority vote of the members of the General Assembly and by a vote of any seven members of the Security Council." Unfortunately the power struggle at the U.N. prevented the holding of such a conference. It was postponed a few times, and the last postponement assigned the sixteenth session of the General Assembly the task of dealing

Lt. Col. R. S. Sial of India, the officer responsible for provisions for the entire ONUC.

Ethiopian unit parading after return from tour of duty in the Congo, bears national and U.N. flags side by side.

with this problem. As in other basic matters, there is the problem of the veto, which makes virtually impossible every effort to adjust the organizational structure of the United Nations to the present-day realities of the world. Suggestions for an increase in the number of members of the Security Council have been rejected by Russia categorically. Russia demands that the representatives of the People's Republic of China be seated in the United Nations organs before it will consider any other change in the composition of those organs.

The problem of China's representation at the U.N., which has been of grave concern almost since the inception of the United Nations Organization, came to a head in recent years. The increase in the number of U.N. members and the growing voting strength of Asian and African members has made the problem more acute. The fact that representatives of a country of over 600 million people—almost a quarter of the human race—are not participating in the workings of the United Nations creates a most acute problem. The standard procedure, practiced for years, of postponing discussion of Chinese representation, the

so-called "moratorium," did not solve the problem. The persistent opposition of the United States curtailed discussions concerning it. How long this policy could be successful nobody could predict. It has been suggested that "two Chinas" be represented at the U.N.—Communist China as well as Nationalist China.

Recently a new point of view was brought into

Lt. Gen. Sean McKeown (*left*), commander of U.N. forces in the Congo, with Dr. Connor Cruise-O'Brien, U.N. representative at Elisabethville, prior to departure for Katanga.

Congolese leaders of the central government in Leopoldville and of the government in Stanleyville sign agreement to convene the Congolese National Parliament.

play on this question when the representative of Pakistan Zafrulla Khan stated that in his country's opinion the admittance of Communist China to the U.N. is only a matter for the Credentials Committee to decide. In this case a decision to seat the delegation of Communist China instead of Nationalist China could be adopted by a simple majority of the General Assembly.

It is hard to say whether this opinion of one U.N. member represents the opinion of the majority. The fact that the United States decided to abandon its policy of supporting the "moratorium" and accepted the challenge of having the problem of Chinese representation discussed in full in the General Assembly, still left open the basic question as to how the decision on this matter should be adopted. It is the contention of the United States and many other countries that the question of Chinese representation is a matter of

Cyrille Adoula, prime minister of the Congo, approved with his government by both houses of parliament (August, 1961).

Dag Hammarskjöld with Prime Minister Adoula standing at attention during the playing of the Congolese national anthem at Njili airport on Hammarskjöld's arrival at Leopoldville (September 13, 1961).

principle, and that therefore any resolution on this matter must be adopted with a qualified majority of two thirds of the U.N. membership. And this is a contention which, by itself, is liable to the assembly's decision. On the outcome of this legal wrangling depends the entire plan of the United States delegation, which hopes that there will be no two-thirds majority for seating the People's Re-

Connor Cruise-O'Brien (*center*), U.N. representative in Elisabethville, during briefing session with staff officers of the Swedish battalion.

public of China in the United Nations. The United States hopes instead that a decision will be adopted to have a committee appointed for a thorough inquiry into the entire problem of Chinese representation. Thus a new delay in the final solution of the problem would be achieved.

Undoubtedly, among the many decisive problems which the U.N. has to face, this is one of the most important, and most explosive.

THE "BLOCS"

In the handling of this and many other problems within the United Nations, a special feature of its workings is becoming more and more evident. This is the evolvement of certain groupings, or, as they are called at the United Nations, "groups" or "blocs" of U.N. member states. The Latin-American bloc, which was in fact the first to make itself felt in U.N. activities, has been surpassed in influence by the Afro-Asian bloc. This development is due largely to the fact that cohesion of the Latin-American bloc has been somewhat hampered by the breaking away from it of

Cuba, and the repercussions which followed. But sheer numbers had their influence as well; the Afro-Asian bloc is numerically twice as strong as the Latin-American bloc, with all the implications of this strength being manifested in their relations. Whether the trend toward the breaking up of the U.N. membership into blocs corresponds with the basic ideas for which it was supposed to stand, is again one of the central problems of the U.N., and the future of these realities is among the important challenges the U.N. has to face.

This bloc structure, which gave birth to the term "Disunited Nations," has been part of the political realities within the U.N., but has not attained any formal recognition within the U.N.'s organizational framework.

It was Russia which, in 1960, turned into a central part of its U.N. policy the idea of giving these blocs formal and official standing. Although elaborate plans for the formalization of the division of the United Nations' membership into blocs (Russia wanted three blocs: the Socialist, the Western, and the neutral) were brought into political play

Mr. Ivor G. Smith, U.N. representative in Elisabethville (*far left*) at meeting with Gen. Sean McKeown (*center*), commander of the UN. force in the Congo.

some years ago, when Russia demanded to make the neutrals a specifically distinguished partner in disarmament negotiations, the formal, insistent demand for the recognition of three blocs within the U.N. did not come until the fifteenth session of the General Assembly. Since then, this issue has been turned into a central principle of Russian policy and diplomatic tactics.

There is, of course, an underlying consideration which could make such a tactic rather agreeable for the so-called neutral nations. The growing number of small member states in the U.N. which do not want to identify themselves with any of the two opposing big powers are certainly in search of some sort of expression of their existence and of the influence they have attained in the United Nations. Every suggestion to increase their influence, to formalize it, could find them receptive. This is one of the birth pains of the U.N.'s march toward universality and the coming years will certainly see a constant jockeying for positions between the adherents of the conception of a "united" United Nations, with a single secretary general, and those who would slowly turn the U.N. into an organization where no individual nations as such can find its expression and means of co-operation with the international community, but rather only through blocs to which these individual member nations would owe their primary allegiance.

It is clear that the whole concept of an organization of sovereign, equal states, of decisions

The people of British Togoland construct their own dwellings from locally obtained materials.

Female members of the Medical Corps of the Indian Army before airlifting to the Congo.

adopted by member states expressing individually their opinions, of a possibility of mutual influence instead of rigid barriers to understanding or a rigid framework for misunderstanding, are all at stake in this discussion—a discusson which embraced the United Nations in the fifteenth year of its existence, and which will certainly keep it occupied for years to come.

COMPOSITION OF THE SECRETARIAT

In this new development another, related problem is becoming evident. This is the problem of the composition of the United Nations Secretariat. The Russian demand for a three-man Secretariat General, that is for three secretary generals representing the three blocs (which implies instituting the veto in the United Nations executive branch), was rejected on the ground that this would in fact paralyze the U.N. and deprive it of any effectiveness. But the Russians seem not to be ready to give up their pressure in this respect, which again involves the entire conception of the United Nations as it was conceived by its founders.

The statements of opponents of this Russian de-

mand, who assert that there could not be a viable United Nations Organization with such a change in its organizational setup, is sufficient proof of the seriousness of the struggle into which the United Nations has been thrown. It is a struggle

President Moise Tshombe of Katanga Province.

While the military force is busy keeping order, the United Nations civilian operations in the Congo are in full swing. Here, U.N. experts take soil samples.

which, even if unresolved, is bound to absorb much of the energies of the United Nations and thus hamper to no small extent the effectiveness of the international organization in matters which it is called upon to handle, by the charter and by the immense practice which has emerged within the sixteen years of its existence.

The struggle over the organizational basis of the secretary general's office, which was expected to reach the decisive stage in 1963, when the second term of office of Mr. Hammarskjöld would have expired, was turned into an immediate, most crucial problem with his sudden death. The United Nations lost not only a most capable personality, who led the international organization into ever improving stages of international cooperation and extension of U.N. activities, but was also thrown into a crisis which has put in danger the very existence of the United Nations as an effective instrument in international relations.

Mr. Hammarskjöld's death became a source of

United Nations experts and a local official study a map of Congo terrain as they make plans to carry out an emergency public works program.

Dr. M. V. Pasechnik of the Ukrainian SSR signs on behalf of his country the statute of the International Atomic Energy Agency.

double crisis—a crisis both constitutional and political.

The constitutional crisis stems from the absence in the U.N. Charter of provisions stating the course of action to be taken in the case of the disease or incapacity of the secretary general during his term of office. In this respect the U.N. Charter is beset by a deficiency similar to the one prevailing in the Constitution of the United States, which does not specify what should be done in case the chief executive becomes incapable of performing his duties. The solutions suggested to fill the secretary general's post have a basis neither in the charter nor in precedent, since the latter does not exist in this instance.

The discussion concerning the character of the secretary general's office thus came to the fore with full force. But within the discussion as to how to provide the U.N. with a leading executive officer, none of the parties suggested having the selection of a new secretary general advanced by two years from the date it should normally have taken place. It is common opinion at the U.N. that the election of a permanent secretary general should be left to 1963, and that at present, a solution on a temporary basis should be found.

But what should this solution be? This is the core of the critical problem. Those who wish to follow the charter argue for a single "interim" or "acting" secretary general, while Soviet Russia and her allies have used the opportunity to press for, even if only on a temporary basis, implementation of their conception of a three-man office of the secretary general.

In the prolonged negotiations for the solution

of this U.N. crisis, the Russians made a few suggestions. One of these suggestions involved the provision of four deputy secretary generals. One of them would be elected chairman and the others would, according to the suggestion, do their utmost work in harmony with him. But in all the Russian solutions, there prevails the basic concept of equality, and the right of any of the four to use his veto. (The four deputies would be chosen to represent the Russian, Western, Asian, and African blocs.)

Acceptance of the Russian demand would of course prejudice the basic struggle for the character of the secretary general's office when it comes up again in 1963, for in that year a permanent secretary general will have to be elected. Although arguments about the paralysis of action which a Russian solution would cause are mentioned constantly, opposition to such a solution is not based solely on considerations of efficiency and practicability. It is the charter, in its articles dealing with the Secretariat, and the papers of the commissions which prepared the basic working rules of the U.N. which are quoted as the main basis justifying opposition to the Russian demands.

The first two weeks of wrangling on this matter provided no solution. The fact that the charter provides for no such circumstances as those which developed after Mr. Hammarskjöld's death during his term of office, leaves, ultimately, the solution of the problem in the hands of the General Assembly, at which a majority of two thirds could have the final say on how the void created in the U.N. by Mr. Hammarskjöld's death is to be filled, and who is to fill it. It could safely be said that never has the death of one man affected so many vital problems of such a large segment of humanity, and never have so many nations cared what would become of the legacy one man left behind.

This was not the last word in the maneuvering for the selection of Mr. Hammarskjöld's successor. Initiatives were taken and a variety of proposals were suggested regarding the solution of the crisis. On November 3, 1961, six weeks after Mr. Hammarskjöld's death, Mr. U Thant of Burma was elected acting secretary general. The vote was unanimous. The 103 members of the United Nations General Assembly voted for, none voted against, and none abstained. As the result of the elections was announced, after nine minutes, the president of the sixteenth session of the General Assembly, Ambassador Mongi Slim, stated briefly: "I declare that His Excellency U Thant has been appointed acting secretary general for a period ending April 10, 1963."

In his first statement as acting secretary general, Mr. U Thant named two U.N. undersecretaries, Dr. Ralph Bunche of the United States and Georgi P. Arkadyev of the Soviet Union, as his advisers, retaining his freedom of choice of any additional advisers he would deem necessary.

"It is . . . my intention to work together with these colleagues in close collaboration and consultation in a spirit of mutual understanding," said U Thant in his statement. Although some saw here an indication of acceptance of the Russian point of view on the organization of the Secretariat, other observers disposed of this contention by pointing out that no veto was involved and

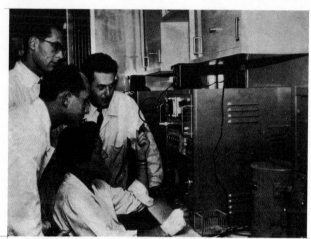

Dr. Traude Bernet, chief of the Austrian Isotope Distribution Center, explains how to handle an oscilloscope.

that the secretary general preserved his full freedom of choice of advisers and freedom of decision on all matters pertaining to the United Nations. For, as he stated in his oath of office, he would "discharge these functions and regulate [his] conduct with the interests of the United Nations only in view and not . . . seek or accept instructions in regard to the performance of [his] duties from any Government or other authority external to the organization."

The grave crisis of the United Nations was thus resolved. The international organization again had a head of its administrative and executive organ. But the question remained open whether this

meant a final solution of the constitutional crisis regarding the concept of the secretary general's office, or only a postponement of the decisive battle on this subject until April 10, 1963, when the U.N. will have to choose its regular secretary general. At this time Mr. U Thant will have served the rest of the term of office to which Mr. Hammarskjöld was elected.

But putting aside, for the moment, the question of the future of this contest at the United Nations, another, related problem is knocking at the doors of the U.N. The composition of the executive branch of the United Nations is being contested not only by Russia, and not only on the grounds mentioned by Russia. Two continents, Asia and Africa, which are growing in importance and in the number of their nations which are members of the United Nations, are demanding a greater share in the U.N. Secretariat. The growth of the U.N. makes imperative modifications in other organizational arrangements as well. As of April 1, 1961, the division of top-echelon and professional jobs in the U.N. Secretariat—undersecretaries, officials of equivalent rank, and directors—was as follows: North America, 22; Western Europe, 18; Asia and the Far East, 11; Eastern Europe, 4; and Africa, 2. These quotas are based on the contributions made by each government to the U.N. budget.

The clamor for changes resulted in the establishment of a Committee of Experts on the Review of the Activities and Organization of the Secretariat, a Review Board on United Nations Reorganization, as well as a committee of three past presidents of the assembly, Lester B. Pearson of Canada, Prince Wan Waithayakon of Thailand, and Dr. Victor Belaúnde of Peru—all of whom handled various aspects of the United Nations organizational setup in view of the changing times.

From the many recommendations these various bodies have made, one conclusion was held in common. All suggested certain modifications in the organization of the United Nations. These suggested modifications included the increase of the quota in the Secretariat composition for East Europe, for Africa, and for Latin America, and it was recommended that populations of member states be considered as well in determining the quotas. It was further suggested that quotas of U.N. officials be allotted on the basis of geogra-

Representatives of the three nuclear powers to the Geneva Conference on the Discontinuance of Nuclear Tests exchange views shortly before the opening of the meeting (October, 1958). They are (*left to right*), James Wadsworth of the United States, S. K. Tsarapkin of Russia, and David Ormsby-Gore of Britain.

phical division to seven regions: (1) Africa, (2) Asia and the Far East, (3) Eastern Europe, (4) Western Europe, (5) Latin America, (6) the Middle East, and (7) North America. Appointments which the secretary general made in 1961, extending the influence of regions other than those which enjoyed predominant representation until recent times, are certainly only a beginning. The problem, once brought up for U.N. debate, will certainly continue to occupy the secretary general, as it did Mr. Hammarskjöld, whose pragmatic approach to these problems took into consideration the changing realities in the world organization.

Even without these problems resulting from newly emerging or newly defined interests and pressures, the scope of U.N. activities demands a growing concentration on the question of co-ordination between the various U.N. agencies, commissions, and organizations. Problems concerning outer space and disarmament may give rise to two new U.N. bodies, apparently now in preparation. The fact that the U.N. has under its supervision—and one could say, command—almost 25,000 soldiers, with all the regular problems of such a military establishment, plus the special problems emanating from the special character of this corps as an army of peace and for peace, acts to complicate even more the already complex framework of

the U.N. If the experience of the United Nations Emergency Force (UNEF), and of the U.N. Force in the Congo (ONUC), could serve as an indication of the role the U.N. is able to fulfill in times of crisis, and if the experience of U.N. observers, the "trouble shooters for peace" located in many countries, could be seen as an encouraging element in the troubled world, then it would seem advisable that some kind of military advisory board be instituted to advise the secretary general on military matters, as he has utilized the counsel of the advisory committees on UNEF and ONUC, composed of representatives of member states which participate directly in U.N. military operations.

CHANNELING AID THROUGH THE U.N.

The military and civilian aspects of the Congo operation will doubtless serve as a precedent for future emergencies in which the U.N. is called upon to intervene. Many practical problems emerged in the Congo operation—an operation which, at least for a years time, prevented the Congo from being turned into an open field of political rivalry by foreign powers, and even, perhaps, from turning into a Korea-type war.

Within this context of prevention of outright foreign intervention in the Congo crisis, another

The technical working group on the detection and identification of high altitude nuclear explosions submits its report to the Conference on the Discontinuance of Nuclear Weapons Tests. In the foreground are W. Epstein of the U.N. Secretariat, and Secretary General Dag Hammarskjöld.

problem gained prominence, namely, the problem of channeling aid through the United Nations. By insisting that it is the sole agency for extending aid to the Congo, the U.N. has prevented involvement of particular powers in Congo affairs, and it set a precedent for future forms of aid to needy countries.

In recent years, this question of aid has been very much in the minds of U.N. delegates. Political observers see in replacing the bilateral forms of aid by aid given through the international organization a decisive remedy in many aspects of the "cold war." They also see in such a change advantages which could benefit the receiving countries by absolving them from being involved in international rivalries. Simultaneously, such a development would consider imponderabilia of national pride, which is, to a certain extent, hurt by the very fact of dependence on foreign aid. And of course there is the further consideration that aid channeled through a central agency such as the U.N. has, according to some, proven by experience to be more efficient.

The Congo was the first example of aid channeled through the U.N. The United Nations Civilian Operations in the Congo had at its disposal, in the first three months of its activities in the

Congo "an integrated advisory and expert team of 170 members brought from six continents and placed within a framework of 11 major fields of United Nations assistance." And since that time, the number of experts has been constantly increasing.

NEW FUNCTIONS FOR THE U.N.

In the atmosphere of crisis, only passing attention was paid to a speech of the delegate of the Netherlands at the sixteenth session of the General Assembly. While speaking on the future of Western New Guinea, which Indonesia claims to be part of her national territory, the representative of the Netherlands, Mr. Luns, announced his country's resolve to terminate its sovereignty over that territory at the earliest possible date and to "transfer its present powers to an organization or international authority established by and operated under the United Nations, which would be vested with executive powers."

Mr. Luns was fully aware that this was a revolutionary initiative, unprecedented in U.N. practices and not provided for in the U.N. Charter. It constituted, as he said, "a form of international administration by a development authority under the supervision of the United Nations. . . . Since these proposals embody an entirely new concept in the history of decolonization, the General Assembly might wish to study them more closely before taking a final decision on them."

This was a new concept in the history of the U.N., as well as in the history of decolonization. If implemented it would turn the U.N. into an administering authority, with attributes of sovereignty over a territory—something the U.N. Charter never envisaged, harboring unprecedented problems and possibilities for the United Nations and its conception. There is no doubt that the Netherlands proposal will come under the scrutiny of U.N. organs and perhaps open a new chapter in the evolvement of U.N. functions and tasks.

THE FINANCIAL BURDEN

Obligations such as those incurred by the U.N. in both the military and civilian aspects of the Congo operation, are burdening the United Nations with an ever-growing budget. Even without such obligations as the Congo operation or UNEF, however, the U.N. activities demand more and more funds.

One must not accept without reservation the concept that a bigger budget is proof of wider operations or greater efficiency, but still the comparison between the budgets of the League of Nations, which did not pass the $6 million mark annually, and the budgets of the United Nations, indicate considerable changes in the scope of the obligations and activities of these two international organizations. Similarly, the budgets of the United Nations, growing with the years, serve as an indication of the ever expanding services which the U.N. furnishes in varying fields.

In this respect it is interesting to note that the U.N. regular budget, which amounted in 1952 to about $48 million, grew by the financial year 1960 to $63,149,700 and by 1961 to $67,437,770. (Of this last figure, the U.S. has contributed $22,332,810; Russia, $9,356,287; the United Kingdom, $5,344,-487; France, $4,396,493; China, $3,441,630; Canada $2,136,421; India, $1,689,902; Italy, $1,545,-642; Japan, $1,504,425; Australia, $1,229,644; and the Ukrainian Soviet Socialist Republic, $1,236,-514. The smallest assessment, $2,287, is to be paid by thirteen African states admitted to the United

Nations at the fifteenth session of the General Assembly.)

But this regular budget does not cover two special tasks of the United Nations—the UNEF and the Congo operation. Both UNEF and ONUC budgets have to be covered by special assessments, which, from the very outset, Russia and the entire Russian bloc at the United Nations have refused to comply with. An idea of the dimensions of U.N. expenses for the Congo operations can be gained from the fact that, for instance, a decision of the General Assembly on the financing of those operations for the period from January 1 to April 21, 1961, authorized the secretary general to incur commitments at a level not exceeding $8 million a month. A second resolution empowered the opening of an *ad hoc* account for the expenses of the Congo operations and appropriated an amount of $100 million for these operations for the period from January 1 to October 31, 1961.

The repercussions of this decision (which was adopted at the last minute, at the very end of the fifteenth session of the General Assembly in the early morning hours, after it became clear that without it the entire U.N. operation in the Congo would collapse) were an additional indication of the problems the U.N. is facing and will continue to face with the expansion of its activities. Russia along with other Communist bloc countries, stated that it would not consider itself bound by any decision taken by the assembly to apportion the costs of the U.N. Force in the Congo, on the ground that the Security Council has exclusive jurisdiction over the financing of military operations undertaken by the U.N. The implication was clear: According to this view, the budget had to be considered by the U.N. organ in which the veto could be applied. In addition to Russia, France stated in 1961 that because of its doubts and misgivings regarding the United Nations' operations in the Congo, it would not be able to support the cost estimates. The financial predicament of the United Nations was outlined by Secretary General Dag Hammarskjöld before the General Assembly's Fifth Committee in the following statement:

The organization will commence the financial year 1961 with a virtually empty treasury; with arrears of assessed contributions totaling approximately $31 million ($8.5 million regular budget and $22.5 million

An exhibit of nuclear energy in Mexico, arranged in connection with the arrival at the University of Mexico of a self-propelled, mobile radioisotope laboratory, which was donated to the International Atomic Energy Agency by the United States government.

on the UNEF budget) and at the same time, the necessity of financing normal budgetary disbursements amounting to some $5 million a month, UNEF expenditures of about $1.5 a month and substantially larger monthly requirements for the United Nations Force in the Congo.

These requirements amount to perhaps $10 million monthly for as long as the force and its supporting services are maintained at their present strength. And it was a dramatic reminder to the committee when Mr. Hammarskjöld stated that estimates quoted in the assembly had put the current cost of armaments at $320 million a day and added, "It may be felt by members that the cost of peace is high, but indeed what is it in comparison to the cost for the preparation of war—not to speak of war itself?"

Is the cost of the United Nations operations a "cost of peace"? This question which has been asked so many times throughout the U.N.'s existence by all those who either thought it to be too influential or else not influential enough, will certainly be asked with increasing frequency in the years to come. The wars which the U.N. has averted (and Secretary General Trygve Lie defined them in 1953, as wars which have saved from the "scourge of war" at least 700 million people) are only part of the role which the U.N. has fulfilled, is fulfilling, and will be called upon to fulfill in

the future. The sheer fact of the U.N.'s presence has, in many instances, made it possible for warring parties to exchange arguments instead of bullets. Further, the U.N. has served as a permanent warning system against the outbreak of war, and it has created, automatically, a kind of coalition against any aggressor.

Being a permanent meeting place of international politics, the U.N. is also a kind of permanent international conference of representatives of all nations, which in our times of personal diplomacy, serves useful purposes for conciliation and negotiation, without these objectives being formally proclaimed. Whoever is familiar with the real workings of the United Nations knows well that the official meetings of its organs, whether public or closed, are only a part of the permanent diplomatic interchange which goes on in the delegates' lounges, at dinner tables, and at parties and other gatherings where diplomats can meet informally without the fanfare of publicity. It has been said by one delegate that the U.N. is for international politics what an airfield is for international air traffic—a comparison which finds its affirmation in many instances of international life.

In the present dynamic days of explosive problems related to the emerging world of developing countries, the U.N. is playing the role of the instrument which stands between chaos and orderly progress within existing realities. Although the spirit of co-operation is often marred by prejudices and divisions, the very fact of sitting permanently together and thrashing out differences in search of a least common denominator of agreement, is a kind of exercise in the responsibility of all for the peace of the world. This responsibility is the more important due to the character of the technological revolution, which is making the world ever "smaller"—a world in which occurrences in one part of it have repercusisons in all the parts of it. The times are over when a revolution in Central America or a struggle for independence in one of the African territories is the exclusive concern of the parties involved. And in such a world of growing interdependence, an international organization is a *sine qua non* of international relations—an extraordinary seminar for the discussion of world interests, at least as qualified by national interests, which every country tries to promote within its framework.

A MIRROR OF WORLD REALITIES

All these considerations have, of course, to be borne in mind whenever an appraisal of the United Nations' activities or importance is being made. The United Nations is not a separate entity; it could not manifest its existence in a way different from that dictated by international political realities. The United Nations is composed of representatives of nations; and it plays the role these nations want it to play. Those seeking remedies in the workings of the United Nations through changes in the charter seem to forget that the United Nations is not a superstate or supergovernment which could act independently of the policies and wills of its members. Therefore all the attempts at finding solutions for certain world problems outside the United Nations, which attempts seem sometimes to be getting the upper hand in international relations, do not diminish the stature and importance of the United Nations. If they are successful, they complement the U.N. efforts. For it should be borne in mind that the U.N. Charter provides for such outer–U.N. arrangements in a special chapter (Chapter VIII) about "regional arrangments," which (in article 52) states: "Nothing in the present Charter precludes the existence of regional arrangements or agencies for dealing with such matters relating to the maintenance of

international peace and security as are appropriate for regional action, provided that such arrangements or agencies and their activities are consistent with the Purposes and Principles of the United Nations." And article 102 states: "Every treaty and every international agreement entered into by any Member of the United Nations after the present Charter comes into force shall as soon as possible be registered with the Secretariat and published by it"—a stipulation which could be a kind of "adoption" by the U.N. of all coming international agreements which could be reached outside the United Nations. Unfortunately, there were few instances where such outer–U.N. efforts proved really successful in a problem area where the U.N. had failed.

The world being as it is, the United Nations, which in a sense reflects it, does not constitute an example of unity and understanding. Critics of the United Nations point to the many disagreements and serious clashes there as proof that the organization is not truly made up of united nations, and, as we have previously mentioned, those with a penchant for sarcasm have even called it the "Disunited Nations." Of course, the disappearance of political and military unity among the big powers —a unity which was at the roots of the thinking of the United Nations' founders—has completely changed the character of the United Nations and the realities and general atmosphere of its working. But there is no doubt that the sixteen years the U.N. has been in existence, in spite of this disruption of the basis of co-operation within the U.N., have proved the vitality of the United Nations idea. They have seen a genuine attempt to create a world of law commanding relations between nations—an attempt which is embodied in an organization which is the only hope for the preservation of the world under the menace of an atomic holocaust. Perhaps one even more striking proof of this validity could be seen in the fact that none of the member states has left the U.N. This situation was different with the League of Nations, where member states used to leave at will, sometimes to return, and sometimes to remain permanently outside the international organization.

The United Nations has attained a variety of names: diplomatic clearinghouse, permanent international conference, framework for creating world opinion, international listening post, town hall meeting of the world. All of them together, and each separately, express the opinions ordinary citizens and professional diplomats hold regarding the United Nations.

There is another name given the United Nations: the central propaganda forum of the world. Whether this is said derisively or in full appreciation of the value of propaganda in today's world, and of a propaganda forum which all U.N. members are entitled to use, it is clear that, being such a forum, it fulfills a vital function in the politics of the second half of the twentieth century. For the founders of the U.N. did not shy away from propaganda, or, let us say, "information."

Ample provisions were made to assure the presence of all facilities which would enable the U.N. to become such a sounding board for national policies. And the role of the press in this respect, the facilities provided for it, and the importance ascribed to its members, are additional proofs of the interest the United Nations has in the dissemination of U.N. ideals, and national aims alike.

The U.N. is, and, in all likelihood will continue for many years to be, a showcase of international coexistence—coexistence which, though generally peaceful, is not always friendly. In this sense, the U.N. is a true mirror of international realities.

PERSONS AND PLACES AT THE U.N.

It did not happen exactly as those who dreamed of a world order had visualized. The site of the headquarters of the United Nations Organization did not become a city of high-minded statesmen who work for world peace and international co-operation, detached from the real problems of the world. Those who wanted the site for the headquarters established "at least twenty-five miles from New York," away from the metropolis of day-to-day work, and away from problems and uncertainties, did not have their way.

San Francisco, Westchester, and Connecticut, which competed to become the site of the "physical embodiment of the United Nations," as the Secretary General called the U.N. Headquarters, had to acknowledge defeat when, on December 11, 1946, Warren R. Austin, the United States permanent representative to the United Nations, announced that John D. Rockefeller, the American financier and philanthropist, who donated millions for the library of the League of Nations, was willing to spend $8.5 million to put at the disposal of the United Nations a site on the East River in New York. Within thirty-six hours the decision was made and the long "trek" of the United Nations organs, from London, Paris, and various locations in Greater New York, had to come to an end.

But years had yet to pass before 1950, when the Secretariat Building would be ready for occupancy. And the General Assembly could not hold its meetings at the permanent headquarters of the U.N. until 1952. London played host to the First General Assembly in January, 1946. Following that, two general assemblies were held in Paris in 1948 and in 1951. Later still, many a New York site had its proud moments of being turned into the "physical embodiment" of the U.N. Rockefeller Center, Hunter College in the Bronx, the

Hunter College, which housed part of the interim headquarters of the United Nations.

United States Marines served as U.N. guards prior to the organization of the U.N. guard unit.

Sperry Gyroscope plant at Lake Success (with the old New York City Building at Flushing Meadows providing supplementary accommodations for the General Assembly, which the Sperry plant lacked), the "social affairs" hall of the Henry Hudson Hotel, where the Atomic Energy Commission listened to the first plans for atomic control—all over town the international organization looked for some hospitable administrator to let it rest for a while until the permanent quarters would be ready.

And like a family on the move, everybody seemed to be close—related not only by the still-glowing spirit of Allied victory and by idealistic hopes for a perfect world order, but also by the very fact of physical closeness dictated by the relatively small conference rooms, the not-too-spacious corridors, and the fact that the delegations were then fewer. It was easy to come across an important delegate ten times a day, and to get acquainted with him. It was easy to find an attentive ear, and, for the newsmen, it was a simple matter to obtain information.

Of course not everything was rosy even then. The plan for atomic energy control was rejected. Russia's Andrei Gromyko walked out of a meeting of the Security Council at Hunter College in 1946,

refusing to debate the problem of Russian troops in Iran. The ideal of big-power co-operation had already been put to hard tests which it did not withstand. The many idealists in the United Nations and the "kibitzers" associated with it in various ways witnessed a somewhat ironic demonstration of the discrepancy between U.N. principles and the facts of power politics, when the Sperry Gyroscope plant, which produced war materials during World War II, and which was put at the disposal of the U.N. afterward, had to

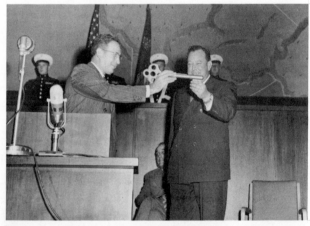

Secretary General Trygve Lie (*right*) receives symbolic key to New York City buildings in Flushing Meadows from Mayor Impellitteri. The buildings were made available for use of the U.N.

Delegates' dining room at Flushing Meadows.

regain some space for war production from the U.N. with the outbreak of the Korean War. It was a sad moment when idealists who rejoiced when the U.N. moved into the Sperry quarters, and saw it as a symbol of the prophesy of Isaiah, "They shall beat their swords into plowshares," had to witness the reversal of the prophesy after only a few years.

Some saw in this reversal a bad omen for the future of the international organization. But others saw in it a useful antidote to utopian idealism concerning future international relations, even so shortly after the horrors of World War II. And so realities of international life were evident to the United Nations during the time it was constantly on the move prior to settling down in its permanent quarters on the East River.

A PERMANENT HOME

The construction of the U.N. Headquarters, which, in contrast to the seat of the League of Nations, nobody christened with the name "palace," took quite a while. From the announcement in 1946 concerning the generous donation of Rockefeller, until 1952, when the General Assembly Hall was ready to seat the members of the Assembly, extensive efforts had been going on to have

the building ready as quickly as possible. An international Board of Design, consisting of architects from fifteen countries and headed by the U.N. director of planning, Wallace Harrison, considered fifty-two designs before one was finally chosen. An interest-free loan of $65 million by the U.S. government, of which over $15 million had already been repaid by 1959, and $2 million from the U.N. budget, provided the funds for the building. In addition, an expenditure of $26 million by the City of New York accomplished a complete transformation of the site. The slaughterhouses, slum tenements, dilapidated docks, the cobblestones of New York's First Avenue, between 42nd and 48th

Press room at interim headquarters.

Ceremony marks the formal transfer to the U.N. of the New York City building at the old World's Fair grounds (October, 1946).

Streets—all were transformed, giving an entirely different appearance to the area of about 8 acres. Gardens, modern buildings, trees, all excellently planned and developed, replaced the shabby neighborhood.

This was the site which once was the hunting place of the Algonquian Indians. Bought in 1620 by Peter Minuet, and later purchased by two English tobacco growers, George Holmes and Thomas Hall, it became during the War of Independence the scene of bloody battles. Near the center of the site stood an apple tree on which the American patriot, Captain Nathan Hale of the Continental Army, was hanged, having been accused of spying for General George Washington.

The historic site was readied, soon to assume again historic significance. On United Nations Day, October 24, 1949, after the Headquarters Agreement between the United States government and the United Nations afforded the site exterritoriality and made it an entity with diplomatic privileges as far as United States authority was concerned, the laying of the cornerstone took place.

Administration building of the Sperry plant at Lake Success, N. Y.

There were spacious, functionally designed buildings, devised to provide convenience and pleasure. The thirty-nine-story Secretariat Building, 73 ft. wide, 287 ft. long, and 544 ft. high, with three of its levels below the street, has blue-green windows made of heat-absorbing glass on the two long sides, and marble on the two ends. It was built to provide working space for over 3,000 headquarters Secretariat officials, besides the 1,300 who are in the field, dispersed over all corners of the world. The glass skyscraper dominates the area and looks out over the East River as if to say to all nations that its gates are open to them in the same way that the seas are open to the ships which pass

Conference area corridor at Lake Success.

A granite block with the words "United Nations" inscribed in English, French, Chinese, Russian, and Spanish, the five official languages of the U.N., was put into place during an outdoor meeting of the General Assembly. Within less than three years the U.N.'s period of wandering had come to an end.

Union Jack flying in front of the U.N. temporary headquarters at Lake Success.

beneath it daily.

The building's floors are especially reinforced to hold the immense weight of almost 14,000 cubic feet of letters, cables, archives, materials from the photo and map sections, and specialized libraries for various U.N. organs (as distinct from the main library). The third floor is occupied by press services, with offices for accredited U.N. correspondents, cable services, the Office of Public Information facilities for the press, a press bar, a press conference room, and racks on which a journalist can

Indian flag being raised as India becomes the fifty-fourth member of the U.N. family of nations (August, 1947).

Plans for the U.N. permanent headquarters take shape on the drawing board.

find "takes" reporting on proceedings going on in all parts of the building, and indeed in all parts of the world where U.N. agencies are operative.

On the fourth floor there is a cafeteria serving thousands of officials, a bank office, on the fifth floor an infirmary, a reading room, and even a shoeshine corner, where one can be understood in any of twenty-seven languages. In short, the building contains a working empire called upon to serve the international organization—to record its activities, to bring knowledge about them to the world, to initiate and to guide projects, surveys, and research undertakings in all matters pertaining to the interests of living men.

But above all these floors, on the thirty-eighth floor of the Secretariat Building, are the offices where, one could say, the nerve center of the entire U.N. operation is located. These are the offices of the secretary general. Offices, conference rooms, living quarters—all are designed to make this place ready for every eventuality in the secretary general's performance of his duties. For he is the chief executive and administrative arm of the United Nations.

To those who walk freely inside the complex of buildings at the United Nations Headquarters, to those who pass from one building to another, through many doors and along lengthy corridors, the U.N. Headquarters appears to be made up of relatively undistinguishable parts. But it is in fact divided into three parts. From the Secretariat Building one can reach the Conference Building. Approximately 400 ft. long, 180 ft. wide, and only 55 ft. high, it houses the chambers of the three U.N. councils—the Security Council, the Trusteeship Council, and the Economic and Social Council. Although not identical in importance in the framework of the U.N. Charter and U.N. activities, each of the three chambers has the same dimensions. Each is 72 ft. wide, 135 ft. long, and

Consultants of the Board of Design of the U.N. permanent headquarters look over model of U.N. buildings prior to a press conference.

has ceilings 24 ft. high. Each of them has glass-enclosed booths along both sides. Here interpreters, cameramen, and photographers view their objects, and the activity is intense. Flash bulbs pop and television cameras, viewed from the floor, sometimes give the impression of gun barrels as they project through the windows of the booths and are aimed this way and that. The cameras may record, for example, the personal struggle of a delegate who tries to "catch the eye" of the operator so that his gesture, the expression of his face, or his shaking hands with some important personality, may be perpetuated and perhaps even relayed to his homeland. This would certainly not harm his political standing and might enhance his chances for political advancement.

The horseshoe table of the Security Council bears the names of the states which are council members. A new president takes over on the first of each month, and this office rotates in the English alphabetical order of the names of the states which are members. The president of the council has the secretary general or his representative on his right side, and the undersecretary for Political and Security Council Affairs or his representative on his left. The president can sometimes prolong considerably the proceedings of the council by not using one of the working languages. In this case,

Secretary General Trygve Lie (*left*) and Wallace K. Harrison, chief architect, applying mortar to seal the cornerstone of the permanent headquarters.

he compels his audience to listen to translations of his remarks into both English and French. This often causes a general exodus of newsmen and advisers who know how to appraise exactly at what time they have to reappear to follow the continuation of the debate.

The three chambers of the three councils are by themselves jewels of architectural and interior decorative art. Providing space for some 400 visitors and 120 newsmen, in addition to the conferees, their assistants, and their advisers, the cham-

Midtown Manhattan seen from a plane flying above the East River. The permanent headquarters of the U.N. is visible at the far right.

Aerial view of the U.N. headquarters and gardens.

bers have many features which the artists adapted to suit the special character of the chamber and the purposes it serves. A mural facing the visitors' galleries in the Security Council chamber by the Norwegian artist Per Krohg, symbolizes the removal of shackles for the institution of individual freedom, and thereby holds the promise of future peace. The marble walls, and especially the inlaid wood on the doors, were designed by the Norwegian, Arnstein Arneberg, as were all the other compositional details of the Security Council chamber.

From a corridor on the third floor of the Conference Building, one can reach the chamber of the Trusteeship Council. Long before the Congo captured the headlines, this chamber was named the "Congo Room" by the somewhat imaginative visitors to the U.N. The coloration and bamboo-like latticework décor are perfectly attuned to the impression made by the nine-and-a-half-foot-tall wooden statue of a child with arms raised, a symbol of mankind's hope for a better future. This chamber was designed by another Scandinavian, Finn Juhl, of Denmark. The statue was carved by Henrik Starche, a Danish sculptor, and the curtains, railings, and doors were made in Denmark as well.

The Economic and Social Council chamber,

The thirty-nine–story marble and glass Secretariat Building. In the foreground, the dome topping the General Assembly Hall.

designed by Sven Markelius of Sweden, is distinguished by a unique, hung ceiling and a white-marble floor. Wood paneling, carpet, railings, and doors, also came from Sweden.

Behind these chambers on a great wall in the corridor which leads from the Secretariat Building through the Conference Building to the Assembly Building, a mural painted by the Dominican artist José Vela Zanetti depicts in strong lines and in red, tan, and black colors, mankind's development from its use of the medieval instruments of torture, toward a world of peace, in which it will attain tranquility, expressed symbolically in the mural by people looking at the world through the image of the United Nations emblem.

Walking further to the north there is the escalator to the delegates' dining room, a place which has seen many a party and many an informal conference. In passing the huge windows in the corridor before the entrance to the General Assembly Building, one can enjoy an enchanting view of the East River and of the U.N. garden, with the Queensboro Bridge in the background. And moving through a narrow corridor which runs along the General Assembly Hall, one arrives at the public galleries of the hall.

One could hardly fail to be impressed by the hall of the General Assembly. It is 165 ft. long, 115 ft. wide, and the domed ceiling is 75 ft. high. The covered lights and the majestic setting of every detail is truly inspiring. As in the council chambers, the two side walls have tiers of glass-enclosed booths for the interpreters, cameramen, television technicians, and film operators. The circular, theatre-like auditorium was initially meant to seat 750 delegates and 1,300 visitors, but the accelerated growth of the U.N. has compelled arrangements for expanded accommodations. The fifteenth ses-

The letters "UN" shine over the skyline of New York, as part of a world-wide celebration of the United Nations' sixth birthday (October 24, 1951).

The heads of press agencies accredited to the U.N. in the U.N. Press Club. Left to right, they are Georges Wolf of France Press, Max Harrelson of the Associated Press, Vladimir Ozerov of Tass, Mike Littlejohns of Reuters, and Bruce Munn of United Press International

sion of the General Assembly, which brought the number of U.N. members up to almost one hundred, compelled the press to abandon its gallery and to be moved to what used to be the lower level of the public gallery, as a special committee of architects had to start work on adaptation of the building to the needs of the growing membership of the U.N. Other victims of the expanding membership were the circular shields on the main wall, facing the assembly delegates, on which the emblems of each member state had been painted. These were removed after it became clear that there would be no room for the emblems of all the members of the U.N. And so a compromise was found. Instead of retaining all the emblems, only one was kept—a huge emblem of the U.N., as if to symbolize as an ultimate goal the arrival of the U.N. at a stage when all nations will see in their actions and discussions there only the United Nations' interests. In that case, the U.N. emblem would visually represent them all.

In front of this wall, on a raised platform, is a green, marble desk. Seated behind it is the president of the assembly and on his right, the secretary general. On his left is the secretary general's execu-

tive assistant, the post held until recently by Andrew Cordier, who resigned in June, 1961, to make room for organizational reforms in the composition of the Secretariat, in the framework of efforts for greater representation, in the Secretariat, of Asia, Africa, and the East European bloc of nations. On a lower level, a smaller, black desk serves as the place from which the speakers at the General Assembly deliver their addresses. The 234 press seats rise gradually toward the rear of the hall, with the seats for the public behind them. On the side walls two murals appear, the work of the French artist Fernand Léger, two nonobjective paintings which architects have christened with the name "scrambled eggs," a description which one not especially fond of abstract painting would be likely to approve.

After leaving the Assembly Hall, one can look down to the main lobby, at the public entrance from New York's 45th Street. Seven nickel doors lead into a lobby whose ceiling—75 feet high—reminds one of a magnificently designed ship. A Foucalt pendulum and a model Sputnik adorn the lobby, giving some taste of men's strivings toward excellence—something which in the setting of the international organization for peace reminds one of the old Roman saying, *per aspera ad astra*—to the stars through hardships.

From the lobby one can easily reach a popular attraction of the visitors to the U.N.—the gift shop —carrying merchandise from all over the world. A bookshop, with United Nations publications, the United Nations Postal Administration sales counter, and a coffeeshop for those who get somewhat weary walking around the eight-acre lot, are also available.

Further features of the U.N. buildings are large conference halls, six smaller committee rooms, a garage for 1,500 cars three stories below the street level, maintenance workshops, a complete fire-fighting unit, a printing shop, a documents reproduction section, and of course air-conditioning installations which keep the building cool and bring relief to all of its offices on a hot summer day. (In order to please every taste, office temperatures can be regulated within a range of twelve Fahrenheit degrees.) All these facilities are appropriate to the physical plant of the United Nations, contributing toward the comfort and convenience of those engaged in its crucial endeavors.

These premises serve one of the busiest office operations in the world. Its 2,300 telephones ring 8,000 times a day, and 12,000 times a day when the General Assembly is in session. One hundred overseas and 1,200 out-of-town calls are made each week during such a period. Six hundred hours a day are spent on the phone by the twenty-one switchboard operators. These operators, representing among them five nationalities, work on rotating shifts around the clock in the Telephone Room on the seventh floor. Four thousand letters a day reach the various departments of the U.N. Sixty-four thousand documents in English and French, over 30,000 in Spanish, 15,000 in Russian and Chinese—116 million pages are being printed every year. Sixteen magazines, hundreds of pamphlets and books, the monthly *United Nations Review,* are published and made available to all information media.

A total of 6,600 windows keep fourteen window washers occupied full time. The elevators travel 250 miles on a working day, along the one and one-half miles of elevator shaftways. United Nations Radio broadcasts in twenty-five languages. Each hour-long speech means 327 hours of work afterward by the various services of the Secretariat.

Regarding the grounds, on the bottom of the

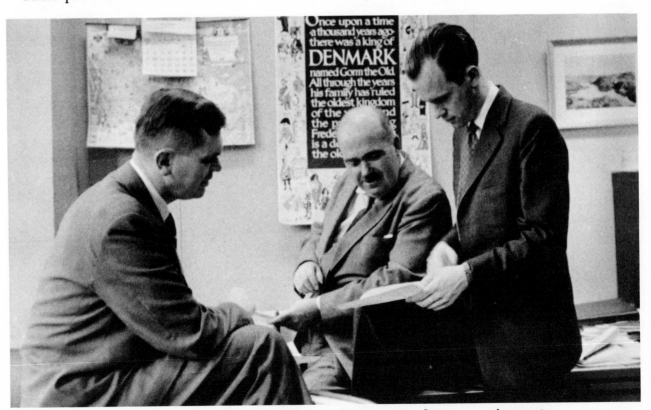

United Nations correspondents exchange views between assignments.

Correspondents at work in the press area.

fountain, at the front of the Secretariat Building, there are forty-five tons of black pebbles from the shallow waters of the Island of Rhodes. Fifteen hundred rose bushes, 185 flowering cherry trees, London planes, English ivy, and sycamore trees adorn the front of the Conference Building, adjacent to the Secretariat Building and the garden. A Japanese pagoda harbors a bell which visitors call the "bell of peace," hoping that its ring will symbolize peace throughout the world. The pagoda

is elevated on a base covered with greenish marble, quarried from the hills of Jerusalem. In front of the three U.N. buildings, facing the United Nations Plaza, is the arc of flags, 400 feet long, at which daily flag-raising and flag-lowering ceremonies are held. The U.N. flag is raised a bit to the rear of the line of flags of U.N. member nations. And opposite these, on the other side of the United Nations Plaza, carved into an imposing wall, large letters proclaim: "They shall beat their swords into plowshares, and their spears into pruning-hooks; nation shall not lift up sword against nation, neither shall they learn war any more." This is the prophesy of Isaiah, which one can also read on a huge statue donated by Russia and placed in the garden which extends from First Avenue to the East River.

A new library building, on the site of the old library building, is being built with a grant of $6,200,000 from the Ford Foundation. The present 200,000 volumes will be increased to 400,000 volumes and it will thus become the richest reference library on U.N. affairs, current world affairs, and on legal, social, economic, and geographical conditions of all nations. Fifteen hundred periodicals and a special set of documents and publications of

Blackboard in the press section helps keep correspondents informed of U.N. activities.

Current newspapers from all over the world are available in the delegates' lounge.

the League of Nations (included in the Woodrow Wilson Memorial Library), and a collection of 50,000 maps, microfilms and bibliographies, will fill the shelves of the new library building, which is expected to have the most modern arrangements, of any library in the world.

THE U.N. POSTAL ADMINISTRATION

Among the many centers of interest at the U.N., the United Nations Postal Administration occupies a special place. The U.N. Post Office, one floor below the street level, and the U.N. Postal Administration sales counter, close to the gift shop, are always extremely busy. Within the almost ten years the U.N. Postal Administration has been in operation, the U.N. stamps have attained, in the world of philatelics, a unique position. Some of its early commemorative issues are among the most wanted and most valued stamps in the world.

Among the many media for promotion of the U.N. idea, the U.N. stamp became a most effective instrument. Tens of millions of stamps of various denominations, many of them commemorating some special occasion in U.N. history—honoring various U.N. organs, or else connected with related U.N. specialized agencies, carry the message of the U.N. all over the world.

Inaugurated on United Nations Day, October 24, 1951, the U.N. postal service was based on an agreement between the United States and the United Nations, which was signed on March 28, 1951. According to the agreement a United Nations Post Office Station was established at the U.N. Headquarters, and was operated by the United States Post Office Department on behalf of

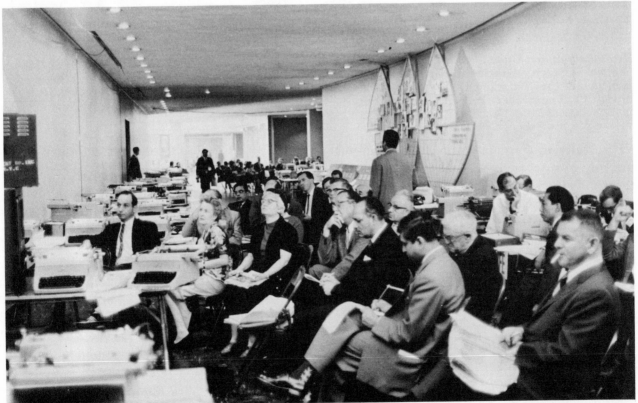

Accredited correspondents follow proceedings of the General Assembly on a television set in the press area.

Presidents of the United Nations Correspondents Association. First row (*left to right*)**: John G. Rogers, Walter O'Hearn, Thomas J. Hamilton, and Jacques Edinger. Second row: Francis W. Carpenter, Krishnamachari Balaraman, Max Beer, Max Harrelson, and John W. Heffernan. Third row: Bruce W. Munn, Pauline Frederick, Paul Sanders, Stanley Burke, and Pierre Huss.**

the U.N. Revenue from the sale of U.N. stamps at the U.N. Post Office Station was to be retained by the United States Post Office Department, which also had to be disbursed for all stamps used on mail dispatched from U.N. Headquarters. Only the revenue from stamps sold for philatelic purposes was to be retained by the U.N.

With time, the sale of stamps became quite a considerable source of income for the United Nations. The budget estimate for the year 1961, for instance, provides for an income, from this source, of $1,066,500 which gives a fair idea of the extent of this operation. Some 279 million United Nations stamps and items of postal stationery have been printed since the U.N. Postal Administration was established.

THE U.N. CARES FOR ITS PERSONNEL

The international personnel of the U.N. is taken care of with respect to its professional interests. The division between the U.N. and the specialized agencies, pertaining to organizational and operational matters, is not preserved in regard to the professional interests of the personnel of these international bodies. The U.N. Joint Staff Pension Board administers the U.N. Joint Pension Fund in which nine organizations participate: the United Nations, the International Labor Organization, The Food and Agriculture Organization, the U.N. Educational, Scientific and Cultural Organization, the International Civil Aviation Organization, the World Meteorological Organization, the Interim Commission for the International Trade Organization, the Atomic Energy Commission, and the Intergovernmental Maritime Consultative Organization. Details about the Fund disclose impressive figures. As of December, 1959, a total of 10,687 people were engaged in a common effort to make the instruments of international co-operation function and fulfill their noble purposes. United Nations personnel alone participating in the fund amounted to 5,386, over half of the entire staff of the international bodies.

Regulations concerning pensions and retirement, withdrawal benefits, disability benefits, and benefits for widows and children are all conceived to give the international official, who sometimes leaves excellent positions in his native country, a feeling of security. As with pension funds in all major institutions, the pension fund of the U.N. has accumulated considerable capital. For the year ended September 30, 1959, the principal of the fund increased from $80,393,303 to $92,627,901.

As is fitting for such a fund, its investment portfolio contains bonds of the International Bank for Reconstruction and Development, in addition to bonds of the United States government, bonds of the Canadian government, and of course bonds of various corporations.

The average yield of all the investments is estimated at 3.8 per cent, which by itself keeps the fund growing, and strengthens this arm of the U.N. operations.

A GREAT TOURIST ATTRACTION

The estimate of the U.N. income for the financial year 1961, from sources other than assessments on member states, shows an interesting entry: Services to visitors and catering services—$631,300.

Such a considerable net income (that is, income after the deduction of expenses for these services), can only be the result of a considerable number of visitors—and the number is very great indeed. On

Press galleries are filled to capacity at a Security Council meeting.

Dr. Eduardo Castillo-Arriola (*left*), permanent representative of Guatemala, is interviewed by newsmen after the Security Council meeting that dealt with the Guatemalan crisis.

June 9, 1961, the seven-millionth visitor entered the United Nations Headquarters. He turned out to be perhaps the happiest visitor among the seven million people who had come to see the United Nations in action. Mr. Phan Thien L. Chan, a twenty-three-year-old student from Vietnam, who studies international affairs, was greeted by the director of the External Relations Division in the U.N. Office of Public Information, Gohl Obhrai—a distinction only he was accorded. A collection of books on the U.N. were presented to Mr. Chan as another part of the greeting ceremony. He confessed that had he not become lost at Times Square, on his way to the United Nations, and thus arrived later than planned, he probably would not have become the lucky visitor.

Since Mr. Chan's visit, hundreds of thousands of new visitors have been at the U.N. The one-hour lecture and tour, costing $1.00 for the general pub-

Members of the Security Council view for the first time the mural painted by the Norwegian artist Per Krohg.

Ceremony marks presentation of the Krohg mural at an informal meeting of the Security Council, the chamber of which is adorned by the painting. Members of the Security Council (*standing, right to left*) are Alexis Kyrou of Greece, Hans Engen of Norway, Oscar Torp of Norway, João Carlos Muniz of Brazil, Secretary General Trygve Lie, artist Per Krohg, Henri Hoppenot of France, Yakov Malik of Russia, Sir Gladwyn Jebb of Britain, and Ernest A. Gross of the United States.

lic, 50¢ for students, and which is free for servicemen, draws over a hundred thousand visitors a month. In May, 1961, a total of 133,868 visited the U.N., this being, along with other spring months, the time of the greatest influx of visitors. The Visitors' Service of the Office of Public Information arranges the tours with a staff of guides which ranges in number between sixty-five and ninety in the peak months of the spring. Some of the guides are an attraction by themselves—some in their colorful native attire and some in the navy-blue uniforms which make them easily distinguishable from the visitors they conduct. And of course, as suits an international organization, visitors from twenty-seven countries can listen to the explanations in their native tongue, if they so desire, in that twenty-seven nationalities are represented on the staff of guides.

WHERE REPRESENTATIVES OF ALL NATIONS MEET INFORMALLY

In these guided tours, the millions of visitors are usually deprived of access to one section of the U.N. Building—the second floor. This is the domain of the U.N. delegates and the press exclusively.

There are certainly many reasons for this restriction, security precautions being not the least important of them. The corridors on this second floor and the two lounges adjoining the Security Council chamber on two of its opposite sides, serve as the real "living rooms" of the delegates. Spread with broad expanses of green carpet, they provide ample walking space between meetings, during lunch time, or, after a day's meeting is closed, when the diplomats are not yet ready to speed home for dinner and would like to exchange views on the session just ended. If the delegates have to stay over for a night-session, or if some emergency meeting calls for their presence, the lounges are again convenient.

The Southern Lounge, which is supposed to provide a quiet space for delegates who really want to rest, affords an atmosphere of relaxation and contemplation. Easy chairs, an excellent view, and a large tapestry by Picasso are some of its features. But for those diplomats who are not especially weary, and for newsmen hunting some

A view of the mural by José Vela Zanetti, on the curved wall on the third-floor lobby of the Conference Building.

"scoop," or at least some exclusive bit of information, the long corridors and the Northern Lounge serve as a kind of a political "coffeehouse," which no other place could afford them. Here friends meet and can hold brief informal conferences; here opponents who only a few minutes before, harshly exchanged arguments at the conference table, engage in friendly conversation. Cameramen photographing such informal conversation sometimes prove a source of embarrassment to the delegates. This once occurred between a Cuban delegate and an American diplomat, and once between United States Ambassador Henry Cabot Lodge, and the Russian representative Andrei Vyshinsky. And sometimes just the opposite occurs—some delegate wants demonstratively to show his country's friendship with another country, and calls for a photographer, some of whom are always near by. Sometimes important political "deals" are made in this lounge, deals which earned it the title of the "diplomatic stock market."

The "living rooms" of the delegations, which unfortunately do not have separate conference rooms for each delegation, are very often crowded

to capacity. In years past, when the U.N. was only at the beginning of its march toward universality, this area was usually rather empty between the General Assembly meetings. One could quietly read newspapers from all over the world, lined up in special racks, or he could look at the works of art gathered in this part of the building—a Gobelin from Belgium, a carpet from Iran or Ghana, magnificent murals by the Brazilian painter Portinari, depicting themes of war and peace, or a large mosaic completely transferred from an old site in Tunis, an archaeological remnant of Roman rule in North Africa. And the contemplative delegate could take advantage of the Meditation Room, which provides a religious atmosphere without religious identification. The small, windowless room, draped in white, contains a polished mahogany log set upright and adorned by a bowl of fresh white flowers. There are a few chairs which can be turned in any direction. In short, the room creates an atmosphere conducive to solemn contemplation, perhaps prior to some historic decision a delegate has to make (although he can only seldom

Delegates' dining room in the permanent headquarters.

act on his own, without clear and direct advice from his government).

HOW THE U.N. GREW

The march toward universality of representation has not been an easy one. Numerous obstacles had to be overcome by many of the present member countries. There were heated discussions at the Security Council meetings. Vetoes were cast. Advisory opinions of the International Court of Justice were handed down. But finally an agree-

Partial view of the General Assembly as a resolution is voted upon. Standing to count the votes is Executive Assistant Cordier.

ment was reached and a "mass" admission of new members took place.

In U.N. diplomatic language it was called a "package deal." And a deal it was. Soviet Russia stopped blocking the admission of the states supported by the noncommunist countries, and in exchange those countries acted similarly regarding the states supported by Russia. In this way, a long view of the admission of member nations since 1946 reveals a rather irregular pattern. Afghanistan, Iceland, and Sweden were admitted on November 19, 1946; Thailand on December 16, 1946; Pakistan and Yemen on September 30, 1947; Burma on April 19, 1948; Israel on May 11, 1949; and Indonesia on September 28, 1950.

Five years passed until a great breakthrough came, when, on December 14, 1955, the following states were admitted in one of the most advertised

Paul-Henri Spaak, of Belgium, president of the First General Assembly.

"package deals": Albania, Austria, Bulgaria, Cambodia, Ceylon, Finland, Hungary, Ireland, Italy, Jordan, Laos, Libya, Nepal, Portugal, Romania, and Spain. Later admissions, with some exceptions, were functionally related to the process of gaining independence by new nations. On November 12, 1956, Sudan, Tunisia, and Morocco were admitted; Ghana came in on March 8, 1957; the Federation of Malaya on September 17, 1957; and Guinea on December 12, 1958. Again in 1960, at the General Assembly session, a big step came when the following countries were admitted to membership: Cameroon, Togo, Malagassy, Somalia, Congo, Dahomey, Niger, Upper Volta, Ivory Coast, Chad, Congo (Brazzaville), Gabon,

Dr. Oswaldo Aranha, of Brazil, president of the Second General Assembly.

Central African Republic, Cyprus, Senegal, Mali, and Nigeria.

At the sixteenth session of the General Assembly, Sierra Leone was admitted to membership. Two other countries—Outer Mongolia and Mauretania—became again subject to political bargaining. With Nationalist China threatening to veto the admission of Outer Mongolia, Russia in turn warned that it would again veto the admission of Mauretania. The breaking away of Syria from the United Arab Republic became a subject of con-

Dr. Herbert V. Evatt, of Australia, president of the Third General Assembly.

siderable discussion as well. Syria was a founding member of the United Nations, and when Syria and Egypt merged into the United Arab Republic, the merged state claimed only one vote, although no formal move was made to cancel Syria's membership. With the one hundred states presently in the U.N., there is good reason to assume that this number will rise soon. For in addition to the above mentioned, new candidates are already in line, some of which will soon be eligible to become U.N. members. Tanganyika, and Western Samoa are among them, as perhaps later will be other presently nonself-governing territories, which are expected to achieve independence in the not too distant future. Once the permanent Security Council members have decided to support the proposal that a certain country be admitted, the country could be considered assured of membership in the United Nations, even before the formal vote of final approval is taken at the General Assembly.

Brigadier-General Carlos P. Romulo, of the Philippines, president of the Fourth General Assembly.

The resolution on admission approved by the assembly is usually very brief, as, for example, is this one, which dealt with the admissions in the fall of 1960: "The General Assembly, having received the recommendation of the Security Council of [date], that [name of country] should be admitted to membership in the United Nations, having considered the application for membership of [name of country], decides to admit [name of country] to membership in the United Nations."

By international usage, political reality, and prevailing beliefs of nations, this act of admission is considered the complete fulfillment of the dream of independence. From the moment of achieving

Nasrollah Entezam, of Iran, president of the Fifth General Assembly.

the status of U.N. member, the countries consider themselves and are considered by others full-fledged members of the international community.

Of course the U.N. Charter contains provisions for expulsion of members as well. Article 5 of the charter states, "A member of the United Nations against which preventive or enforcement action has been taken by the Security Council may be suspended from the exercise of the rights and privileges of membership by the General Assembly upon the recommendation of the Security Council. The exercise of these rights and privileges may be restored by the Security Council." Article 6 goes even further, speaking about complete expulsion: "A member of the United Nations which has persistently violated the principles contained in the present Charter may be expelled from the organization by the General Assembly upon the recommendation of the Security Council." Thus far in the history of the U.N., it has not been necessary to invoke either of these provisions.

MAKING A NAME AT THE UNITED NATIONS

With the admission of a new nation to the U.N., the great game of international politics and diplomacy is opened to its representatives. The committees, the councils, and primarily the Gen-

eral Assembly, give ample opportunity to every representative to draw the attention of his fellow delegates not only to his country and its problems, but also to himself as an individual, as a diplomat.

The representative of a great power—of, say, a permanent member of the Security Council—need expend no special effort to become known in the U.N. Being a representative of a major power gives, by itself, special weight to everything he says, every statement he makes. Delegates from other countries must gain attention and standing through their diplomatic abilities, their eloquence, their wit, and their legal schooling. The presentation of his credentials to the U.N. secretary general, who is accompanied on such occasions by the chief of U.N. Protocol, is only a beginning for the permanent representative of a given country. The delegates are fully aware of this, and they are also aware of the fact that their performance at the U.N. could well serve as a steppingstone in their political careers at home. The prepared speeches, carefully elaborated with the assistance of advisers and experts, sometimes include not only the text, but even remarks on the art of delivery as well. In one instance, for example, a delegate left his text on the conference table after his speech had been delivered, and the text was later discovered to be full of remarks and symbols to remind the distinguished delegate what modulations of voice he was supposed to produce. At one point a marginal notation said: "Weak point—shout." On an-

Dr. Luis Padilla Nervo, of Mexico, president of the Sixth General Assembly.

other occasion, a delegate reminded himself to make a long pause to "let the listeners absorb well" his wisdom.

But these are of course rather exceptional manifestations of the care delegates take for the impression they make on fellow delegates and the public in general. The regular work of a U.N. diplomat is considered a kind of high point, a kind of a peak in the diplomatic art, in the same way that any international conference is considered ideally to involve the greatest refinement of diplomatic technique. Perhaps this is the reason why it so often happens that the most important leaders of countries venture from time to time to appear before the forum of the United Nations. These are

Lester B. Pearson, of Canada, president of the Seventh General Assembly.

Eelco N. Van Kleffens, of the Netherlands, president of the Ninth General Assembly.

Mrs. Vijaya Lakshmi Pandit, of India, president of the Eighth General Assembly.

"transient" U.N. diplomats as compared with the permanent representatives, the ambassadors every member nation has at the United Nations. Presidents, prime ministers, and foreign ministers of all nations have addressed the highest forum of the U.N., the General Assembly, at one time or another. The list of personalities who have appeared at the U.N. is a "who's who" on the highest levels of world politics. Truman, Eisenhower, Kennedy, Khrushchev, Macmillan, Nehru, Mollet, Sukarno, U Nu, Nasser, Tito, Nkrumah, Castro, Sekoú Touré, Queen Elizabeth, King Saud, King Hussein—the list is almost as long as the list of

José Maza, of Chile, president of the Tenth General Assembly.

U.N. member states.

But the temporary presence of these statesmen, however important it may have been to world affairs, does not make it part of the U.N. "landscape." For these are not personalities who reached or asserted their stature in the halls of the United Nations. Without a pretense of presenting a complete list of these permanent U.N. personalities,

Prince Wan Waithayakon, of Thailand, president of the Eleventh General Assembly.

some of them will be reviewed in order to fill out this picture of the U.N. by the introduction of some of its principal actors.

Certainly of central importance is the name of Lester Bowles Pearson of Canada. Throughout nearly all the years of the U.N.'s existence, until a general election in Canada unseated his Liberal-party government, Mr. Pearson was in one capacity or another connected with the U.N. Even in the beginnings of the U.N., he was no novice to the concept of international co-operation. As far back as in 1930, the then thirty-three-year-old Pearson participated in the London Conference for Naval Disarmament, and later in the League of Nations Disarmament Conference, in 1933-34. The former

Sir Leslie Munro, of New Zealand, president of the Twelfth General Assembly.

assistant coach of varsity football and hockey, who collected, due to his fame at the U.N., an immense number of honorary degrees from United States universities, learned well what war means as an officer in the Royal Flying Corps in World War I. He later lent his experience to the UNRRA administration, participated in the United Nations Conference on International Organization in San Francisco, signed the NATO Treaty in Washington, D.C. in 1949, and had his services on behalf of the idea of international organizations acknowledged by his election to the post of president of the Fifth Session of the General Assembly, in 1950.

Dr. Charles Malik, of Lebanon, president of the Thirteenth General Assembly.

As to whether this was the high point of Mr. Pearson's diplomatic career in the framework of the international organizations, not all of Mr. Pearson's friends and admirers agree. There are some who think that he left a much more lasting mark on United Nations history in the year of the Suez crisis, 1956, when, as Canadian foreign minister, representing his country at the General Assembly, he proved that not only a big power, not only a permanent member of the Security Council, could influence decisively the events in

the U.N., and through it, on the entire world scene. The idea of the United Nations Emergency Force, UNEF, which gave rise to hopes that a United Nations police force was within reach, is due largely to Mr. Pearson's efforts. For he had put this idea forward in open diplomacy, arguing for it at the U.N. councils, in personal contacts with the U.N. delegates, and closeting himself for hours with Secretary General Hammarskjöld. "Peace is far more than ceasing to fire," said Mr. Pearson in a 4:00 A.M. speech before a night-session of the General Assembly. Only half an hour later, Mr. Pearson sat with the wary secretary general, trying to convince him that this force was the only solution to the crisis. When the two met again for lunch, little more persuading seemed to be necessary—the idea of a United Nations police force arm started to enter its implementation phase.

Frederick H. Boland, of Ireland, president of the Fifteenth General Assembly.

This was a unique opportunity and a unique achievement. But as it was, it could have been achieved due to a second factor. For this project won support from other powers, and primarily from the United States and its permanent representative for eight years, Henry Cabot Lodge.

"The most youthful-looking grandfather at the United Nations," as delegates used to call Mr. Lodge, is over six feet tall. His figure was one of the most familiar at the U.N. With a flair for dramatic gestures, he was always eager to repulse attacks by the Russian representative.

Mr. Lodge regarded it an important and rewarding aspect of United States policy to court the friendship of the African and Asian nations in the

Dr. Victor Andrés Belaúnde, of Peru, president of the Fourteenth General Assembly.

Mongi Slim, of Tunisia, president of the Sixteenth General Assembly.

U.N. A grandson of Senator Henry Cabot Lodge, who once advocated United States participation in the League of Nations, but later became a bitter opponent of President Wilson and was considered responsible for the United States' absence from the League, Henry Cabot Lodge, Jr. (who dropped the "Jr." during his term of office at the U.N.), seemed to want to demonstrate his devotion to in-

ternational co-operation even more than he would have, had he not perhaps felt it necessary to contradict the notion which the name Lodge evoked in the minds of those who knew something about the history of the United States' relation to international co-operation within the framework of international organization.

Educated at Harvard, Mr. Lodge was a newspaperman, a member of the Massachusetts legislature, and was twice elected a member of the United States Senate. He resigned from the Senate in 1944 to join, at age forty-two, the European Theatre of Operations. Mr. Lodge assumed his post as United States representative to the U.N. in January, 1953. At the time of his tenure of office, this post was elevated to the highest possible standard within the framework of national government. Lodge was a member of the Cabinet of President Eisenhower, and, as was rumored at the U.N., he could directly, without turning to the secretary of state, approach the President himself on major policy decisions at the U.N. And when the term of office of President Eisenhower came to an end, Ambassador Lodge provided a good ex-

South lobby of the General Assembly Building as seen at night from the piazza in front of the Secretariat Building.

F. Van Cauwelaert, minister of state of Belgium, and the Reverend L. J. C. Beaufort, of the Netherlands, exchange views in a lobby at the U.N.

ample of how a United Nations post could serve political advancement well, when he was chosen to be the running-mate of the Republican candidate for the Presidency, Richard M. Nixon.

Lodge's successor at the U.N., Adlai Ewing Stevenson, has also done great credit to the high esteem a United Nations representative enjoys. "The United Nations is the listening post of the human race," he said on one occasion, and complemented this statement with another expression of devotion to the idea of the United Nations: "On a dark scene, in dark times of troubles, New York's guest, the U.N., is proclaiming by deed as well as word, that men can live, not by violence and brute strength, but, at least by reason and law."

The United States representative to the U.N., who assumed his post after the new Democratic administration took over in 1961, also holds the rank of a Cabinet member. The grandson of the Democratic vice-president of the same name as his own, Mr. Stevenson became, when the Democratic National Convention elected him to run in 1952, the first drafted presidential candidate since 1888. He was defeated by General Dwight D. Eisenhower, who defeated him a second time when,

in 1956 at the age of fifty-six, he again headed the Democratic ticket.

No doubt these experiences in United States politics greatly enhance Mr. Stevenson's stature at the U.N. He is no stranger and no newcomer to the international organization. Ambassador Stevenson served as adviser to the United States delegation to the U.N. Conference on International Organization in San Francisco, 1945, and thus participated in the framing of the U.N. Charter. A year later he served as senior adviser to the United States delegation to the First General Assembly in London.

In the contests at the United Nations, where arguments count, eloquence is the most prized attribute and wit the deadliest weapon. Mr. Stevenson puts all these qualities, which he has in abundance, in the service of the cause he expounds. When it becomes known that Stevenson is going to speak, there is an atmosphere of expectation and anticipation. And his speeches have always measured up to the expectations of his audiences.

In this quality of presenting an outstanding appeal to listeners, and of evoking special interest in both the content and the manner of delivery of a speech, Mr. Stevenson had a competitor of high standing years ago in the first decade of the U.N.'s history. This was the representative of Soviet Russia and close colaborator of Stalin, Andrei Yanuarevitch Vyshinsky.

Born in Odessa in 1883, Mr. Vyshinsky was a familiar figure in the early days of the U.N. As head of the Russian delegation from the first to the fifth session of the General Assembly, he was a most outspoken U.N. diplomat. Sharp, uncompromising, to the point, and always ready with a penetrating analysis, Vyshinsky was invariably interesting and sometimes convincing, even from his opponents' point of view. He had at his disposal many personal abilities, which he proved in a challenging life at the time of the Russian revolution. Among the many delegates of important stand-

Four members of the United Nations Security Force. Their blue-gray uniforms are familiar to the innumerable delegates and visitors. Shown (*left to right*) are Robert Herman and Arthur Lotze of the United States, Lt. Gerhardt Litzmann of Norway, and Constantine Lupu of Romania.

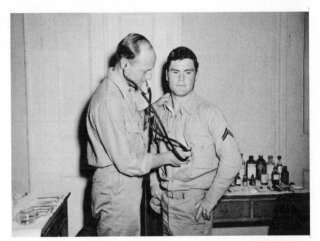

The United Nations infirmary provides quick medical care.

ing in their countries, Vyshinsky was a personality of the first importance. For six years—six fateful years for Soviet Russia, from 1940 until 1946—Vyshinsky stood at the helm of Russian foreign policy, and was thus directly responsible for Russia's participation in the preparations for a world organization.

From the viewpoint of the international diplomatic community, which used to assemble for the General Assembly, Vyshinsky's presence at these meetings used to be considered a proof of the importance Soviet Russia ascribed to the existence and role of the United Nations. The former chief prosecutor in Russia's great trials, the codifier of many of the laws of the new Russian regime, manifested daily the potentials of his legal mind. He understood how to twist a resolution, almost ready for adoption, to make it better suited to his taste

Millions of pages are mimeographed annually at U.N. Headquarters.

Guards enjoy a respite with the newspapers of their countries of origin.

and what he considered to be in the interests of Soviet Russia. He knew how to blister opponents discreetly and how to charm friends and admirers. His appearance on the floor always caused a small sensation and his speeches drew large numbers of visitors who wanted to have a look at Stalin's "right-hand man" in his struggle for power.

But this general atmosphere of respect, which Vyshinsky used to enjoy, did not make him immune to strict rules of procedure at the U.N. meetings. Old-timers at these meetings remember well how the omnipotent Vyshinsky had his speech cut off in the middle by the assembly president when he failed to leave the platform after having used up the time allotted to him for his speech. The button which the president of the assembly can press, shutting the speaker's microphone and preventing his words from reaching the translators and the public address facilities, was used against Mr. Vyshinsky, who then had no other choice but to comply and leave the platform. This incident provided another illustration of the fact that in the U.N. General Assembly, all countries are equal, whether large or small.

The president of the General Assembly who shut off Vyshinsky's microphone in 1953 was no

other than the sister of Prime Minister Nehru of India, Madame Vijaya Lakshmi Pandit. The only woman to date to be the president of the assembly, Madame Pandit brought wit and charm to her high duties—duties which men generally performed with functional dryness and in a matter-of-fact manner. Swarup Kumari (Beautiful Princess), her given name, was changed by her husband according to Indian customs to Vijaya Lakshmi (Goddess of Victory). Madame Pandit demon-

The U.N. Fire Department.

THEY SHALL BEAT THEIR SWORDS INTO PLOWSHARES. AND THEIR SPEARS INTO PRUNING HOOKS. NATION SHALL NOT LIFT UP SWORD AGAINST NATION. NEITHER SHALL THEY LEARN WAR ANY MORE

A permanent reminder to U.N. diplomats by the first who dreamed of a United Nations. The City of New York built this section of granite wall as part of a program of improvements in the U.N. area.

strated daily that she knew how to combine the qualities associated with both these names. With a vast background of political experience, she was the first Indian woman to hold a ministerial post. She was a devoted follower of Mahatma Gandhi and she served successively as Indian ambassador to Soviet Russia and to the United States. Madame Pandit presided over the assembly with firmness and understanding many an experienced diplomat would follow with respect. She demonstrated this firmness when the head of the delegation of her own country, Mr. V. K. Krishna Menon questioned from the floor one of her rulings. Madame Pandit immediately solved the problem by asking from the president's chair, "Does the distinguished representative from India challenge the ruling of the chair?" thus silencing, amidst laughter, the stormy delegate from India.

But on other occasions, the presidents of the U.N. organs, be it of the General Assembly, the Security Council, the Political, or the Credentials Committees, did not succeed so easily in disposing of Mr. Krishna Menon's inquisitive initiative. V. K. Krishna Menon, the minister of defense in the government of India, who almost always heads the

Dr. Henry T. Heald (left), president of the Ford Foundation, gives a check for $6,200,000 to Secretary General Dag Hammarskjöld to be used for construction of the new U.N. library.

View of the library building, named after the late Secretary General Hammarskjöld.

United Nations Radio broadcasts daily in twenty-five languages.

Indian delegations to the assemblies, is often the most prominent personality in the United Nations chambers. A former lawyer in London, who ran for a city office there, Mr. Menon manifests his legal education on every occasion. When the question arises as to what is and what should be considered a "point of order," it is Mr. Krishna Menon who always has an original thought, a special point of departure, or a different approach. Skilled in the intricacies of legal argumentation, Mr. Krishna Menon is often, in fact, the most outspoken representative of the uncommitted bloc of nations at the U.N. His initiatives are numerous, and he presses diligently toward what he considers to be right and appropriate in a given instance. Always on the move in the long corridors and the big

Mexican youths watch a film on U.N. activities, which was made available by the U.N. Information Center.

United Nations official publications.

special care for periodic contacts with the press, and his luncheons with members of the U.N. press corps became a highlight in mutual relations between diplomats and accredited correspondents at the U.N.

Another personality who has distinguished himself at the U.N. should be mentioned. He is Brigadier General Carlos Romulo. Editor, lecturer, historian, expert on American literature, and a soldier who accompanied the forces of General MacArthur in the campaign for the liberation of Leyte, Romulo succeeded early in his diplomatic career at the U.N. in capturing the attention of the world organization. The short, sixty-year-old scholar, soldier, and prolific orator, never refrained from proclaiming openly his views, even if they did not sound "neutral" to his friends among the Afro-Asian bloc. His books *My Brother Americans, Changing Tides in the Far East,* and *Mother America,* give a clear picture of his political preferences, which he has presented outspokenly many times as the head of the Philippine delegation of the U.N.

Among the old-timers at the U.N.—diplomats whose life career is in fact part of the U.N. history

lounges of the U.N. Headquarters, Mr. Krishna Menon, leaning on the cain which he never puts aside, gives the impression that he never needs a rest. He is a kind of a diplomatic "perpetuum mobile," who likes to mix with people and whose bushy gray hair can seldom be missed. Many look to him for consultation, advice, or information.

A complete contrast in character, behaviour, and mood is another well-known personality from Asia —Prince Wan Waithayakon of Thailand. Many delegates and journalists call him the "most affable personality in the United Nations."

Belonging to the older generation of diplomats (he was born in 1891), Prince Waithayakon has behind him long experience in the workings of international organizations, As permanent representative to the League of Nations from 1926 to 1930, Prince Waithayakon always serves as an example of conciliatory and friendly contacts.

As president of the assembly, the highest honor the international community can bestow upon a devoted servant to the idea of international cooperation, Prince Waithayakon turned the assembly president's office into a center of conciliation and understanding. Conscious of the role of the press in the formation of the U.N. image among peoples of the world, Prince Waithayakon took

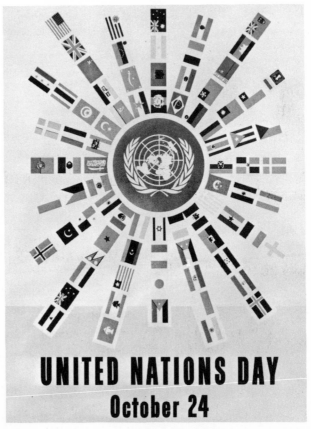

United Nations Day poster for 1957, designed by Olav Mathiesen of U.N. Graphic Presentation.

Performers from seven nations in a program on international co-operation.

Artistic performances are given annually at the General Assembly. Musicians and dancers of the Japanese Imperial Household pose with Secretary General Hammarskjöld and Koto Matsudaira, Japanese representative to the U.N.

The six top winners of a children's contest for U.N. stamp designs hold their entries.

—two other names must be mentioned. They are those of the Latin American diplomats Dr. Victor Andrés Belaúnde of Peru and Professor Enrique Rodriguez Fabregat of Uruguay.

Dr. Belaunde, born in 1883, made a name for himself as a scholar of excellent standing long before he came to the United Nations as head of the delegation of Peru to the Fifth General Assembly. The author of books on philosophy, history, and law, who was elected president of the Fourteenth General Assembly, used to demonstrate his wide legal training at meetings of the Security Council, when the country he represents was given a non-permanent seat in that body. Even those who do not understand Spanish enjoy the flow of his oratorical phrases, tinged with deep moral convictions to which he never fails to appeal in his presentation of the causes he defends.

His fellow Latin American, who is among the delegates longest representing their countries at the U.N., is Professor Fabregat of Uruguay. Known as an excellent mediator, Professor Fabregat has had a hand in many an important U.N. decision—

not the least important of these being the reports, and, later, decisions, which led to the U.N. resolution on the establishment of the state of Israel. As chairman of the Peace Observation Commission, Professor Fabregat heads a U.N. organ which, although for the time being dormant, could at any minute assume decisive importance in world-wide developments.

Stamp collectors lining up at the U.N. Postal Administration selling counter for first-day covers.

Secretary General Hammarskjöld presents Dr. R. A. Metall (*left*), director of the International Labor Organization's Liaison Office with the U.N., with a souvenir folder of U.N. postage stamps honoring the ILO. At right is Walter Hoffman, acting chief of the U.N. Postal Administration.

And speaking of the U.N. decision to establish the state of Israel, a U.N. observer cannot fail to mention the name of the Israeli representative to the U.N. for ten years, since the first day of Israel's admittance to the U.N., Mr. Abba Eban. Among the youngest of U.N. diplomats, Mr. Eban was born in 1915 in Capetown, South Africa, he soon evidenced, in the U.N., a kind of brilliance not many demonstrate. An expert linguist, who lectured on Hebrew, Arabic, and Persian at Cambridge and other institutions of higher learning, his mastery of the English language has been a source of admiration even among his bitterest opponents. Israel's permanent representative has had the floor at the U.N. more than any other delegate, one can safely assume, even when compared with the representatives of the major powers. It was Israel's permanent preoccupation with her relationship with the Arab U.N. members which caused Mr. Eban to fight numerous verbal battles at the U.N. Whenever he

spoke, he demonstrated that language can be used as an instrument of conflict sometimes even more potent than any physical weapon.

As his opponent, Mr. Eban had often to counter a formidable diplomat representing the Arab position toward Israel. Ahmed Shukeiry, an Arab from

A special issue of Ghana stamps commemorating United Nations Day is presented to Andrew Cordier.

Palestine, who serves at present as the Saudi-Arabian permanent representative to the U.N., has demonstrated the kind of efficiency in terms of diplomatic "production" that sometimes makes it difficult to believe that it is really accomplished by one man. It often happens that Mr. Shukeiry has before him as often as twice a day as many as forty pages of prepared text for his speeches before the U.N. bodies—speeches mainly aimed against Israel, but sometimes dealing with other matters considered by the U.N. as well. His power of delivery is considered outstanding, and although many consider his language harsh and often undiplomatic, he never changes his approach.

Of course the list of prominent U.N. personalities is much larger. Valerian Aleksandrovitch Zorin, the Russian deputy foreign minister, who at this writing represents his country at the U.N., has, within the short period of his activity at the U.N., proven himself a most formidable opponent of the United States representative, Mr. Stevenson. And his predecessor Arkady Sobolev, who prior to the assumption of the post of Russian U.N. representative got acquainted with the workings of the U.N. as one of the secretary general's assistants, never avoided an argument, and never failed to

answer questions put to him by newsmen, even if his answers were sometimes evasive.

In frequent clashes with the Russian representatives, the permanent representative of China, Tingfu F. Tsiang, serves as an example of stubbornness in the face of adverse odds which perhaps no other representative has had to withstand to such a degree. Holding the permanent seat of China at the Security Council, and being a permanent target of the growing number of delegates who demand his replacement by a representative of the People's Republic of China, Mr. Tsiang does not always try to be pleasant, but defends eloquently the position that the mainland of China is under occupation, and that the legal government is the one which he represents, with its seat on Taiwan. Born in 1895, he does not show his age, and is among the diplomats whose experience at the U.N. goes back as far as the second session of the General Assembly. A former ambassador of China in Russia, during the years 1936–1938, he likes to demonstrate his acquaintance with history, in which he is quite apt as a scholar and authority on the history of his native country.

From the days of the Korean conflict many remember the speeches of Sir Hubert Miles Gladwyn

Signing of the Postal Agreement between the United Nations and the United States. Seated from left to right are Albert Goldman, postmaster of New York; Warren Austin, United States representative to the U.N.; Secretary General Trygve Lie; Jesse Donaldson, United States postmaster general; and Bertil Renborg, head of the U.N. Postal Administration.

Junior U.N. artists exhibit their talents.

Jebb, the representative of the United Kingdom who contributed most to the British diplomatic offensive at the time of the Korean conflict. The Russian representative at the time, Jacob Malik, had in Mr. Jebb a formidable opponent who knew how to argue well, and how to seize an advantage from Russian arguments. This ability turned him into one of the best-known and best-liked diplomats at the U.N. among the visiting public which did not approve Russian attitudes in regard to the Korean conflict.

And the British representative who followed Jebb, Sir Pierson Dixon, who spoke for his country until 1960, was another example of the British school of diplomacy in the accuracy of his definitions, the exquisite language, and the gallantry which everybody who had contact with him greatly enjoyed.

The Algerian conflict has somewhat hampered French diplomats at the U.N. from making their full contribution to the debates there. Mr. Armand Berard, the present representative of France at

the U.N., an old-time diplomat whose erect figure stands out among the many members of the U.N. diplomatic corps, is held in esteem by all. The French logic and *esprit* is well represented in Mr. Berard as is the art of convincing oratory. Another aspect of U.N. activities—disarmament negotiations —finds in the French representative Mr. René Meyer, an excellent contributor and a voice which is always heard with respect.

Among the representatives of smaller nations, Ireland's Frederick H. Boland has shown outstanding diplomatic qualities. As president of the fifteenth session of the General Assembly, he proved his skill in handling special problems created by the great influx of world figures in the first weeks of the fifteenth session. In time, he turned the office of president of the assembly into an institution far more influential than his formally stipulated prerogatives would indicate.

Among delegates from the African nations, especially the new ones, the most characteristic feature is their youthfulness. Almost all of these delegates are in their early thirties, and some are even in their twenties. Graduates of European schools of public administration or politics, they prove daily that the new nations of Africa entered the international organization fully prepared to play their role in the development of international relations.

Among these diplomats, two have already found their way to diplomatic distinction. The permanent representative of Ghana, Alex Quaison-Sackey, has proven in many debates on African crises to have the ability to define and to understand a problem, and to make suggestions leading toward its solution. Also a colorful and important personality is the Nigerian representative to the U.N. Conciliation Commission for the Congo, Jaja A. Wachuku. And there are many others who are daily surprising the "old hands" in the diplomatic skill with which they demonstrate their understanding for the inner workings of the international organization.

It might be mentioned at this point that there is a special category of diplomats at the U.N. These are the diplomats who represent states which are not members of the U.N.—the Federal Republic of Germany, South Korea, Monaco, Switzerland, and Vietnam. The status of these diplomats is that of observer.

Not only professional diplomats serve with the United Nations delegations. Parliamentarians and leading citizens of all walks of life can be met in the corridors of the U.N. during the assembly sessions—and they, by themselves, could fill a sizable volume of *Who's Who* in the world of politics and social and economic endeavors. There is no doubt that outstanding among them, not only among members of United States delegations to the U.N., but among this category of U.N. delegates in general, is Mrs. Eleanor Roosevelt, whose relationship with the United Nations is a permanent one regardless of whether, at a given time, she happens to

The United Nations International School was founded in 1947 for children of members of the U.N. Secretariat and delegations. Here third-grade students study the globe in a geography class.

Class at the school for interpreters in Geneva (founded in 1940).

be a member of the United States delegation to the U.N.

Since the establishment of the U.N., Mrs. Roosevelt lent her name to every effort aimed at strengthening the U.N., and at popularizing the idea of international co-operation. The moving spirit, for many years, of the United States Committee for the United Nations, and its chairman in 1950, Mrs. Roosevelt initiated and participated in many actions on behalf of the U.N. or one of its agencies. Since the days of the United Nations Conference

Visitors in the main lobby of the Assembly Building. In the foreground is a statue of Zeus, a gift of the Greek government.

on International Organization in 1945, in which Mrs. Roosevelt participated as a member of the United States delegation, Mrs. Roosevelt in fact became a kind of symbol of American faithfulness to the U.N. idea. In her wide lecturing activity, and in many publications, Mrs. Roosevelt has expounded the importance of the U.N., and her appearance in a U.N. committee, or in the U.N. delegates' lounge, is always a kind of a demonstration by the former first lady that she has managed to stay important, as many delegates put it, as the "first lady of the world." The Universal Declaration of Human Rights, adopted by a U.N. commission under Mrs. Roosevelt's chairmanship, will no doubt remain the most lasting monument of her service to the great causes of humanity.

And while speaking of services to humanity within the framework of the U.N., it is fitting to recall the name of Raphael Lemkin, who was head

Twenty-seven languages are represented among U.N. guides, who conduct tours of the building at permanent headquarters.

of a "one-man lobby" in the United Nations, a lobby which had one objective: to assure the maximum number of ratifications for the Genocide Convention. When on September 24, 1959, the Legal Committee of the General Assembly observed a minute of silence in memory of Lemkin, who passed away in his fifty-eighth year of life, the official *United Nations Review* wrote: "Raphael

Bartenders at U.N. Headquarters.

Lemkin had the distinction, more than any other person, of being responsible for a large number of accessions to or ratifications of the Convention on the Prevention and Punishment of the Crime of Genocide." All his immense legal knowledge and his bottomless energy he devoted to the idea of prevention of Genocide. As early as in 1933, in the days of the League of Nations, Lemkin appealed to the league to ban mass extermination. The mission which failed at the forum of the League of Nations was successful at the United Nations. There is no doubt that if there is any single person who can be credited with the achievement of turning extermination into a crime to be prevented and punished by clear international legal obligations through an international convention, it is certainly Raphael Lemkin, the man who himself lost his entire family in the holocaust in Europe, and whom every delegate knew, since he approached them all in his plea to have all the U.N. member states ratify the Genocide Convention.

This gallery of U.N. personalities is of course of a passing character. Delegates come and go. New delegates come with new governments assuming power; they leave when recalled by their governments for new assignments. The U.N. has seen many instances, for example, when a delegate had his credentials questioned when another delegate of his country appeared at the U.N. forum after a violent change of government had taken place.

If one compiled comparative lists of U.N. diplomats and the people who attained positions of importance and leadership in their countries, he would surely become aware of how many of these public servants were able to use their service at the U.N. as an important step in their political careers.

But there are other personalities in the U.N. who, by virtue of their function, are called upon to be a permanent link between all delegates, delegations, and, indeed, all phases of U.N. activity. The office which these personalities have held is of course the office of secretary general of the United Nations.

When, on a Saturday, February 2, 1946, at 11:00 A.M., the president of the first session of the General Assembly performed the formal ceremony installing Mr. Trygve Lie as secretary general, he was not installing someone unknown in the international community of diplomats. Clearly, Trygve Lie did not come from a major power, and perhaps was not internationally known to the general public, but his fellow diplomats had had many occasions to meet him at his work. He had served as minister of justice and as minister of foreign affairs of Norway, and had headed the delegation of Norway to the U.N. Conference on International Organization, at which he served as chairman of the committee which drafted the part of the charter concerned with the Security Council. The head of Norway's delegation to the first session of the General Assembly, Lie was the unanimous choice for the highest post in the U.N.

The fifty-year-old first secretary general of the U.N. repeated solemnly after the president of the

View of the main delegates' lounge, at the time of the fifteenth assembly session.

Another view of the lounge. Seated in center is Mongi Slim of Tunisia.

assembly, Henry P. Spaak of Belgium, the oath of office: "In accepting the appointment, I, Trygve Lie, solemnly undertake to exercise in all loyalty, discretion and conscience the functions entrusted to me as Secretary General of the United Nations, to discharge those functions and regulate my conduct with the interests of the United Nations only in view, and not to seek or accept instructions in regard to the performance of my duties from any Government or other authority external to the Organization."

After almost eight years, on May 7, 1953, Mr. Trygve Lie was on his way back to Norway. The resignation which he had handed down some time earlier, surprised at that time only one man—the representative of the very power which forced his resignation, Andrei Vyshinsky of Russia. To other leading personalities at the U.N., Lie's decision had been known for months. The Russian boycott of the secretary general, after he was accused by Russia of excessive zeal in pursuing resolutions during the Korean war, seemed to be unbearable for Mr. Lie, a good-humored man who enjoyed a political discussion, but seemingly could not stand an unceasing attack coming from a great power, a permanent member of the Security Council. In the only interview he gave after his resignation, which appeared in the Norwegian newspaper *Arbeiderbladet,* he said, "I have often had the evil feeling,

that a possibility to solve a conflict somewhere in the world had been spoiled because one of the member nations did not accept me as Secretary General." An example of this attitude of Russia toward Mr. Lie could be found in a 1951 article in *Izvestia,* the leading Russian official newspaper, which attacked Mr. Lie's annual report. *Izvestia* commented: "The entire report of the Secretary General of the United Nations is construed so as to help the American aggressors."

Thus came to an end what certainly had been a pioneering effort. The first secretary general had to organize the Secretariat, to choose its members, to establish rules and usages, to make the entire

Shelves located in the lounge provide safekeeping for delegates' briefcases.

United Nations and Tunisian officials stand before an old mosaic, a gift of Tunisia to the U.N.

machinery of the U.N. work. Even such a problem as location for various U.N. organs was quite an important concern of Mr. Lie's. Members of the Secretariat from its first days remember his briefings, held in the long corridors of the Sperry Gyroscope plant, where his loud voice was an important asset. An affable co-worker and understanding boss, he was honored at his departure by the staff of the information services, which presented him with a commemorative gold medallion depicting the U.N. Headquarters, which had in the leather box it was encased in, a metal plaque with the inscription: "To the First Secretary General of the U.N., Mr. Trygve Lie—creator of the Secretariat, builder of the permanent Headquarters, spokesman for peace —the Department of Public Information whose aims he staunchly promoted and forcefully served, presents this token of abiding affection and heartfelt thanks."

The U.N. was now without its chief executive officer, but it could not remain so for long. Candidates had to be found. Names had been mentioned—Brigadier General Carlos P. Romulo of the Philippines, Nasrollah Entezam of Iran—but only a few mentioned the name of the then forty-eight-year-old head of the Swedish delegation of the U.N., Dag Hjalmar Agne Carl Hammarskjöld. The *New York Times* mentioned Mr. Hammarskjöld as the "dark horse candidate." But he won the confidence of the big powers to become, in April, 1953, the second United Nations secretary general. (His

service earned him, in September, 1957, an extension of his term for another five years, which began in April, 1958.)

Mr. Hammarskjöld was no newcomer to the art of diplomacy. Although not very well known on the international political scene, he had already

The Meditation Room. Fresco painting is by the Swedish artist Bo Beskow.

Michel Gallin-Douathe (*right*), representative of the Central African Republic, presents his credentials to the secretary general.

China's veto barred admission of Outer Mongolia to U.N. membership in 1955.

Sir Leslie Munro talks informally with Arkady A. Sobolev of Russia.

Queen Elizabeth, accompanied by her husband Prince Philip, visited the United Nations in October, 1957. Left to right in foreground: Jehan de Noue, chief of U.N. Protocol; Queen Elizabeth; Sir Leslie Munro, president of the General Assembly; Secretary General Dag Hammarskjöld; and Selwyn Lloyd, chairman of the British delegation. During her visit, the Queen addressed the General Assembly.

Representatives of the permanent members of the
Security Council voted for the admission of sixteen
nations to the U.N. (December, 1955).

V. K. Krishna Menon, minister of defense for India
and chairman of his country's delegation.

Premier Nikita S. Khrushchev at a luncheon given him by the United Nations Correspondents Association (October, 1960).

Presentation to the U.N. of the complete papers of Abraham Lincoln. Attending, left to right, are Undersecretary Ralph Bunche; Secretary General Dag Hammarskjöld; Henry Cabot Lodge, United States representative; Senator John Sherman Cooper of Kentucky, chairman of the Lincoln Sesquicentennial Commission; and Charles F. Willis, chairman of the United States Committee for the U.N.

Adlai Stevenson of the United States converses with V. A. Zorin of Russia with the aid of a Russian interpreter.

Andrei Vyshinsky of Russia and Madame Pandit of India in friendly conversation prior to a meeting of the Security Council.

Prince Wan Waithayakon (*left*) of Thailand, president of the eleventh session of the General Assembly, hands over the gavel to Sir Leslie Munro of New Zealand who, in September, 1957, was elected president of the twelfth session.

Dr. Victor Andrés Belaúnde, representative of Peru, addresses the Security Council on the Suez Canal question.

Abba Eban (*right*), of Israel, is seen exchanging views with Arkady A. Sobolev before a meeting of the Security Council.

Ahmed Shukeiry (*left*), Syrian representative to the U.N., exchanges views with delegates of other Arab nations prior to a December, 1955, meeting of the Security Council in which Syria sought U.N. sanctions against Israel for her alleged attacks near the Israeli-Syrian border.

Arkady Sobolev (*right*), Russian representative to the U.N., converses with Egypt's Omar Loufti in the Security Council chamber.

Tingfu F. Tsiang representing China at a Security Council debate.

attained standing in his native Sweden and in other Scandinavian countries. A son of the Swedish prime minister in the war years 1914–1917, he soon proved a man of manifold abilities and talents. An expert economist, he became so valuable that even a Socialist government retained him in a key position in the Ministry of Finance, even though he was not a Socialist party member. Titles and important positions came easily to him. His brilliance was well known. Minister of state, member of the Swedish Academy, professor of economics, governor of the State Bank, he became known also for his devotion to literature, philosophy, and the arts.

Sir Pierson Dixon (*center*) and Allan Noble (*left*) of Britain are seen, prior to a meeting of the General Assembly, in conversation with Selim Sarper of Turkey.

But many delegates at the U.N. had still to learn who their new secretary general was. When his name came up for the vote, many asked, "Who?" expressing thereby their astonishment and their curiosity alike. But their curiosity was soon to be rewarded. The "boy wonder of Swedish officialdom," "a realist who pricks balloons," the "most wanted bachelor around town," were all expressions which the British press used to refer to Hammarskjöld.

The new secretary general soon became highly esteemed. Being of assistance in diplomatic contacts and keeping himself out of the limelight became his first trademark. In time these characteristics were pinpointed by a diplomatic term

Armand Bérard representing France at a recent meeting of the General Assembly.

which seems to have been coined by Hammarskjöld himself—"quiet diplomacy." In an organization which stands for open diplomacy by its very character, this was an innovation which proved to be workable and very useful. Many a problem has been solved in this way up on the thirty-eighth floor of the U.N. Building, in the secretary general's office, instead of being aired at the Security Council, or in another U.N. organ's meeting. Quiet diplomacy worked because it had a well-thought-out political conception behind it. In one of his rare political significance of incomparable standing. "Mr. U.N.," as many called him, had also been labeled the "prime minister of the world." There was no crisis, no international problem, in which his initiative, his action, was not significant. Diplomats stood astounded at the volume and quality of his work, and the U.N. staff looked up to their chief as to an unattainable example of performance.

This devotion to the U.N. did not deprive Mr. Hammarskjöld of his other interests, however. At one of his press conferences, a reporter, who seemed

Alex Quaison-Sackey of Ghana, photographed as he presided over a 1961 session of the General Assembly in the absence of Assembly President Mongi Slim.

interviews, Mr. Hammarskjöld confided "The Secretary General must build the delegations' trust in him. The importance of his initiative is based on his political signficance."

And indeed, the secretary general achieved a

Eleanor Roosevelt, for her tireless activities on behalf of the U.N. since its inception, has been called by delegates "the First Lady of the World."

to follow Mr. Hammarskjöld's interests closely, asked somewhat inquisitively,

We are all, I believe, aware of the widened responsibilities throughout this whole year, which have held you close to a dawn-to-midnight schedule: the continuous waves of crisis in the Congo, the necessity to defend the U.N. under siege, and a long extraordinary Assembly. Yet, this year is marked by the emergence of Dag Hammarskjöld in other fields: as translator of Nobel Prize winner St. John Perse's volume *Chronique;* as co-translator of the English play in verse *The Anti-*

Jaja Wachuku, chairman of the Nigerian delegation, addresses meeting of the sixteenth session of the General Assembly.

Secretary General Trygve Lie accepts from John D. Rockefeller III, acting for his father John D. Rockefeller, Jr., a check for $8,500,000 for the purchase of a six-block Manhattan site for the permanent headquarters.

phon which had a world premiere in Stockholm in February; as author of *New Look at Mt. Everest,* complete with some strikingly beautiful pictures by photographer Hammarskjöld. My question is: How did you manage it all and what about sharing with us this magical formula for extension of time?

Perhaps the best answer to this question was given by Mr. Hammarskjöld at another time. The secretary general, the busiest diplomat on earth, needed some diversion. And his main diversion was reading. It is necessary as a mental exercise, Mr. Hammarskjöld said, "a kind of intellectual calisthenics." As he explained it, to read was also his profession. As a member of the Swedish Academy, he had to read the works of candidates for the Nobel Prize for Literature. "If one read only U.N. reports," he once said, "one would develop rather a curious mentality." And when there was no time for reading, music supplied the diversion. During the Suez crisis, Mr. Hammarskjöld confided, he listened to Bach's "Sixth Brandenburg Concerto"—"and it is in a way like reading an extremely good

An impromptu press conference as members of the Security Council leave chamber after having appointed, by a vote of ten to none (with one abstention), Swedish Minister of State Dag Hammarskjöld as secretary general.

Henry Cabot Lodge, United States representative, has an informal discussion with Secretary General Hammarskjöld before a meeting of the Security Council.

book or poem."

In his eight years of office, the secretary general created a complete philosophy of public service as an official of an international organization. Discussing this problem some years ago, before the attacks against him and against the entire conception of a neutral official of an international organization were started, Mr. Hammarskjöld said, "The qualities of an international official [are] heightened awareness combined with an inner quiet, also a certain humility, which helps [him] to see things through the other person's eyes to reconstruct his case, without losing himself, without being a chameleon."

It seems, however, that this continual effort to "see things through the other person's eyes" did not exempt Mr. Hammarskjöld from severe criticism by Russia, one of the permanent members of the Security Council. But Mr. Hammarskjöld did not duck the challenge. In one of his speeches at the General Assembly, in which he defended his conduct as secretary general against Russian attacks, he stated bluntly, that "it is easy to resign" and made clear that he intended to stay on in his post

as long as the smaller nations found his service useful.

His sudden death has proven more than his life the extent of affection he enjoyed among diplomats and hundreds of millions the world over. His disappearance from the U.N. scene was felt as a tragic blow to mankind's hopes for a world of law and international co-operation. The soldier of peace fell while on a U.N. mission, leaving a gap which will be hard to fill for years to come.

The third man to assume the post of secretary general, U Thant of Burma, symbolizes the change the United Nations has witnessed in the last six to seven years. The fact that non-European nations are in the overwhelming majority in the U.N., and that the number of the neutral or nonaligned nations grows constantly in the international organization, has found dramatic expression in the selection of the personality to head the U.N. Secretariat. As a Buddhist, U Thant subscribes to a religion with the strongest tradition of pacifism, and seems suited for his high post. Head of the Burmese delegation to the United Nations for four years (since 1957) he served with his country's delegation as early as in 1952. In his years of service at the U.N., U Thant made many friends but no enemies. The fifty-two-year-old former teacher who turned to political writing and entered politics in 1947 as press and publicity director of the Anti-Fascist

The United Nations flag flies at half-mast following confirmation of the death of Secretary General Hammarskjöld.

The body of the late secretary general is carried to a waiting plane at Salisbury Airport in Rhodesia, for its journey to Uppsala, his home town in Sweden.

People's Freedom League of Burma, showed early in his career interest for the efforts to organize the international community for the preservation of peace. When, at the age of twenty-three, he wrote his treatise about the League of Nations, neither he nor his friends could have guessed that after twenty-nine years, he would be chosen to head a new, improved version of the League of Nations and that he would reach a point where he could put to test his peacemaking abilities and his theories on co-operation of men for the advancement of all.

It is natural that in the extremely wide scope of U.N. activities, at headquarters and around the world, the secretary general must have a group of high officials on whose devotion, loyalty, and abilities he can rely. The Executive Office of the Secretary General, the Office of Legal Affairs, the Office of the Controller, the Office of Personnel, two undersecretaries for Special Political Affairs, the Department of Political and Security Council Affairs, the Department of Economic and Social Affairs, the Department of Trusteeship and Information from Nonself-Governing Territories, the Office of Public Information, Conference Services and General Services—all these principal sections in the organizational framework of the Secretariat are headed by officials whose distinguished records of service have entitled them to assume these wide responsibilities at the United Nations.

Among these top officials of the U.N. Secretariat, Andrew Wellington Cordier has assumed highly exposed functions as the secretary general's assistant. Holding the post of executive assistant to the secretary general, Mr. Cordier has been, in fact, in one way or another, part of every development which has taken place at the U.N. Providing continuity in the Secretariat's high echelons, Mr. Cordier has been fulfilling his functions in that body since the inception of the United Nations Organization. After assisting in setting up the machinery of the U.N. in 1945, he became responsible for co-ordinating U.N. activities and programs, and soon became a kind of personal envoy for the secretary general whenever and wherever a "trouble shooter" was necessary.

With the exception of the secretary general, Mr. Cordier is the best-known official at the U.N. Participants in the General Assembly meetings are used to seeing Mr. Cordier sitting at the left side of the assembly president, as he is consulted by the president on matters of U.N. procedure and usages. And when election-time comes, it is again Mr. Cordier who conducts the voting procedure, who calls the names of member states, and who announces the results of the voting.

A stocky, broad-shouldered man, Mr. Cordier never ducks a dangerous situation, and when on one of his missions to a troubled area a sniper's bullet missed him by a fraction of an inch, he wasn't shocked at all, and remarked, "It must have been a very poor sniper, if he missed such a visible target."

Born in Canton, Ohio, in 1901, Mr. Cordier has behind him a distinguished career in teaching history and political science. He visited Europe to get acquainted with such critical areas as Danzig and Sudetenland. Upon joining the United States Department of State in 1944, Mr. Cordier started a new career, which brought him into association with the international organization. A technical expert on the United States delegation to the U.N. Conference on International Organization, Mr. Cordier served also as an adviser to the late Senator Arthur H. Vandenberg, the leading Republican who contributed a great deal to America's firm support of the U.N. idea. After sixteen years of association with the U.N., Mr. Cordier resigned, in June, 1961, evidently to make the secretary general's plans for a reorganization of the U.N. Secretariat easier to implement. As of August 1, 1961, Mr. Cordier assumed the post of undersecretary in charge of

General Assembly Affairs, relinquishing the functions of executive assistant to the secretary general.

In June, 1961, part of the tasks previously performed by Mr. Cordier were assigned to Mr. C. V. Narasimhan of India, who had served as undersecretary for Special Political Affairs since December, 1958. The character of this new assignment has been defined by the secretary general as follows: "Mr. Narasimhan will be, as an additional assignment, something which I might perhaps most properly call *chef de cabinet.*"

Associated with the U.N. for as long as Mr. Cordier is another of its distinguished high servants, Dr. Ralph Johnson Bunche. Among the many souvenirs he treasures as reminders of his activities on behalf of the world organization, there is one which is of a highly unusual charactor—a vase given to him by both the Arabs and the Israelis in recognition of the decisive role he played in achieving the armistice agreements which stopped the Arab-Israel war. This same achievement gave Dr. Bunche another distinction of the highest order. In 1950 Dr. Bunche received the Nobel Prize for Peace,

The coffin with Hammarskjöld's body arrives at the cemetery in Uppsala, followed by dignitaries from many lands.

Funeral services at Uppsala. Among the overseas visitors present are Adlai Stevenson, Trygve Lie, and Madame Pandit.

which he always regards as given not only to him personally, but also to the United Nations as well, in recognition of the U.N. contribution to the preservation of peace.

As is the case with Mr. Cordier, Dr. Bunche has a teaching career behind him. He also has a series of books to his credit, some of them dealing with race relations, a problem to which Dr. Bunche's origin made him especially sensitive. *A World View of Race* and *Africa—the War and Peace Aims* are two of his works.

These are only a few of the many who deserve to be mentioned. If a biographical history of U.N. officials was written, it would be a history of the achievements of outstanding personalities from all countries. At the U.N. these people have found their "front" in the struggle for peace. Here many of them have found an excellent milieu for pursuing outside interests. When one passes the big

bulletin boards on the fourth floor he can easily learn what a variety of interests these U.N. officials have, for he can read the notices announcing activities of the various clubs. In addition to the announcements of the U.N. Co-operative, which affords many benefits to its members if they buy at least one share for ten dollars, there is the news from the various clubs—clubs geared to such outside interests as cricket, golf, dancing, hiking, boating, flying, horseback-riding, chess, photography, and languages (including Esperanto). Here the enjoyment of life is increased as those with common interests meet.

It is clear that great care has been taken to bring the message of the U.N. to the public. "We the peoples of the World" are the opening words of the Preamble to the U.N. Charter, and the peoples of the world have to be informed of what is going on in their organization. The unanimous declaration

Ambassador U Thant acknowledges congratulations shortly after the Security Council unanimously recommended to the General Assembly that he be appointed acting secretary general.

In this gallery of U.N. servants, special mention should be given to the scores of individuals who have lost their lives in the service of the U.N.—either those killed in accidents while on service, or those who were victims of direct attacks on them while on a U.N. mission. "Died for the United Nations"—these simple, brief words to honor those who sacrificed their lives for the U.N.'s aims and purposes, are the dramatic manifestation of the vitality of the international organization. One need not subscribe to the saying, "An idea which has found people ready to die for it must live and be victorious," to acknowledge that those graves of U.N. servants, spread all over the world, are and will remain eternal monuments of humanity's strivings toward international co-operation and peace.

Newly appointed Acting Secretary General U Thant taking the oath of office in the General Assembly Hall (November 3, 1961). Assembly President Mongi Slim administers the oath.

of the first session of the General Assembly in London, which states: "The United Nations cannot succeed unless peoples of the world are fully informed of its aims and activities," became of principal concern to the U.N. Secretariat. The Office of Public Information, entrusted with the implementation of this task, is doing so by providing facilities for dissemination of knowledge concerning the U.N. through radio, television, the press, films, photographs, and other information media. Thirty regional centers of the Office of Public Information, spread all over the world, are serving as direct instruments of these U.N. efforts.

And in these efforts, radio, television, and the press have become an inseparable part of the U.N. The United Nations Correspondents Association (UNCA), with its periodic luncheons for leading diplomats at the U.N., or visiting it, became a kind of unofficial U.N. institution. The election of its presidents and members of the executive are sometimes as heated as the election of heads of U.N. organs. For the UNCA also tries to preserve the principle of regional distribution in the selection of its officers.

Unveiling of a plaque commemorating men of sixteen countries who lost their lives while fighting with the United Nations command in Korea.

INDEX